"I have had an opportunity to use the BREATHE program with a cohort of first semester college undergraduates. The move to college creates unique challenges, and the BREATHE program, which can be adapted for this population, provides powerful tools to help emerging adults manage this transition. Learning the basics of mindfulness, strengthening emotion recognition and emotion management skills, and developing compassion for self and others, are all extremely important skills for college students. . . . As Broderick writes, 'there is a difference between knowing *about* emotions and knowing your own emotions *as they are experienced.*' The BREATHE program allows this distinction to emerge brilliantly."

> —**Sandra Kerr, PhD**, professor in the department of psychology, West Chester University, PA

"As a longtime instructor of mindfulness-based stress reduction, currently teaching instructors in two school districts, Broderick's book, *Learning to Breathe*, is a welcome gift. It is filled with clear information about mindfulness, from both the educational and neurological perspectives, and presents an excellent, thorough, and complete curriculum for adolescents. This book will be welcomed, used, and gratefully received by teachers and students."

> —**Ferris Buck Urbanowski, MA**, mindfulness instructor, South Burlington, Vermont School District, and Washington West School District, Waitsfield, VT

"*Learning to Breathe* is an invaluable resource for those looking to share mindfulness with adolescents. Broderick has carefully crafted a professional and wonderfully straightforward mindfulness curriculum that can be used in a variety of settings. Highly recommended!"

> —**Doug Worthen**, mindfulness teacher at the Middlesex School in Concord, MA

"*Learning to Breathe* couldn't have come at a better time! Educators are seeking new ways of meeting a rising tide of societal challenges. Compelling new research supports the benefits of learning a mindfulness practice. With a focus on adolescents, Broderick has intelligently created a flexible mindfulness curriculum that is user-friendly, evidence-based, and age-appropriate. Through this achievement she offers the opportunity to 'experience burgeoning self-awareness, self-regulation, and the emotional balance that supports fully engaged learning and well-being.' Ideally, all schools would teach these practices."

> —**Marilyn Webb Neagley**, education consultant, coeditor of *Educating from the Heart*, and author of *Walking through the Seasons*

"Engaging, varied, and user-friendly lessons make this an essential resource for any educator who wishes to bring mindfulness into the curriculum. From theory to practice, this guide provides teachers with the necessary information to make mindfulness come to life in their classrooms and in the lives of their students. A must-have for all those committed to the social and emotional health of adolescents."

> —**Karen Bluth,** research fellow at the Program of Integrative Medicine at the School of Medicine at University of North Carolina, NC

"*Learning to Breathe* is an extraordinary curriculum, grounded in a deep understanding of adolescent learning, adolescent growth, and the daily experience of adolescent life. The brilliant design of the BREATHE program provides teachers with ease in implementation and flexibility to adapt for the uniqueness of each class, while at the same time providing the quintessential elements of mindfulness-based well-being in each lesson. Educators and school systems that adopt this creative program will be giving a gift to themselves and to the adolescents in their care for a healthier, more positive and productive future.

—**Irene McHenry, PhD**, licensed psychologist, author, international speaker and workshop presenter, and currently executive director of Friends Council on Education

"The unfolding field of mindfulness education for tweens and teens is most fortunate to be gifted with Broderick's theoretically grounded and pragmatically written step-by-step guide. Broderick offers first-hand experiences and clear insights to encourage teachers and therapists teaching mindfulness practices to deepen their own practice while teaching and learning alongside youths. When offered in the spirit with which it is written, the *Learning to Breathe* curriculum opens a conversation around the often overwhelming stressors that are simultaneously unique and universal to preadolescents and adolescents while offering them an array of exercises to meet the stressors with more clarity and care. In doing so, these exercises for youths can introduce a new way of being in the world that frees young people from automatic avoidance and risk-taking behaviors that often compound their stress—thereby decreasing experiences of distress and increasing experiences of empowerment. Let the exploration begin!"

—**Laura J. Pinger, MS**, senior outreach specialist at the Center for Investigating Healthy Minds at the Waisman Center on the University of Wisconsin-Madison

"I have seen first-hand the transformational potential *Learning to Breathe* has for a wide range of students in the high school setting. Broderick has done an amazing job of creating a mindfulness-based universal prevention program for high school applications. Those looking for a program to use to bring mindfulness to high school students in a curricular way need not look further than *Learning to Breathe*."

—**Todd D. Cantrell**, house principal at Central Bucks High School West in Doylestown, PA

"I am delighted to provide an unequivocal endorsement of Broderick's *Learning to Breathe*. This program for adolescents is beautifully designed and hits all the right notes for teaching mindfulness as a tool to navigate the ups and downs of adolescence. Grounded within a developmental framework and clinical understanding of adolescent issues, Broderick's book is user-friendly and will resonate with clinicians, educators, and parents alike. As a school social worker with experience of successfully implementing [the program] within a very diverse population, it is gratifying to have a program of this integrity that is compatible with multiple areas of the curriculum."

—**Marjorie James, MSW, RSW**, social worker with the Toronto District School Board

"School reform is doomed to failure until it faces the reality of kids as they come: stressed-out, overwrought, and inattentive to school work. This marvelous book fills this gap with a curriculum that helps teenagers reduce stress, handle their emotions, and master their attention. A step-by-step guide for teachers and clinicians, *Learning to Breathe* is clear, inventive, and practical, and it can be implemented starting tomorrow. This inspiring book is also a timely wake-up call for the nation."

—**Jerome Murphy**, Dean Emeritus at Harvard Graduate School of Education

"*Learning to Breathe* offers a time-tested, research-based solution to assist young people in cultivating positive qualities, such as mindful awareness and compassion for oneself and others. [The book will] inspire young people to use these qualities in the service of the greater good in the twenty-first century. I hope we see this curriculum in all of our schools."

> —**Robert W. Roeser**, professor of psychology and human development in the department of psychology at Portland State University, Portland, OR

"Even when we have an inside familiarity with the practice of mindfulness it is challenging to make it accessible and meaningful to others. Broderick's book and program have done just this—translated the practice into a practical, accessible program for both teachers and students. The result is a curriculum that maps beautifully onto both the opportunity and the vulnerability that are inherent in the teenage years."

> —**Rebecca Crane**, director at the Center for Mindfulness Research and Practice, Bangor University, UK

"*Learning to Breathe* is truly a gem that fills a critical gap in social and emotional learning programs for adolescents. With a deep commitment to helping young people navigate the social and emotional challenges of this developmental period, Broderick has artfully crafted an outstanding mindfulness-based program supported by rigorous research. The program is unique among its peers. Rather than functioning as an 'add-on' that places extra burdens on teachers, it has been successfully integrated into existing curricula and meets standards in the areas of science and health. This program is a proven method for promoting well-being and resilience among young people."

> —**Patricia A. Jennings, MEd, PhD**, research assistant professor in human development and family studies at the Prevention Research Center at Pennsylvania State University, PA

"*Learning to Breathe* is an excellent program for teachers or practitioners interested in teaching mindfulness to adolescents. The instructions and lesson plans are easy to follow as an instructor, and they allow for enough flexibility to make the program fit your needs. Our students readily engaged in the activities during class and kept up with a home practice as well. Most told us that they noticed differences in their lives and reported that the mindfulness practices they learned would be helpful in their classes at school to help relax them before tests or keep them alert, as well as being helpful for sports. We heard from several students that it was their favorite part of their summer and that they were very glad to have taken the course."

> —**Kristen Lyons, PhD**, assistant professor of developmental psychology at Metropolitan State University of Denver, Denver, CO

"*Learning to Breathe* is a superb guide for helping adolescents manage their emotional lives. Broderick draws from the finest knowledge in psychology and mindfulness education to craft this extraordinary book—it is sure to become a classic."

> —**Richard C. Brown**, founded Naropa University's Contemplative Education Department in 1990, and recently co-developed Garrison Institute's mindfulness-based Care for Teachers program

"This is experiential learning at its best. The teacher facilitates a journey of discovery from which both students and teachers alike come back hungry for more!"

> —**Bruce Glick**, teacher who has worked with special needs children and youth in myriad settings

"Drawing on her expertise in developmental psychology and mindfulness, Broderick has crafted a comprehensive, beautifully designed, mindfulness-based curriculum for adolescents. *Learning to Breathe* details a multitude of simple yet powerful mindfulness practices for teens as well as clear, concise, step-by-step instructions for teachers and clinicians to implement this wonderfully rich curriculum. This book is a tremendous resource—a must for educators and clinicians who want to bring the transformative power of mindfulness to teens."

> —**Diane Reibel, PhD**, director of the Mindfulness Institute, Jefferson Myrna Brind Center of Integrative Medicine, and coauthor of *Teaching Mindfulness*

"Broderick's years of real-world experience with teenagers shine through on every page of her wonderful new book, *Learning to Breathe*. When it comes to teaching mindfulness, adolescents can be an especially challenging group and Broderick has developed wise, practical, and time-tested methods that help teens manage stress and develop attention as they integrate mindfulness into their daily lives."

> —**Susan Kaiser Greenland, JD**, author of *The Mindful Child*

"Know thyself. Building not only on the accumulated wisdom of the ages but also on the pioneering work of Jon Kabat-Zinn, Broderick has created an extremely well-pitched curriculum for helping teens through what may well be tumultuous years. Practicing mindfulness, a sustained state of nonjudgmental self-awareness, has well-documented salubrious effects. In this well-written and insightful book, Broderick explains clearly what mindfulness is, why it is important, and how to teach it to our youth."

> —**Philip David Zelazo, PhD**, Institute of Child Development, University of Minnesota

"I wish that I had had this resource when I was principal of my high school. I can't think of a more important gift than to teach students to work with their emotions at such an important period of transition in their lives."

> —**Rona Wilensky,** founding principal of New Vista High School, Boulder, CO

"*Learning to Breathe* is a gift to educators and therapists who are committed to supporting the resilience and well-being of the young people they serve. Well-researched, with lessons that are well designed and accessible, it enhances and contributes to the field of social and emotional learning."

> —**Pamela Siegle,** executive director at Courage and Renewal Northeast

LEARNING
TO
breathe

A Mindfulness Curriculum for
Adolescents to Cultivate Emotion Regulation,
Attention, and Performance

PATRICIA C. BRODERICK, PHD

NEW HARBINGER PUBLICATIONS, INC.

Publisher's Note

This publication is designed to provide accurate and authoritative information in regard to the subject matter covered. It is sold with the understanding that the publisher is not engaged in rendering psychological, financial, legal, or other professional services. If expert assistance or counseling is needed, the services of a competent professional should be sought.

Distributed in Canada by Raincoast Books

Copyright © 2013 by Patricia C. Broderick
New Harbinger Publications, Inc.
5674 Shattuck Avenue
Oakland, CA 94609
www.newharbinger.com

"Emotion Faces" artwork in Appendix D appears courtesy of Alexa Nippa.
All other artwork in Appendices C and D appears courtesy of Jill Design Studio.

Cover design by Amy Shoup
Acquired by Catharine Meyers
Edited by Nelda Street

Library of Congress Cataloging-in-Publication Data

Broderick, Patricia C.
  Learning to breathe : a mindfulness curriculum for adolescents to cultivate emotion regulation, attention, and performance / Patricia C. Broderick, PhD.
      pages cm
  Summary: "The breakthrough book Learning to Breathe presents a research-based curriculum for teachers and clinicians who are seeking ways to help improve behavior and bolster academic performance in adolescents. Drawing on a combination of mindfulness-based therapies, the brief interventions outlined in the book have a strong theoretical basis in both education and psychology, and are proven effective when it comes to dealing with adolescent students who act out in the classroom"-- Provided by publisher.
  Includes bibliographical references.
  ISBN 978-1-60882-783-1 (pbk.) -- ISBN 978-1-60882-784-8 (pdf e-book) -- ISBN 978-1-60882-785-5 (epub) 1. Behavior modification. 2. Adolescent psychology. 3. Behavior disorders in adolescence--Prevention. 4. Mindfulness-based cognitive therapy. I. Title.
  LB1060.2.B73 2013
  370.15'28--dc23
                              2013006044

Printed in the United States of America

16   15   14

10   9   8   7   6   5   4   3   2

With gratitude:

To Jon Kabat-Zinn, for bringing mindfulness to the mainstream

Contents

Part 3   Eighteen-Session Program

Part 4   Supplementary Information

Foreword

This is a much needed, extremely well-thought-out, and beautifully constructed curriculum. It is commonsensical, user friendly, and straightforward to implement. Most importantly, it engages you, the teacher, in developing your own mindfulness practice so that you are not asking things of your students that you are not actually exploring and experiencing for yourself. This element of honing your own personal mindfulness practice can provide great benefits in terms of your well-being and sense of ease and presence in your work.

Bringing this curriculum to life in a nonmechanical way can have profound effects on your students. It can catalyze the development of embodied self-awareness and, with it, the potential for greater self-understanding, self-confidence, and emotional intelligence. This process is made easier by the inclusion of extremely effective "scripts" for each lesson, offset from the rest of the text, which can support you on the steep slope of your own learning curve. Through the systematic cultivation of attention, awareness, self-compassion, and kindness toward others— all capacities that adolescents already have and that can be strengthened through training—a set of fundamental and highly beneficial life skills are developed. These skills can help teenagers navigate more effectively through a time in life that can be confusing, filled with uncertainties, and exceedingly stressful. These life skills form the basis for building successful relationships, beginning with oneself. They can also contribute to optimizing the classroom environment and learning.

Even great musicians have to first tune their instruments. It is the same with learning. For many students, before they can engage fully in the more academic aspects of the curriculum, they may first need to tune their own "instruments" by learning how to pay attention and then sustain attention over time—in other words, to calm, stabilize, and focus the mind and the body. Mindfulness is the premier vehicle for that attunement to oneself and to everything else. Moreover, there is a large and rapidly growing body of scientific evidence showing that mindfulness training can be instrumental in reducing stress and its negative consequences on the body and the mind in adults. Early studies suggest that the same is true for children. Stress has been shown to have negative effects in adolescents on the development of regions of the brain that are involved in executive function, working memory capacity, and emotion regulation.

Since these functions influence learning and behavior, it makes sense to give children mindfulness-based tools to promote effective self-regulation, stress reduction, and the ability to sustain attention.

Mindfulness in education is now a growing movement that is bringing mindful awareness and contemplative practices into K–12 schools, both public and private, throughout the United States, as well as other countries, for the benefit of teacher and students alike. This curriculum is a signature addition to that effort.

In the past decade or two, social-emotional learning (SEL) has become established as an important element of classroom learning and culture. SEL teaches children to recognize their own emotions and those of others, and develop the skills necessary to communicate them more effectively. However, there is an important difference between learning about emotions and actually being able to recognize them in the present moment. Here is where mindfulness comes in.

Mindfulness adds value to SEL because it goes beyond cognitive understanding and is grounded in an actual practice that can be sustained or evoked throughout the day. Training in mindfulness provides embodied and very practical and simple exercises for cultivating the recognition of emotions as they arise; the felt experience of emotion and mood, whether it be anxiety, sadness, elation, boredom, anger, or irritation; and the thoughts and body sensations that invariably accompany them. These mindfulness exercises form a living practice repertoire that is always accessible to the student and can be cultivated in everyday-life situations before emotionally or socially challenging situations even arise. Mindfulness training also helps integrate different aspects of experience into a coherent whole, and makes emotional intelligence and mindfulness, as opposed to mindlessness, much more likely to become a "way of life" for the student, both in the classroom and beyond.

Teenagers are particularly vulnerable to the negative consequences of destructive emotions that can lead to hurtful actions toward themselves or others. As we have said, important areas of the brain are still in the process of developing. These areas are associated with the capacity to self-regulate and to control impulses, particularly when in the grip of strong emotions. And since teenagers often have much more exposure and access to the negative influences of society and culture as they move beyond the normally protective buffers of parents and home, they are particularly vulnerable.

Deep down, most teenagers are explorers and seekers, yearning to feel more connected, have a sense of belonging, and find meaning in their lives. Their potential for growing and changing, and for contributing to the world is enormous. When we see them caught in habits of mind and behaviors that don't serve them and that may actually be harmful, we empathize with them and want to be of help in some way. Yet there is a particular kind of inner work that no one else can do for them. It requires befriending oneself—and that is exactly what this curriculum has to offer on so many different levels.

Trish Broderick has created a program that gives teenagers a range of simple mindfulness practices, nested within a coherent framework that can empower them inwardly and outwardly. The Learning to BREATHE curriculum provides a precious opportunity to develop greater awareness and self-compassion at a crucial phase of life, and the ability to make wiser choices and to respond more appropriately in difficult situations, rather than to react in habitual and often harmful ways.

We hope that this curriculum connects in a deep way with teachers as they begin this exploration and adventure for themselves and for their students. May it alleviate in some small way some of the more painful aspects of adolescence, and empower both teachers and students alike to know themselves and what they are capable of in ever-deepening and more and more satisfying ways.

—Jon and Myla Kabat-Zinn
August 18, 2012

Acknowledgments

I owe much gratitude to those who have been a part of this curriculum, directly or indirectly, over the years of its development. These acknowledgments will only scratch the surface of that debt.

Without Jon Kabat-Zinn, whose brilliant Mindfulness-Based Stress Reduction (MBSR) program invites everyone to experience a more mindful life, this book would not exist. He and Myla Kabat-Zinn have been gracious, generous, and tireless advocates for so many of us in the field of mindfulness in education. I am grateful to my teachers at the Center for Mindfulness, Florence Meleo-Meyer and Melissa Blacker, for their guidance and example, as well as to all of my friends in the Philadelphia mindfulness-teachers group for supporting my practice.

As a professor and psychologist by training, I have always been captivated by the work of researchers, especially those with a soft spot for the well-being of children and youth. Little did I know that in a totally unexpected stroke of good fortune, I would be collaborating with some of them. I am deeply grateful to Mark Greenberg, director of the Penn State Prevention Research Center; to Tish Jennings, a leader in the contemplative education movement; and to Richie Davidson, founder of the Center for Investigating Healthy Minds, for their ongoing support and encouragement. This work has also been influenced by the incredible contributions of my colleagues on the Educational Leadership Council of the Garrison Institute, whose creative and heartfelt efforts to support contemplative teaching and learning continue to inspire me. I am especially grateful to the staff and students of Villa Maria Academy High School, who were supportive of my efforts to translate mindfulness into something young people could understand as I began to develop this curriculum in their school.

At this point in time, there are many educators and clinicians bringing mindfulness to youth in many different ways, and there are many researchers who are committed to studying its benefits. To all of you, thank you. To those of you who have had a more direct hand in helping me over the past decade of work on the various iterations of this curriculum, I am deeply grateful.

I also owe sincere thanks to the staff at New Harbinger for their warm and enthusiastic support. Catharine Meyers, acquisitions director, and Jess Beebe, editorial manager, have been consistently encouraging and helpful as this process unfolded. Heather Garnos, prepublication director; Margo Beren, special sales manager; and others were wonderful to work with and showed remarkable energy and commitment to making this project successful. Nelda Street's expert copyediting and mindful attention to detail has contributed greatly to the clarity of the work.

Finally, I am always grateful for the love and support of my husband and children. Their presence in my life keeps me going and reminds me of what this work is all about.

Part 1

Introduction and Overview

Chapter 1

A Message for Teachers and Therapists

This book describes a curriculum for adolescents that is probably very different from other curricula or programs you have previously used. Typically, a curriculum manual, whether it be for academic subjects like math or social studies or for psychoeducational topics like social skills or violence prevention, provides an outline for teaching content. It generally offers guidelines and activities for helping adolescents use their attention to comprehend and retain information. Traditional curricula often focus on performance, judged right or wrong by a teacher who is expert in the domain and who may possess the answer key. In Learning to BREATHE (L2B), *attention*, as opposed to specific content, is the core of the curriculum. Thus, teacher and students alike must settle into present-moment awareness by slowing down and practicing a new skill set for paying attention. Although there is a structure to the lessons and activities, this curriculum allows for openness and flexibility on the part of the teacher or therapist.

Teaching mindfulness means facilitating adolescents' recognition of their own personal experience, at the moment of that experience. This is best accomplished through your connectedness to your own inner and outer experience and to your students. Mindfulness is the opposite of being "zoned out," asleep, in denial, or unaware of what's happening. It is open, moment-to-moment awareness, held without judgment, even when what is occurring may be unwanted. So in this teaching, each new moment provides the experiential material that is the heart of this curriculum. Mindfulness practice is for each person in the room.

Research in this burgeoning area of study suggests that mindfulness offers great benefits to health and well-being by shifting the nature of our relationship to experience. Although the scientific account of underlying neural circuitry is still being worked out, we know that cultivating an even-handed and openhearted stance toward life can strengthen emotional balance, resilience, and interpersonal effectiveness. These are skills we all can use. Thus, mindfulness education may be useful as universal prevention as well as intervention for specific populations. Throughout this book, use of the word "teacher" refers to classroom teachers engaged in social-emotional learning programs; to school-based specialists like counselors, school psychologists, and social workers; and to therapists who work with adolescent groups. For clinicians who treat adolescents individually, the structure, language, and exercises offered here might be helpful when they are skillfully adapted to suit individual needs.

Although mindfulness is a construct that has a definition, simply emphasizing the cognitive understanding of the concept is not sufficient. Understanding must incorporate experience. Jon Kabat-Zinn, in his book *Full Catastrophe Living* (1990), makes an apt comparison to eating. It makes no sense to ask someone to eat your food for you; you must eat it yourself to derive both pleasure and benefit. Similarly, each person must experience mindfulness to reap its rewards. Consequently, the pedagogical tradition of providing teachers and clinicians with skills and techniques in a curriculum manual may only be useful if such techniques are employed within the context of the instructor's own mindful awareness.

So what are some recommendations for teachers and clinicians who will teach this program? Several are listed here that, although general, cover the main points. I recognize that teachers and therapists have diverse background experiences and training. It is not my intention to restrict the program to those with a specialized degree or field of study. However, some prerequisites appear to be very important for successful implementation.

First, some basic training in mindfulness is strongly encouraged, particularly when you are teaching adolescents about mindfulness of thoughts and emotions. Ideally, this would come from participation in a course like Mindfulness-Based Stress Reduction (MBSR) or other mindfulness-based programs. MBSR is an eight-week empirically supported group program that incorporates practice in various mindfulness techniques, classroom discussion, and homework. Engaging in other contemplative disciplines can also provide a foundation for teaching. Mindfulness is becoming better known, and retreats and workshops are becoming more easily available, regardless of geographic location. You may also want to seek out some type of in-service training or personal supervision to provide you with guidance in this work.

Second, it is strongly recommended that instructors who teach L2B to students or clients continue to practice mindfulness or some other contemplative practice on a regular basis. As the message to adolescents goes, we are all "in training" to develop inner strength. It is difficult for teachers and therapists to embody the qualities of mindfulness in groups unless they themselves do their own inner work. For example, it is particularly difficult to practice silence in the group without feeling at ease with silence yourself. It is difficult to respond to adolescents' questions about practice without some personal experience of what that practice is like for you. Furthermore, the attitudes that are the foundation of mindfulness—nonjudging, patience, beginner's mind, trust, nonstriving, acceptance, and letting go (Kabat-Zinn, 1990)—are nurtured through sustained practice.

Third, L2B teachers should have appropriate credentials to work with children and adolescents. Professionals in this category might include classroom teachers, counselors, psychologists, social workers, health professionals, and others who are appropriately certified for their positions. The rationale is that L2B is a program that requires some expertise in group work and adolescent development. Issues such as facilitating group discussion, group management, classroom or group organization, establishing a supportive environment, careful management of social-emotional issues, and understanding developmental needs and tasks represent important areas of expertise that contribute to the success of the program. Classroom teachers should be sufficiently trained to recognize when students might need more intensive support, especially with youth who have experienced trauma, and should be able to refer these students for appropriate services. Therapists might repeat certain themes or support the curriculum with other therapeutic techniques, if needed.

Fourth, those interested in presenting the program with fidelity should be mindful of how this applies to implementation. "Competence is one component of treatment *integrity* (the extent to which the approach is carried out as intended); the others being *adherence* (the extent to which the teacher applies the appropriate 'ingredients' at the appropriate time point and does not introduce intervention procedures which are not recognized as a part of the approach) and treatment *differentiation* (how the approach can be distinguished from other approaches)" (Weck, Bohn, Ginzburg, & Stangier, 2011). This means maintaining the orientation, structure, and essential messages of L2B without removing or adding elements. Although this book provides detailed lesson scripts, it is more in the spirit of mindfulness teaching that they be used as guidance rather than as a rigid narrative, provided the essence and sequence of the program is delivered faithfully. Teachers and therapists may want to stay abreast of developments in research related to teacher training in mindfulness-based programs (see for example, Crane, Kuyken, Hastings, Rothwell, & Williams, 2010).

Finally, mindfulness practice is a moment-by-moment experience. Each of us begins over and over again, in each new moment, regardless of what the moment holds. It's important to set the intention to be present, as fully as possible, and keep the intention in mind. It's equally important to be accepting of yourself, not expecting perfection but remaining curious about the process and open to the possibilities. Thus, every moment of every day in the classroom or in the therapy office is an opportunity to start wherever you happen to be and to work with whatever happens to be here.

Chapter 2

Making a Case and a Place for Mindfulness in Education

What do children and adolescents need to be successful in life? When this question arises, a common answer is "a good education." Academic success is the goal that is emphasized in standards-based movements about education reform, and it is currently in the forefront of public consciousness. The most typical benchmarks of academic success include outcomes such as test performance, progress through the educational system, and mastery of content knowledge. However, teachers and therapists who work with youth on a day-to-day basis, and who witness their progress and their struggles, know that there is more to this story. There is little doubt that in addition to academic success, we also want our youth to be happy and well.

These goals are far from being disconnected: we now realize the fundamental role that social and emotional well-being play in the attainment of academic outcomes (Elias, Wang, Weissberg, Zins, & Walberg, 2002; Goleman, 2006). Learning to channel attention to productive tasks, to sustain motivation when work becomes demanding, and to handle the frustrations of sharing, learning, and communicating with peers are skills that depend on the ability to understand and manage emotions. These are competencies that children and adolescents learn alongside more traditionally academic ones. Demands for these types of interpersonal, intrapersonal, and problem-solving skills increase as students progress through the school years.

Although the emphasis on academic achievement often captures most of the attention in debates on school reform, important inroads are being made by those who take a more holistic approach to education. Wang, Haertel, and Walberg (1993) reported that among eleven factors most important for classroom learning, social and emotional factors accounted for eight. Decades of research on empirically based social and emotional learning programs have consistently shown that well-designed and well-implemented prevention programs offer a means of reducing problem incidence while building skills for mental health, improving classroom behavior, and enhancing achievement (Durlak, Weissberg, Dymnicki, Taylor, & Schellinger, 2011; Greenberg et al., 2003; Zins, Weissberg, Wang, & Walberg, 2004).

Many prominent voices have joined together to call for inclusion of social and emotional learning within K–12 school curricula. The mission of the Collaborative for Academic, Social, and Emotional Learning (CASEL, 2003) is to promote social and emotional skill development in schools through comprehensive programming. Personal, social, and emotional learning goals are included within the framework for nationally recognized school counseling and violence-prevention programs (American School Counselor Association, 2005; Mihalic, Irwin, Fagan, Ballard, & Elliott, 2004).

Neuroscience, too, has offered evidence to support a holistic message about cognitive, social, and emotional development. Recent scientific advances have led to rejection of a cognitive versus affective framework to describe human cognition (Damasio, 1994; Siegel, 1999). Evidence shows that the prefrontal cortex, considered the center of higher-level cognition in the brain, also plays a dramatically important role in emotion processing and regulation. Thus, the operation of the brain is more like an orchestra than a number of soloists. This paradigm-shifting evidence has forced us to rethink the relationship between reason and emotion (see Davidson, 2012). Not only does academic learning depend on social and emotional skills, but also it is virtually impossible to disentangle the two. A report from the National Scientific Council on the Developing Child (2004, p. 3) put it this way:

> When feelings are not well managed, thinking can be impaired. Recent scientific advances have shown how the interrelated development of emotion and cognition relies on the emergence, maturation, and interconnection of complex neural circuits in multiple areas of the brain, including the prefrontal cortex, limbic cortex, basal forebrain, amygdala, hypothalamus, and brain stem. The circuits that are involved in the regulation of emotion are highly interactive with those that are associated with "executive functions" (such as planning, judgment, and decision making), which are intimately involved in the development of problem-solving skills during the preschool years. In terms of basic brain functioning, emotions support executive functions when they are well regulated, but interfere with attention and decision making when they are poorly controlled.

Reports of student academic performance often find their way into local newspapers in features that compare schools within and across districts. What garners less attention is the fact that schools are also charged with oversight and management of students' emotional and behavioral problems. Counselors and therapists, both inside and outside of schools, know all too well the toll that such difficulties take on young people's development. Recent large-scale epidemiological studies paint a dramatic and disturbing picture of the state of youth mental health. The landmark report in 2000 by the US Surgeon General (US Department of Health and Human Services, US Department of Education, & US Department of Justice) revealed that one in ten of our young people suffers from a mental health condition that meets diagnostic criteria, and one in five suffers from problems that significantly impair day-to-day functioning, including academic achievement and social relationships. Ten years later, the first national representative sample of over ten thousand US adolescents, the NCS-A (Merikangas, Avenevoli, Costello, Koretz, & Kessler, 2009), reveals an even starker view. Approximately half of adolescents sampled (49.5 percent) met lifetime criteria for at least one diagnosed (*DSM-IV*) mental disorder, and 40 percent of these individuals met criteria for at least one additional mental disorder. Of this affected group, about one in four or five experienced symptoms so severe as to significantly impair their functioning across the life span (Kessler et al., 2012).

Most major mental illnesses have their start in childhood and adolescence. The NCS-A study (Merikangas et al., 2009) revealed that the earliest onset occurred for anxiety disorders (age six), followed by behavior disorders (age eleven), mood disorders (age thirteen), and substance-abuse disorders (age fifteen). Anxiety disorders, highly influenced by the experience of stress, are the most common mental health issues of adolescents and adults. Regrettably, severe emotional and behavior problems are even more prevalent than the most common chronic illnesses of adolescence, asthma (approximately 5.4 percent) (Akinbami & Schoendorf, 2002) and diabetes (0.26 percent) (American Diabetes Association, 2011). The annual economic cost of mental health problems to adolescents and their families is estimated to reach a quarter of a trillion dollars, making adolescent mental health a major public health issue, and strengthening the argument for effective prevention and treatment (Merikangas et al., 2009).

But even those adolescents without major risk factors who look, from the outside, as if they are doing well may also benefit from a little help. We now know that the physiological changes of puberty usher in a host of hormonal changes that render this period of life extraordinarily sensitive to stress (see Blakemore, 2008; Casey, Getz, & Galvan, 2008). During the adolescent period, the brain is engaged in a widespread remodeling project, one that will ultimately shape its adult contours in areas related to cognition and emotion (see chapter 17, "The Adolescent Period: Challenges and Opportunities"). The fact that so many major mental illnesses that cause suffering throughout life begin in adolescence begs for greater attention to the conditions of modern adolescence, especially those conditions that pose risks to well-being. The good news is that the developing brain is malleable and responsive to experience, a phenomenon called *neuroplasticity*. Thus, the potential for reducing risk and providing beneficial experience that can positively alter the developmental trajectory is encouraging. This period might even be a time for "interventions and opportunities to reduce or reverse the adverse effects accumulated from earlier insults" (Romeo & McEwen, 2006, p. 210).

Mindfulness has the potential to be a very useful component in prevention and treatment efforts because of its effectiveness in reducing emotional distress and promoting emotional balance, improving attention, and contributing to motivated learning. Virtually all social-emotional learning (SEL) programs and many therapeutic modalities recognize that adaptive development rests on the child's maturing capacity for emotion regulation. Emotion regulation is increasingly viewed by contemporary researchers as a foundation for well-being and positive adjustment throughout the life span (Gross & Muñoz, 1995). *Emotion regulation processes* may be defined as those strategies used to moderate affective experiences in order to meet the demands of different situations or to achieve certain goals (Campos, Frankel & Camras, 2004). Such processes can include identification, differentiation, and acceptance of emotional experiences; ability to manage distress and modulate excitement; capacity to sustain motivation; prioritization among competing goals; and adaptive adjustment of behavioral responses (Cole, Michel, & Teti, 1994). Difficulties in emotion regulation are at the root of many adolescent disorders, including depression (Garber, 2006), eating disorders (Czaja, Rief, & Hilbert, 2009), deliberate self-injury (Sim, Adrian, Zeman, Cassano, & Friedrich, 2009), substance-abuse disorders (Sher & Grekin, 2007), and greater reactivity to stress (Degnan, Henderson, Fox, & Rubin, 2008).

Emotion regulation skills have their foundation within the context of a secure emotional relationship with loving caretakers (Sroufe, Egeland, Carlson, & Collins, 2005). In such relationships, both positive and negative emotions are tolerated and managed. With continued experience of predictably responsive care, children learn to tolerate longer and longer periods of discomfort, because they have had the experience of what it is like to be cared for with sensitivity. They gradually come to understand, based on this experience, that feelings will not overwhelm them and that they can care for themselves. This is the foundation of distress tolerance. As previously noted, these capacities continue to develop in the adolescent brain as greater self-regulatory skills emerge.

The ideal outcome for the individual is an affective structure that can handle both positive and negative (uncomfortable) feeling states without resorting to chronic repression or tuning out on the one hand, or chronic acting out in aggressive or self-destructive ways on the other. Emotional resilience is poised in the middle of this continuum. A central feature of emotional resilience is the ability to find a way to rebalance after the experience of discomfort or what is commonly called "stress." The ability to manage distress, from the normal day-to-day unpleasantness of not getting your own way or being bored with schoolwork to more difficult life circumstances, is built on the practice of tolerating distress without necessarily acting on it. As mentioned before, many SEL programs and therapeutic interventions are very effective in increasing adolescents' awareness of feelings and in helping them identify ways of coping. Often the information about emotions is delivered using didactic, top-down methods. Even interactive exercises might require, for example, that adolescents reflect on past experiences and plan ways of coping with future challenges.

It is suggested here that there is a difference between knowing *about* emotions and knowing your own emotions *as they are experienced*. In addition to learning about emotions, there is a distinct advantage in learning how to notice what's happening in the present moment. Attending to and identifying emotions can mitigate the emotional reaction and increase emotional balance and clarity (Silvia, 2002). This practice offers the opportunity to develop hardiness in the face of uncomfortable feelings that otherwise might provoke a response that could be harmful (for example, "acting out" by taking drugs or displaying violent behavior, or "acting in" by becoming more depressed). Learning to attend to your present-moment experience, called "mindfulness," offers adolescents a tool to manage emotions as they are perceived and potentially increase in magnitude. Mindfulness training can complement and strengthen other approaches and therapies that promote emotion regulation, reduce stress, and develop attention.

Mindfulness has been defined as a certain way of paying attention: "on purpose, in the present moment, and nonjudgmentally" (Kabat-Zinn, 1994, p. 4). Mindfulness provides a means of handling distress with intention and nonjudgment via several proposed mechanisms. First, bringing attention to the present-moment experience of thoughts, emotions, and physical sensations shifts cognitive focus away from the past (such as a memory of a troubling incident) and the future (such as apprehension of impending trouble), thereby disrupting the connections between automatic cognitive interpretations and patterns of reacting. Second, focus on present-moment internal and external experience broadens attention and allows for suspension of previously practiced patterns of reacting (avoidance or overengagement), sometimes called *decentering*. Third, the quality of nonjudgment that is essential to mindfulness permits the observation of your experience without judgment or evaluation. The practice of orienting to experience with curiosity and acceptance strengthens tolerance for distress by altering automatic response patterns described previously. When practiced regularly, mindfulness can provide a powerful tool for restoring emotional balance and preventing engagement in harmful behavior.

To understand mindfulness and its role in child and adolescent development, it is also important to consider the nature of attention and the ways in which we typically construe it. We often think of attention as a traitlike characteristic that is relatively immutable or inborn. For example, students might be described as having "short attention spans" or as "highly attentive." Or attention is viewed as so fragile and subject to distraction that it has to be "caught" by creative teachers or engaging clinicians. As noted earlier, attention is often seen as something separate from emotion, despite evidence from research and personal experience that shows how emotional states significantly affect the quality and the objects of our attention. In addressing emotion regulation through the teaching of mindfulness, attention is viewed as a skill that can be trained to observe the whole range of cognitive and emotional experiences that present themselves. It is a capacity that can be refined with practice so that it can be directed and maintained, intentionally and with greater stability, on objects of your choosing.

Mindfulness is attentiveness to the present as it is happening. This is quite a different way of using the mind from what we typically experience. Most of the time, children and adolescents use their minds to manipulate ideas or concepts, to recall information from the past or from their storehouse of knowledge, to imagine future circumstances, to plan, to calculate, or to schedule. These are just some of the important functions of mind that improve as children age and that are enhanced through schooling. But there is also a present-moment mind that is aware of unfolding thoughts, feelings, and sensations. This quality of mind allows for meta-awareness of those circumstances, plans, and calculations as they unfold. Mindfulness allows the individual to gain entrance to the workings of the mind such that, as some adolescents put it, it's possible to have "space in my mind," allowing them to see that "changing thoughts and feelings are nothing but travelers stopping by for a quick stay." This realization can be deeply empowering as students come to recognize their potential for riding the waves of experience with greater equanimity. The inner reserve of mindful awareness is available to everyone, and these faculties of mind, developed with practice, have direct relevance to burgeoning self-awareness, to self-regulation, and to the emotional balance that supports fully engaged learning and well-being.

Chapter 3

Objectives and Theoretical and Developmental Foundations of Learning to BREATHE

The Learning to BREATHE program described in this curriculum manual was created to facilitate the development of emotion-regulation and stress-management skills in late childhood and adolescence. There are two versions of the program included, potentially useful for younger (such as fifth through eighth or ninth grade) and older (such as eighth or ninth through twelfth grade) groups of adolescents. L2B is intended to help adolescents recognize the nature of emotions in order to act on them more carefully, apprehend the nature of thoughts in order to let go of the ones that are harmful to self and others, and improve awareness of physical sensations in order to foster health and well-being. Specifically, Learning to BREATHE provides adolescents with fundamental knowledge, tools, and opportunities to practice skills that cultivate present-moment attention, support emotion regulation and emotional balance, foster positive self-development, improve stress reduction, and support academic performance.

The program adapts mindfulness-based techniques in a format that is interactive and developmentally appropriate. The specific goals of the program are:

1. To provide universal, developmentally appropriate mindfulness instruction that fosters mental health and wellness

2. To enhance capacity for emotion regulation

3. To strengthen attention and support academic performance

4. To expand the repertoire of skills for stress management

5. To help students integrate mindfulness into everyday life

Theoretical Foundations of Learning to BREATHE

This program is derived from the seminal work of a number of researchers and clinicians and is deeply indebted to their conceptual and empirical contributions. First and foremost, Learning to BREATHE integrates themes of Mindfulness-Based Stress Reduction (MBSR), developed by Jon Kabat-Zinn (1990), into a program that is shorter, more accessible to students, and compatible with school curricula. However, the emphasis of L2B differs somewhat from the traditional stress-reduction orientation used with adults in MBSR. Learning to BREATHE, designed as universal prevention, is presented to students as a way to empower them as they grapple with the psychological tasks of adolescence. The major program goal, represented by the "E" at the end of the word "BREATHE," refers to "empowerment/gaining an inner edge."

Learning to BREATHE also provides a way for adolescents to develop social and emotional learning (SEL) competencies. Currently, many schools have implemented SEL requirements within their academic programs, because they have come to recognize the interconnectedness of academic, emotional, and social learning (see appendix B, "Links between L2B and Educational Laws and Standards"). Learning to BREATHE explicitly addresses two of the major domains of SEL (see CASEL, 2011):

- Self-awareness (recognizing your emotions and values as well as your strengths and limitations)

- Self-management (managing emotions and behaviors to achieve your goals)

L2B also supports other SEL competencies, like fostering empathy, relationship building, and responsible decision making.

This curriculum also rests on theoretical developments from therapies that focus on emotion-regulation skills, notably acceptance and commitment therapy (ACT) (Hayes, Strosahl, & Wilson, 1999), mindfulness-based cognitive therapy (MBCT) (Segal, Williams, & Teasdale, 2002), and dialectical behavior therapy (DBT) (Linehan, 1993). Learning to BREATHE attempts to promote the development of emotion regulation by facilitating awareness of sensations, thoughts, and emotions; by encouraging decentering from thoughts and feelings in ways that allow for simple observation and less experiential avoidance; by learning to defuse the intensity of emotions and the subsequent drive to act on them automatically; and, finally, by reducing negative rumination, which has been shown to be a risk factor for the development and maintenance of depression (Broderick & Korteland, 2004; Morrow & Nolen-Hoeksema, 1990). Finally, Learning to BREATHE reflects the important influence of affective neuroscience (Davidson, 2012; Siegel, 2007) and positive psychology (Seligman, 2002) in its emphasis on training the mind and practicing a wholesome emotional skill set.

Developmental Assumptions

In order to understand the rationale for the lessons and the manner in which they are presented, it is helpful for clinicians and teachers to understand some basic assumptions about adolescent development and learning. Over the past few decades, an enormous amount of research attention has been paid to adolescence in particular and child development overall (see Broderick and Blewitt, in press). Much of what we have learned has confirmed traditional views of adolescence, while recent findings, particularly about the brain and stress, have illuminated the inner workings of the adolescent mind in new and helpful ways (see chapters 17 and 18 for more information). Built on a strong developmental framework, Learning to BREATHE rests on the following assumptions about the adolescent period.

- Cognitive and emotional development are inextricably linked. Both kinds of development support and influence each other. Therefore, academic success, which is a primary focus of schooling, depends on the foundation of emotional wellness. While academic achievement may not be the primary goal of therapy, clinicians also recognize the bidirectional nature of emotional and cognitive functions and work to support clients' success in school.

- Adolescents are involved at a deep psychological level with constructing an identity and developing autonomy from adults. They do best in reasonable, autonomy-granting environments that support the growth of competence and enhance relationships with peers. The need for autonomy in adolescence sometimes gets expressed as resistance. Disinterest, questioning authority, and other challenging behaviors may be some of its manifestations. Understanding the developmental context for this behavior helps reduce the chances of coercive interactions that can be counterproductive. L2B instructors should build on adolescents' needs for self-management.

- Adolescents' ability to reason abstractly typically increases with age and education. In addition, adolescents' capacity for introspection ("emerging introspection") increases, and they are able to profit from learning about how their minds work. Whereas young children might not have the cognitive capacity to recognize thoughts, identify them, and note their qualities, such abilities become more possible at adolescence. Programs and interventions can capitalize on this emerging skill to help adolescents recognize patterns of helpful and unhelpful thoughts and emotions. In this way, ruminative and reactive patterns might be modified.

- Adolescence is a time when emotions can become overwhelming and confusing. Healthy emotion regulation (understanding and managing emotions) is critical for success in school and in life. The ability to understand and manage emotions can advance as children reach adolescence, yet training in this area has often been neglected, particularly in school settings. Many adolescents come to therapy for problems related to emotional dysregulation. Mindfulness programs strengthen emotional balance and support this fundamental protective factor.

- Stress is a common problem in the lives of children and adolescents today. Adolescent brain development is marked by significant structural and functional changes that make it vulnerable to permanent stress-related alterations, rendering adolescence a period of unique sensitivity to stress. The onset of many major physical and mental illnesses—like anxiety, depression, addictions, eating disorders, and so on—often occurs in adolescence. However, this period is also potentially receptive to interventions that support healthy development.

- Adolescents experience strong internal pressure for social conformity and sensitivity to social comparison. Pressure to disclose vulnerability is counterproductive, particularly in groups. However, normalizing the experience of the "worrying mind" or the experience of stress, without putting individuals on the spot to disclose specific details, can facilitate self-discovery within the peer context.

- Children and adolescents are more likely to learn new behaviors and absorb new information when they are actively participating. A practice-based program thus allows for a greater chance of generalizability to other settings and greater motivation to participate.

In recent years, a wealth of information about the various topics presented in this chapter has become available. In many ways, we now have a well-articulated theory of adolescent development, a richer understanding of the interconnectedness among academic, social, and emotional learning, and an initial scientific understanding, based on psychology and neuroscience, of the contributions of mindfulness to well-being. Because a complete review cannot be done in a book of this nature, mindfulness teachers may want to do some background reading in this extensive research and clinical literature to help support their teaching. A number of references and short chapters on stress and the adolescent period are offered at the end of the book as an introduction to some of these exciting developments.

Chapter 4

How to Use This Manual:
Teaching Learning to BREATHE

In part 2 of this curriculum manual, you will find complete descriptions of sessions for L2B. The program covers six themes that correspond to the letters of the word "BREATHE." The last letter, "E," does not stand for a separate theme or set of lessons per se, but rather for the ultimate goal of the program: Empowerment/gaining an inner Edge.

Theme	Letter	Focus
Theme 1	B	Body
Theme 2	R	Reflections (thoughts)
Theme 3	E	Emotions
Theme 4	A	Attention
Theme 5	T	Tenderness; Take it as it is
Theme 6	H	Habits for a healthy mind
Overall program goal	E	Empowerment/gaining an inner Edge

As previously noted, there are two versions of the L2B program. Each version has the same architecture and themes. Both versions cover all six themes, but one version covers them in six sessions, and the other version covers them in eighteen shorter sessions. It is also possible to adapt the program for an alternate number of sessions, depending on time. How should you choose which version to use? There is quite a bit of flexibility in the curriculum, so the decision may be made on the basis of available time and the characteristics of the adolescents. It may be that older adolescents could benefit from the six-session curriculum, and younger ones might need shorter, more frequent sessions. The choice of curriculum should not be made solely on age but should also reflect maturity level and needs of the group. It is useful to retain the thematic integrity of the program regardless of the version used, primarily because it unpacks the acronym "BREATHE." Thus, it's best not to skip session themes or change their order. Regardless of the number of sessions offered, adolescents should be encouraged to practice the skills taught in this program between sessions and to apply them to their lives.

For school-based programs with older and more mature groups of adolescents (for example, ninth or tenth through twelfth grades), six sessions of forty-five minutes each may be appropriate. A general recommendation is that no more than two L2B sessions (if using the six-session version) be held per week. This allows time for students to practice at home and at school between sessions. When class sessions are shortened due to school schedule changes, it is strongly recommended that teachers retain the mindfulness practice period that comes at the end of each session. When class sessions are extended or when it is possible to teach the program in longer blocks of time, more activities and varied periods of practice may be included. Between class sessions, short periods of mindfulness practice should be part of each school day.

For younger students (fifth through eighth or ninth grades), shorter, more frequent sessions may be preferable. The eighteen-session version essentially expands elements of the six-session version and allows for more in-class practice, reinforcement of concepts, and activities. These eighteen sessions might take approximately fifteen minutes each and may be offered once, twice, or three times per week. Nothing in these recommendations should prevent teachers from using the eighteen-session versions with older adolescents, if time allows. Teachers are the best judges of the needs of their students, and repeated practice is often the best way to learn. Clinicians, as well, should make adaptations based on the needs of clients.

This book provides ways to understand the structure and objectives of the program and the links between lessons. There are suggested ways to discuss various parts of the program and segues into other areas. These scripts are not rigid but serve as guidelines. Each session, whether it is part of the six-session or eighteen-session version of the program, has a common structure. This simple structure is provided to establish some continuity across lessons and to create a rhythm that includes content, activities, and mindfulness practice. Each session includes three elements:

1. Review/presentation of the lesson theme

2. Activities that facilitate understanding of the lesson theme

3. In-class mindfulness practice

In addition to lesson descriptions, this book is designed to provide additional resources to support teachers in parts 1 and 4. It is not uncommon for readers to skip over sections describing theoretical foundations of a curriculum to get to the actual implementation chapters, but it may be very useful to read these sections to understand the roots of the program. Each of the lesson themes is supported by scientific research, especially literature on emotion regulation, stress reduction, cognitive science, and mindfulness; and understanding the interrelationships of these fields can support effectiveness and flexibility of instruction.

In school settings, L2B has been offered as part of health, English, math, science, social skills, and music classes. It has also been offered during advisory and study-hall sessions. Thus, the choice is really up to you, the teacher, to find the best fit for the program within the school day. The objectives of L2B may be linked to objectives of existing curricula, such as health or counseling. Thus, the program could provide an opportunity to meet certain standards within an existing educational curriculum. In appendix B, examples of possible connections between L2B and performance standards are provided. It is very important to note, however, that L2B was never intended to be a one-shot opportunity to learn and practice mindfulness in a school or other setting. To be meaningful, mindfulness must be integral to the life of the organization. L2B might offer a structured way of introducing mindfulness to adolescents that can then be incorporated into daily life in creative ways.

Mindfulness, Manuals, and Working with Adolescents

Teachers and clinicians are very familiar with manualized curricula. Some of you who are reading this might appreciate their structured support, while others might be highly skeptical of a "mindfulness" curriculum. Both appreciation and skepticism are understandable. In some contexts, a high level of detail can be useful. For example, researchers need a clear understanding of what's actually being done in order to assess outcome effectiveness, so highly detailed manuals are required. Research has shown that manualized, empirically supported treatments for youth have an advantage over other forms of treatment in terms of outcome effectiveness (Weisz, Jensen-Doss, & Hawley, 2006). However, it can be difficult for some teachers and clinicians to accept this kind of program. So, it's preferable to think of this program as "manual guided" instead of "manualized." The hope is to offer a kind of trellis to support and contain the specifics of the program while providing room to breathe and respond mindfully to what is happening in the group. The first and foremost principle of mindfulness is that we show up for whatever is unfolding. With practice, you will find your own way of working with the curriculum. It is always best not to memorize any script but, rather, once you understand it, to find a way to make it authentically your own.

This attitude of openness is especially important when working with adolescents. Mindfulness is offered as an *invitation* to experience what's occurring with greater skill and clarity. It's not uncommon for adolescents to be skeptical, ambivalent, or even uncomfortable with something new. Therefore, the advance work of creating and then maintaining a safe space is critical. This means that you really mean it when you *invite* students to participate. In past implementations of L2B with certain groups of students, group members were allowed to sit in the back of the room or otherwise not participate (provided they respected others' participation) until and/or if they became comfortable. A very small number of students acted on this, but after about two or three sessions, they engaged with the group. Sometimes this advance work means getting to know the students before launching into the curriculum. Whereas classroom teachers or clinicians may already have developed relationships with group members, the potential for resistance can be higher for instructors who are new to the group. The literature on working with adolescents in groups has a venerable history, and one time-tested observation is that adolescents have "a special sensitivity to premature attempts to establish closeness" (Rosenthal, 1971, p. 361). The importance of teacher authenticity can't be overstated. It's important to be able to handle various manifestations of adolescent insecurity with some equanimity and without personalizing or coercing.

Having emphasized the importance of a nurturing and safe context, it's equally important to establish guidelines for groups. Students in schools are familiar with this, and guidelines help foster a context for learning (Weinstein, 2007). Class guidelines can be developed by adolescents themselves, who often do a marvelous job of articulating key dimensions of a safe environment like mutual respect and cooperation. Discussing and agreeing on core guidelines at the beginning of the program is an investment that is well worth the time it takes.

In teaching L2B, use a process of guided discovery. The structure of the sessions builds on progressive themes that are best suited to inductive methods that support inquiry and experiential learning. You can scaffold students' understanding by making connections explicit when appropriate; using real-time, present-moment examples; assisting students in noticing relationships; and supporting the application of ideas and practices to their lives. Most important, it is your own embodiment of mindfulness that is the best teaching resource.

The Best Setting for Learning to BREATHE

The importance of a quiet, comfortable environment cannot be overstated. An ideal environment is one that is carpeted, where lights can be lowered, and that is relatively free from distracting noise. Spaces like this are often difficult to find in schools, but sometimes a carpeted area in an auditorium, library, or empty classroom may be available. Each lesson may be delivered in the classroom if necessary, and teachers should try to make this environment as conducive to the intent of the program as possible. The aim is to create a space that supports calmness and engaged attention. It may be helpful for participants to sit in a circle on the floor or on cushions and yoga mats, or, if the session is held in a classroom, to have chairs configured in a circle. If there are no cushions available, it's best not to sit on the hard floor, as this may become an uncomfortable distraction. At a minimum, there should be space to lie down on a yoga mat or blanket for some of the mindfulness practices. Additional throws or light blankets are very useful to keep participants warm as they practice and are highly recommended. Prior preparation of materials and physical space can greatly enhance the impact of the program.

Using Learning to BREATHE Program Materials

All of the elements described below are available for download at www.newharbinger .com/27831. See back of book for more information.

The student workbooks (printed here as appendices C and D) are designed to accompany the class sessions and were an integral part of research implementations of Learning to BREATHE. They provide journal space for writing responses to in-class activities and a reference to the fundamentals of mindfulness practice. When time permits, instructors may choose to use the workbook pages for a short period of journal writing at the beginning or end of the class or therapy session. Students can write about their experiences or note questions they want answered. Sometimes youth may need reminders of what was discussed in session or in class. The workbooks contain one-page "Tips to Take Away" that recap the main points of the lessons.

As in the program versions, one student workbook corresponds to the six-session version (appendix C) and another corresponds to the eighteen-session version (appendix D). Students should have their own copies of these materials. You may wish to collate the workbook pages either by photocopy or by download; you may also contact the publisher for information about possible bulk purchase, which may be helpful for large groups. We've also provided downloadable audio files for home practice (at the URL above).

Downloadable posters for each of the letters in "BREATHE" are useful visual reminders of the lesson themes. Each poster contains one of the letters in the acronym together with its core message. The first session introduces the first and last letters "B" and "E." Over the course of the program, instructors add letters each time a new theme is introduced. Ideally, the posters should be displayed in the room so that previous messages can be reinforced.

You may wish to give group members small wallet cards at the completion of the course. A template with the acronym BREATHE and the key messages of each letter is provided for download.

Practicing Mindfulness between Sessions

The practice of mindful awareness offers a way to perceive every experience and every task of the day with full attention, interest, and compassion. Mindfulness is not something that can be learned, like a list of facts, from a teacher, book, or curriculum manual. To be authentic and useful, mindfulness practice must be tried, experienced, applied, and incorporated into your day-to-day life. Thus, every moment of every day in the classroom is an opportunity to practice being mindful. In thinking about how to bring mindfulness to your classroom or therapy session, instructors are invited to reflect on these questions: *How could I be more present to what is happening in this classroom? How might being mindful change the nature of what my students/ clients and I experience here? How might mindfulness affect the ways in which my students/clients and I communicate with each other?*

Teachers who are able to meet with adolescents between sessions might want to incorporate some small practices that support the goals of the program. One example might be to lead a short awareness-of-breath practice at the beginning of the school day or at transition times during the day. You might use the *Learning to BREATHE* audio file for a brief period of mindfulness practice with the whole class. Or, teachers or students might ring a bell or use another sound to bring attention to the present moment at various times throughout the day. Students could also be encouraged to keep a log or diary of their experiences with mindfulness practice. Students might be given five minutes to use the journal portion of their workbooks at the end of the class day or therapy session. Other reflective activities such as mindful listening, mindful walking, mindful eating, and so on can be explicitly connected to the objectives of *Learning to BREATHE*.

You might decide to keep a list of key words to reinforce words and concepts that are part of the language of this program. Gradually, adolescents will build a mindfulness vocabulary to help them understand the core messages of the curriculum and to remind them to practice. Teachers may choose to write the key words on the blackboard or post them on a bulletin board as a way of linking the course to the life of the classroom. These words and phrases may not be totally new or unfamiliar, but highlighting them provides a visual reminder of program themes.

Suggested Key Words

mindfulness	neutral
present moment	concentration
attention	sticky thoughts
sensations	"notice and let go"
five senses	emotions
inner-strength training	feelings
"inner edge"	nonjudgment
empowered	positive emotions
mindlessness	negative/uncomfortable emotions
automatic pilot	mindfulness of feelings
mindful zone	stress
mindless zone	acute stress
inattention	chronic stress
curiosity	mindful movement
interest	self-compassion
body scan	tenderness
practice	"take it as it is"
chattering mind	loving-kindness
focused attention	attention muscle
broad attention	self-care
zoom lens	"re-mind"
perception	practicing meanness
pleasant	gratitude
unpleasant	appreciation

Beginning Each Session: Opening Mindfulness Practice

Each L2B session (after the introductory session) should begin with a brief mindfulness practice period. Very often, tension builds up in the body that makes it difficult for the mind to settle and pay attention. This may be particularly true for children and adolescents. The transition from whatever has happened before in the young person's day to the mindfulness lesson may be eased by some initial movement practice. This can be as simple as standing with full awareness of the body, or it may involve something more active. The short movement practices may be done in any setting without any special equipment (see activity on page 24). These are primarily standing movements, but if space and facilities (such as carpet) permit, other, lying-down positions may be used as well. Invite students to notice the ways the body feels and the sense of space around the body as it moves. Movement practice can transition into the following opening mindfulness practice, or it can take the place of the practice.

The opening mindfulness practice may involve a short (such as one to five minutes) period of breath awareness or attention to sounds, and later alternate with short versions of other practices from the lessons. A suggested narrative for a breath-awareness practice is provided next. Notice the emphasis on relaxing the body and releasing tension at the beginning.

Let's start with a few moments of mindfulness practice. Let go of anything you might be holding. Find a comfortable position in your chair, with your feet flat on the floor, your back straight but not stiff, your shoulders relaxed, your facial muscles relaxed, and your hands resting comfortably on your thighs or in your lap.

(pause)

Now take a deep breath through your nose, and let the breath come out through your mouth so that you can hear it like a soft sigh. Try to make the out-breath slow and long. Do this two or three more times to help you relax.

(pause)

Now let your breath move into and out of your nostrils soundlessly, and just pay attention to the in-breath and the out-breath.

(pause)

There's only one thing to do right now: feel the breath move; notice the sensations of breathing.

(pause)

Pay attention to the in-breath and the out-breath until the sound of the bell.

(bell)

Another variation on the opening mindfulness practice is a short period of writing in a mindfulness journal. If group members have access to a journal or notebook, invite them to write about what they are experiencing at this moment, what stands out for them from an earlier session, or what questions are arising for them right now. Soft music might be played during journal writing, if desired. Journals are private and should not be shared with instructors or other group members.

. . . .

ACTIVITY: Mini-Mindful Movements to Begin Sessions or for Practice between Sessions

1. **Around the room.** Split the class in two; half the class comes to the front of the room, and the other half stands in the back. This may need to be adjusted depending on the size of the class.

   The object is for each of you to make one trip from your spot to the other side of the room and back mindfully, that is, in silence and without touching anything (desks, people, and so on). Movement can be fast, slowed down, normal, or a mix of each. You'll be walking slowly and silently from one side of the room to the other. Try to pay attention to your breath and your movement as you walk, not touching anybody or anything as you mindfully make your way across the room. Notice any thoughts and feelings that you experience during this practice.

2. **Holding the world.** *Stand in a stable position, feet hip-width apart and toes facing forward. Unlock your knees very slightly and take a deep, full breath. Now bring your arms into a circle in front of you, as if you were holding the world. Let your fingers come close together but without touching. Hold the posture, become aware of your breath, and mindfully notice any sensations in your shoulders and in your hands and fingers. After a short period, slowly move your hands down to your sides.*

3. **Forward bend/rag doll.** *Stand with your feet hip-width apart. Slowly and mindfully bend over at the hips and let your arms hang in front, perhaps swaying from side to side like a rag doll. Your fingers might touch the floor. Stay in this position for a brief period and notice the sensations of breathing. Come up very slowly to a standing position. Be mindful of your breath as you straighten up with intention.*

4. **Wake up your body.** *Start from a standing position. Using your right hand, make a soft fist or use the tips of your fingers to tap from the top of your left shoulder all the way down your arm and hand. Keep tapping from your left side at your waist down the left side of your leg. Now use your left hand to repeat this process on your right side. When you are done, take a few minutes to feel your body. You can also stop between left-and-right–side tapping to sense any difference between the left and right sides.*

5. **Tree in the wind.** *Stand with your feet slightly apart and your arms at your sides. Begin to rock slowly from front to back on your feet while keeping your balance. Move from side to side. Slowly move in a circle as you maintain balance; vary the speed and direction of movement as much as you want, all the while keeping a centered balance. Now, try this with your hands in the air to vary the movements.*

6. **Crescent.** *From a standing position, slowly and mindfully extend your arms toward the ceiling. Keep your arms straight overhead while slowly bending from your waist to the right. Your arms stretch to the right side, making a crescent shape. Hold this position, feeling the stretch and noticing the breath in your body. Repeat on the left side.*

7. **Step up and reach.** *Begin from a standing position and tune in to your breath. Take a step forward with your right foot as far as is comfortable. Your right knee should be directly over your right foot, and your left leg is extended behind you. Lift your left heel up and balance on the toes of your left foot. Reach your arms up overhead and look up. Hold this position and tune in to the breath. Come back to a standing posture and now step out on your left foot. Now, let's repeat this process.*

8. **Bell ringer.** *Stand and breathe to get balanced. On the in-breath, clasp your hands together above your head as if you were grasping a heavy rope, and on the out-breath, imagine pulling the rope down to the floor, slowly and mindfully. The motion involves clasping your hands above your head and bringing them down as far as you can, bending at the waist. Repeat at different speeds. Notice the muscles used in this movement. Feel the sensations in your body.*

9. **Winding the clock.** *Begin in a standing position with your feet about hip-width apart. Imagine that there is a large clock in front of you. Raise both your hands, palms facing out, as if to touch the top of the circle. Take a few in-breaths, and then on an out-breath, sweep both arms in a clockwise motion, keeping your palms extended, to wind the clock in a large circle. Bending from the waist about 90 degrees, circle upward again on the in-breath. When you get to the top of the clock, exhale and sweep back down the circle from one o'clock to six o'clock. Keep the circular motion going in a smooth, sweeping, broad movement. In-breaths and out-breaths should be steady and regular. Your hands should "touch" the clock face all the time, as if you could move the clock's hand, making a big, complete circle. After six circles, change direction and repeat.*

10. **We are the world.** Invite the students to stand in a circle facing each other. *Tune in to the breath. If you're comfortable, close your eyes and see if you can become aware of the students standing next to you on both sides. Now open your eyes and slowly raise both arms, extending them in front of you toward the middle of the circle. Hold this pose while tuning in to the breath. Take an in-breath and imagine moving the breath through your body to the tips of your fingers. On the out-breath, allow the breath to move out from your fingers into the middle of the circle.* (Repeat a few times.)

In summary, adolescents who have participated in L2B frequently state that the experience was particularly helpful for one important reason: "People always tell us not to stress out," many report, "but nobody tells us how." Yet it may not be simply a matter of telling adolescents to breathe or even leading them in breathing exercises. As the experts tell us, mindfulness is a way of being in the world. Contextualizing the practices within a program structure that makes sense may help adolescents understand the intricacies of their minds and bodies and the reasons why it's important to find inner balance. A framework and a rationale for practices (like mindfulness of breath) can support adolescents as they learn to make more autonomous decisions about how to live well. No single program is a silver bullet, but a program may contribute by providing a planned sequence of practices and discussions that help ground its message. However, even a well-designed sequence is not enough. Mindfulness needs to be embedded in a system that cultivates its practice and stands behind the intention to foster inner balance. Thus, practitioners should regard the suggestions in this chapter as ways that might be helpful in implementing a program, but they should also remember the importance of creating and cultivating a mindful context in which such a program can take root.

Part 2

Six-Session Program

Chapter 5

Theme B: Body

Key Point: **Listen!** Your body is trying to tell you something.

Essential Message of Theme B: Mindfulness is a way of paying attention, and mindlessness is inattention. Mindfulness increases calmness, balance, and inner strength, and reduces stress. We can start our practice of mindfulness by paying attention to the body.

Class Objectives:

- To introduce the program's acronym, BREATHE

- To describe what mindfulness means and how it is related to wellness and health

- To experience the way the body holds tension and to practice awareness of the breath and the body

As noted in the previous chapter, each session consists of three elements: introduction and presentation of theme, activities to develop the theme, and practice.

Introduction and Presentation of Theme B

1. Welcome the students.

2. Introduce the program.

3. Present the definition and main purpose for practicing mindfulness. Stress the concept of being "in training."

4. Discuss class guidelines.

B *This course is called Learning to BREATHE, and it's about how mindfulness can help us in our day-to-day lives. During our time together, we will be learning and practicing how to become mentally stronger and more balanced by being more mindful. We hear a lot about mindfulness in the media, on TV, in some exercise programs, and so forth.*

What have you heard about mindfulness?

Wait for students to give some examples.

Sometimes the meanings can be confusing. One way to think about mindfulness is as a way to calm our minds so that we can be relaxed, refreshed, and more attentive. It is also a way of building our inner strength and being more balanced.

In each class, we will be discussing one aspect of building personal strength through learning and practicing ways to handle the good things and the bad things that happen to us in life. In sports, a person develops physical strength. In mindfulness practice, a person develops inner strength. So this program is like "inner-strength training." We'll be paying attention to the inside and the outside. We will be practicing mindfulness together every time we meet, and I encourage you to practice on your own whenever you wish.

Each letter of the word "BREATHE" represents a lesson in our program, and each time we meet, we'll add another letter to spell out the word "BREATHE." Each letter will add another piece to our understanding of what mindfulness means and how it can help us. So right now, we'll start by putting up the last letter "E." The last "E" stands for the goal of the program, which is to help us be empowered and gain an inner edge.

Put the "E" poster on the blackboard or in an appropriate place in the room. The posters reinforce the main message of each lesson and help students integrate the overall themes in the form of the acronym "BREATHE." If possible, the letters can be kept on the wall in between sessions as a visual reminder.

Sometimes when we are asked to do something new or unusual, we may feel awkward or a little uncomfortable.

Sometimes we have reactions that make us want to act silly or laugh. It's okay if you feel these things. See if you can just notice these feelings without acting on them and distracting others. It's important for you to try to participate fully in order to gain the benefits of the program. If at some time, you do not wish to practice some of the mindfulness exercises, remember to respect your classmates who might want to participate, by remaining still and quiet.

If you are the classroom teacher or a clinician with an existing relationship with group members, there may be less need for warm-up activities or establishing class guidelines.

However, when you are new to the class, there should be ample time to establish connection with the students and to allow student participation in establishing class guidelines before beginning the curriculum. You may choose to remind the class about guidelines from time to time as needed.

Activities to Develop Theme B

1. Introduce mindful listening practice.

2. Distinguish mindfulness and mindlessness (automatic pilot).

3. Note the particular quality of mindful attention: nonjudgment. Nonjudgment means attending with curiosity and openness.

4. Illustrate automatic pilot using the "My Mindful/Mindless Life" activity (see the student workbook).

5. Experiment with other ways of being mindful: eating and sensing.

6. Another activity, the "Mindful Walkabout," is described in this section but may be used at any point in the program. It is an outdoor activity that blends mindful walking, mindful observation, art, and poetry.

Let's begin by learning a little about what mindfulness is and how it might be helpful in our lives.

ACTIVITY: Mindful Listening

MATERIALS: Bell or chime, paper, and pencil (optional)

This mindfulness practice involves paying attention to sounds and can be used as a first experience of mindfulness. Begin by inviting adolescents to sit comfortably and close their eyes for a few minutes without any specific instruction.

Let's begin by learning a little about what mindfulness is and how it might be helpful to us. Start by finding a comfortable sitting position. Feel free to close your eyes if that's comfortable for you. If not, then just let your gaze soften and rest on the floor in front of you. Just remain seated like this until I ring the bell.

Allow a short period of silence. Ring the bell after about two minutes.

Invite group members to open their eyes and share any sounds they heard during the first listening period. Group members can write them down if they wish.

Now let's do this again, but this time, pay very close attention to all the sounds that come and go. Notice sounds close to you and sounds farther away. Notice how they appear and then disappear.

Ring the bell after about two minutes of silence.

Invite group members to open their eyes and share any sounds they heard during the second listening period. Make a list if desired.

What did you notice? How was the first listening period different from the second?

This was a practice exercise in mindfulness. Mindfulness means paying attention—on purpose—to what is happening in the present moment. It also has a special quality of not judging the experience. An attitude of openness and interest in present-moment experience is fundamental to mindfulness.

You may refer to Jon Kabat-Zinn's definition of mindfulness: "Mindfulness is paying attention in a particular way: on purpose, in the present moment, and nonjudgmentally."

Is this how we usually pay attention in our day-to-day lives? How is it different? Did you notice any tendency to like certain sounds or dislike certain sounds? Can you give some examples? Notice how we "judge" our experiences automatically.

Experiencing something "without judgment" involves perceiving it with curiosity and openness, and without preconceptions. This way of experiencing, rooted in these fundamental attitudes, can be cultivated intentionally. We all have well-established preferences and preconceptions that we use to help us make sense of the world. These can often be helpful, but they also serve as blinders that restrict the fullness of experience.

So just as we missed a number of sounds the first time we sat quietly, we often do things without awareness, or mindlessly. It's as if we're on automatic pilot. Let's try to identify the things we do mindlessly and the things we do mindfully.

• •

Point out how the quality of attention is different when attention is focused on the present moment. Tie in the concept of "automatic pilot." This refers to the idea of acting mechanically and without real awareness. So much time in our lives is spent mindlessly (without mindfulness). You can use an activity in the student handbook called "My Mindful/Mindless

Life" to help adolescents reflect on the idea of automatic pilot. Students may work alone, or in dyads or small groups to identify things they do mindfully and mindlessly. Class discussion could focus on the benefits and drawbacks of acting mindfully and mindlessly. You might suggest that group members practice being curious about their experiences and start paying attention to what they might be missing in their experiences. The following mindful-eating activity is a good way to support this exploration. See Jon Kabat-Zinn (1990) for more background.

One of the disadvantages of mindlessness is that we miss a lot of what's going on in our lives. Let's practice to see how it feels to eat mindfully.

. . . .

ACTIVITY: Eating Mindfully

MATERIALS: Raisins, napkins or small paper plates, bell (optional)

Jon Kabat-Zinn (1990) introduced this awareness activity in his groundbreaking book, *Full Catastrophe Living.* The "raisin exercise" is a simple eating practice that illustrates how mindfulness involves doing something ordinary with great awareness. Students are given three raisins to eat as directed. Directions are given slowly, with pauses in between. Some teachers may prefer to vary the food item and use other types of fruit, candies, and so on, or even a bag of various items with different tastes. Make sure that students are not allergic to the sample foods provided. The point is to fully experience the richness of eating using all the senses.

Sit comfortably in your chair, and I will come around the room and pass out a few objects to each of you.

I'd like you to focus on one of the objects as if you've never seen it before. Imagine that you've arrived here from another planet and the object is completely new.

Now take the object in your hand and turn it around.

Become aware of what you see: the shape, texture, color, size, temperature, hardness or softness.

And if you notice that you're thinking something—perhaps thoughts like Why are we doing this? *and* This is pretty silly—*just notice them as thoughts and let them go. Bring your attention back to the object.*

Now, being aware of the movement of your arm, bring the object to your nose and smell it.

Place the object in your mouth, without chewing or swallowing. Become aware of all the sensations you are experiencing.

Then when you're ready, consciously take a bite and notice the taste. Notice the texture. Notice the rest of your mouth and the sensations there.

Now slowly and consciously chew the object and, when you're ready, allow yourself to swallow.

Students may choose to eat the other raisins mindfully. Or they may choose not to do so. Note the process of making this choice.

Ring the bell or chime to end the activity.

Now, discuss the activity.

What were some things that you noticed as you looked at the raisin? Some smells? Some textures? Some colors? Some tastes? Some movements?

Add other dimensions if desired.

What was it like to hold the raisin in your mouth without chewing it?

Is this the way we normally eat?

Where was your attention during the activity? What happened when it wandered?

Can you think of some ways to eat more mindfully?

. . . .

You may choose to use another type of mindfulness practice that does not involve eating, or use the raisin exercise in combination with mindful sensing. The "Sense Doors" activity is described next.

. . . .

ACTIVITY: Sense Doors

We experience the world through the senses in the present moment. In place of or in addition to the raisin activity, the "sense doors" activity can be used to practice sensory awareness of various objects. Collect a variety of objects that have different features (color, shape, sound, smell, weight, texture, and so on). Put them all in a large plastic bag or a box, pass them around the room, and allow group members to select an object. Try to do this in silence so that participants can pay attention to their selection process.

Once everyone has an object, adapt the raisin activity script to explore the sensory characteristics of the objects: brightness, dullness, pungency, roughness, smoothness, heaviness, lightness, sharpness, coolness, warmth, sweetness, and so on. If they wish, group members can call out the characteristics or make lists of as many sensory characteristics as they notice. They can also discuss any awareness of the selection process that they remember. Some possible objects can include pieces of fabric, bells, stones, small toys, jars of spices, glitter balls, keys, tape, sandpaper, elastic, pieces of wood or metal, fragrant oils, and so on.

Sit comfortably in your chair, and I will come around the room with a box of objects.

I'd like you to choose something from the box. Notice what it feels like to make your choice. Pretend that your object is something that you've never seen before. Imagine that you've arrived here from another planet and the object is completely new.

Now take the object in your hand and turn it around.

Become aware of what you see (read items slowly): *shape, smoothness, roughness, color, size, temperature, hardness, softness, weight, smell, sound.*

And if you notice that you're thinking something—perhaps thoughts like Why are we doing this? *or* This is pretty silly—*just notice them as thoughts and let them go. Bring your attention back to the object.*

Turn the object around in your hand.

Notice its features from every angle.

Be curious about this object.

Turn your whole attention to it.

Ring the bell or chime to end the activity.

Afterward, discuss the activity.

What were some things that you noticed as you looked at the object? (Review the previous dimensions and ask for examples.)

Is this the way we normally experience things?

Where was your attention during the activity? What happened when it wandered?

What did you notice about this object that you've never noticed before?

Another component may be added to the activity that involves mindful observation of form and function. This was developed by Richard Brown of Naropa University and is reproduced here with permission.

B Second-Generation Names

Observe the object and create a new "name" for it based on its features (shape, size, color, and so on) and function. The new name should include both. So, a pencil becomes a "skinny yellow letter maker," or a watch is a "time-telling silver wristband."

· ·

ACTIVITY: Mindful Walkabout

This activity can be used at any point in the six- or eighteen-session version of the program when an outdoor exercise is appropriate. The objective is to observe something in nature closely and mindfully and share it with the group through art or poetry. This activity works best when an outdoor park or natural area is available, although it could also be done in other settings.

Provide each group member with a pad of paper and a pencil. Invite them to take a mindful walk around the area and notice the natural world. When they come to something of interest, perhaps something that they have never noticed before, instruct them to stop and observe mindfully (notice shape, color, texture, movement, context, size, and so on). Encourage them to observe with appreciation and interest. Ask them to use the paper and pencil to draw a "map" of the walk and a sketch of the objects of mindful observation. The entire activity might take ten to fifteen minutes, or longer if desired. No particular expertise in art is required. Ring a bell to return to the group setting.

After the walkabout, observers might share their experiences with the whole group. This could include describing the map of the particular path. You may also invite group members to complete a couplet (two-lined poem) based on their experience of mindful observation. Choose one opening line for the whole group, or assign different ones to each member. It's helpful to print out the first line on a piece of paper and allow group members to write the second line of about seven to nine syllables. Members can then read their couplets aloud individually or chorally, adding their lines to create a whole-group poem.

Some possible opening lines include:

Happy for the chance to stop and look

_____

Still for a while, I pause and look

_____

Holding in my steady gaze

_____

What have I seen on my journey?

_____

What is more beautiful than this?

_____

Walking the path, I see what's hidden

_____

Here's an example from a complete couplet:

> *Holding in my steady gaze*
> *A cloud drifting all day through the sky*

. . . .

Moving to Practice

1. Emphasize that we're learning to pay attention in a particular way.

2. Start by paying attention to the body. (Add the "B" poster to the wall, leaving space for the letters that will come between the "B" and the last "E.")

3. Introduce basic awareness of breath and move to the "Body Scan" (later in this section).

4. Introduce real-life mindfulness. (See the list of possibilities in the student workbook, for example, "Mindfulness in My Life" in the workbook.)

This program will enhance mindfulness skills to balance the ways that we practice being mindless. Practicing paying attention in an open and interested way is the first step. We can start our training in mindfulness by paying attention to the body. Sometimes, as we shall see, our minds are stuck in the future or in the past, but the body is always in the present. Much of the time we don't pay very much attention to our bodies. Sometimes we pay too much attention to one aspect of the body, but neglect the whole. So we begin our mindful awareness training by focusing on the body as a whole.

B

Place the letter "B" on the wall in the appropriate place.

Let's start by paying some attention to our breath. Sometimes we breathe from the chest. Put your hands on your upper chest, right near the top of the rib cage, and breathe in and out from there.

After a short period, ask what this experience was like:

What did you notice about this type of breathing?

This is often called "shallow breathing" and is associated with anxious states. Shallow breathing can result in reduced oxygen intake and can make you feel fatigued.

Now place your hands on your belly and breathe from there. Notice the movement as the breath comes in and leaves the belly.

After a short period, ask what this experience was like:

What did you notice about this type of breathing? How was it different?

Belly breathing feels more relaxing. The body can be trained to breathe in a healthier way.

Now let's try a complete breath. Put one hand on your chest and the other on your belly, and allow the breath to move in from your nostrils, fill your lungs, and expand your belly. Then exhale through your nostrils. Notice how the whole body was involved. This is the kind of breathing we'll be practicing in the "Body Scan."

PRACTICE: Body Scan

MATERIALS: Mats and/or blankets for lying on the floor, throws for warmth

Take time to prepare the group members for this mindfulness practice. You might demonstrate positions for sitting or lying down. The "Body Scan" is easiest to do while lying down, if possible. If this is not possible for space reasons, a seated position is fine. When lying down, adolescents should have mats (for carpeted floors) or both mats and blankets (for hard floors). Something to cover up with for warmth is helpful. Allow for space between each member to limit distractions. Try to set a relaxed, contemplative mood by considering the choice of room (lighting, noise, and so on) and logistics. Adolescents may feel comfortable in a circle during discussion but may feel self-conscious during practice.

Using a soft bell or chime to signal silence is very helpful. If possible beforehand, remind the students to dress comfortably for the classes. Light blankets or throws are very useful to keep warm during practice and are highly recommended.

Allow the group to move into the lying or seated position for the "Body Scan" practice. Lead students in this guided body-scan practice slowly and reflectively. Allow time for silent periods between instructions. This scan is a complete body scan, moving from the feet to the head area. If time is limited, instructors may limit the focus to a few areas (such as feet, lower back, shoulders, and head) or use the version of this practice from the eighteen-session program.

This "Body Scan" is designed to help you relax and pay attention to how your body feels and what it might be telling you.

It's a time to listen to your body and to be in your body as fully as possible.

> **If students will be lying down:** *So now, lie on your back on the mat or blanket, with your feet about hip-width apart and falling away from one another, and your arms at your sides.*

> **If students will be seated:** *Sit with your back straight but not stiff, with both feet on the floor, and your hands comfortably in your lap.*

Close your eyes if that's comfortable for you.

Listen to and follow my instructions as best you can. Try to stay awake and alert.

Remember to breathe completely and let the breath flow freely into and out of the body.

When you notice your mind wandering, as it will, gently bring it back to focus on the instructions.

Now become aware of your belly rising as the breath moves into your body and falling as the breath moves out of your body,

…not controlling the breath in any way, just letting it find its own rhythm,

…feeling your body sink deeper into the mat or your chair on each out-breath.

(pause)

And now on the next in-breath, direct your attention all the way down through your body to the soles of both feet,

…becoming aware of your toes, the arches of your feet, the place where the heels meet the floor,

…noticing any feelings in your feet, any warmth or coolness, pressure, tingling, or tightness.

B

And now, direct your breath to your feet, imagining that you can breathe right into your feet: first into your right foot and now breathing into your left foot,

…and on each out-breath, letting go of any tiredness, any tension, right from the soles of both feet.

(pause)

Now gathering up your attention, moving it away from the feet, and focusing your attention on your legs,

…notice any feelings in your legs, being aware of the skin, the bones, the muscles,

…perhaps the pulsation of circulation,

…perhaps warmth or coolness.

Now, notice the contact your legs make with the mat or the chair, allowing your attention to explore any feelings in this part of your body.

And on the next in-breath, use your attention to direct your breath all the way down your entire left leg, and next, breathe down your entire right leg.

Now, direct the breath down both legs, breathing in relaxation and breathing out any tiredness, any tension.

Remember that whenever you find your mind wandering, just let go of the thoughts as gently as you can, and come back to focus your attention once again on your body.

(pause)

So now move your full attention to your lower back,

…just observing any feelings in this part of the body,

…perhaps tightness,

…perhaps tingling,

…aching,

…any feelings at all.

And allow your attention to move slowly up your back,

…all the way up your spine

…so that you are aware of each vertebra,

…aware of the muscles,

...aware of the skin of your back,

...aware of your contact with the chair or the mat.

And on the next breath, breathing into the whole back area,

...allow the muscles to ease and release with each breath,

...letting go of any tiredness or fatigue,

...and breathing openness and relaxation into the entire back.

(pause)

Moving your attention now to the belly,

...feel the movement of the abdomen as it rises and falls with each breath,

...and take a deep breath in,

...allowing the abdomen to really expand on the in-breath,

...and then release, breathing out, and noticing the feeling of the abdomen deflating.

(pause)

Moving your attention up to the chest area, be aware of the heart, the lungs,

...aware of the movement of the chest,

...perhaps aware of the heart beating.

Breathe into the chest and abdomen, breathing in new energy and letting go of any tiredness or tension.

(pause)

Now gathering your attention again and focusing it on both arms and hands, let your attention come to rest on the fingertips of both hands,

...aware of sensations of tingling and air touching the fingertips,

...possibly feeling moisture or dryness;

...aware of the sides of the fingers,

...the knuckles,

...the palms of the hands,

...the tops of the hands.

(pause)

Now move your attention up your arms, allowing it to settle on your shoulders.

Notice the muscles here, really exploring any sensations in the shoulders:

...perhaps burning,

...tightness,

...tension,

...heaviness,

...or lightness.

Just breathe deeply into the shoulders, releasing any concerns and allowing your shoulders to completely soften.

(pause)

Next draw your attention to your head area. Notice any feelings at the top of your head,

...your forehead,

...your eyes,

...your nose,

...your cheeks and mouth,

...your jaw,

...your neck.

As best you can, notice any and all feelings in this area of your face and head.

Then, letting the next breath fill this entire region of your body,

...breathe in new energy and relaxation;

...breathe out any tightness,

...any tension,

...any fatigue.

(pause)

Now opening up your awareness,

…see if you can feel your breath moving easily through your whole body as you lie here,

…noticing the movement of the breath from your head to your feet.

Notice how the breath moves freely and easily from your feet to the top of your head.

(pause)

As we conclude this practice, be fully aware of your body as a whole:

…complete, strong, at ease.

(bell)

Allow group members to share some of their experiences with the "Body Scan" if time permits, and provide them information about how to access an audio file of the "Body Scan" for home practice (see audio downloads at www.newharbinger.com/27831). Adolescents often fall asleep during this practice, which is a good time to point out the benefits of nonjudgment. It's the experience that is important, whatever that may be, not any particular achievement. You may point out that this is an example of the body trying to tell us something: that we are fatigued and need to care for ourselves.

. . . .

At the conclusion of the first session, note that mindfulness can be practiced in every moment of the day. So invite group members to use the examples in the workbook (for example, "Mindfulness in My Life") to choose one activity as their personal opportunity to practice mindfulness outside of the session. You might choose to copy the activities on slips of paper and allow group members to select their practices randomly out of a hat.

Another way to encourage mindfulness practice outside of sessions is to use "Mindful Dots" (included with permission of Diane Reibel, Jefferson University): Give each participant three simple stickers (for example, simple dots) and ask them to put each of the stickers someplace where they will see them frequently, such as on a computer screen, locker door, notebook cover, and so forth. Each time they notice the sticker, ask them to take a mindful breath.

B

Invitation to Home Practice

1. Practice mindful breathing for at least three breaths at a time, three times per day. Use "Mindful Dots."

2.. Practice the "Body Scan" with the audio file (see audio downloads at www.newharbinger. com/27831). (Instructors may choose the number of times to suggest this depending on the sequence of sessions.)

3.. Try the "Three-Minute Body Scan," described in the student workbook, each day in school or in some other setting.

4. Practice your own special activity (from "Mindfulness in My Life") mindfully. Write about it in your workbook (see "My Home Practice: Theme B").

Chapter 6

Theme R: Reflections

Key Point: **Thoughts (reflections) are just thoughts.**

Essential Message of Theme R:

The mind constantly chatters. We can work with the chattering mind by paying attention to thoughts and watching them come and go. We don't need to believe everything we think.

Class Objectives:

- To understand the way the mind typically chatters (inner self-talk)

- To comprehend the interrelationships between thoughts and feelings

- To investigate the effects of mind chatter on attention and performance

- To work with thoughts by observing them and letting them go

Review of Previous Theme and Introduction of Theme R

1. Use the "Opening Mindfulness Practice" (see chapter 4).

2. Review theme B if time allows (mindfulness, nonjudgment, awareness of body, and so on).

3. Add the letter "R" to "B" and the final "E."

4. Reinforce the intention to do "inner-strength training," and call attention to "inner chatter."

5. Introduce the importance of understanding thought (mental activity) and the way our minds work.

Lead the "Opening Mindfulness Practice" (see chapter 4).

Recall that mindfulness is a special way of paying attention. It's paying attention, on purpose, to whatever is happening right now, without judging it or immediately needing to change anything. We've practiced mindfulness by paying attention to sounds, to sensory experiences, and to what our bodies were telling us.

Today we're going to practice mindful awareness of our thoughts.

Did you notice any thoughts in your mind during the brief period of silence at the beginning of the class? What was that like? Were there a lot of thoughts? A few? Were they the same thought? Can you describe the experience?

Wait for responses and pause between questions. Students should not be asked or expected to disclose any specifics about their thoughts unless they choose to do so.

Our brains are amazing. They help us think, solve problems, plan ahead, remember information, communicate with others, feel certain things, and do what we want to do. Most of the time, our brains are generating thoughts. Usually we're not aware of the brain's constant chatter, but we can become more aware. This lesson is about learning to pay attention to thoughts in a mindful way, and we'll discuss how this can be helpful to developing inner balance.

Activities to Develop Theme R

1. Use "The Big Event" activity to explore how thoughts are related to feelings and behavior.

2. Observe thoughts, and notice their variety and universality.

3. Notice the tendency to evaluate thoughts as pleasant, unpleasant, or neutral.

4. Use "My Mind Is a Cast of Characters" to illustrate the relationships among thoughts, feelings, and performance.

5. Note the difficulty of trying to deal with unwanted thoughts by suppressing them.

The following is a standard CBT activity.

To help us understand a little more about the nature of our thoughts, let's begin by listening to a short story called "The Big Event."

....

ACTIVITY: The Big Event

MATERIALS: Student workbook, and pencils or pens

Please open your workbooks to the page that says "Big Event Circles" so that it's ready for you to write down your thoughts. In a moment, I'm going to ask you to close your eyes and listen carefully as I read you a story. I want you to imagine yourself as the character in the scene I will describe. As best you can, try to notice what thoughts and feelings are occurring for you.

Imagine that your school is sponsoring a big social event. It could be a dance, a party, or something like that. Lots of people your age will be there from many different schools. You asked some friends to go with you, but they had something else to do and didn't want to change their plans to go with you. You feel excited about going and a little nervous because you are going alone. When you get there, you enter the hall and see someone you know across the room. You look at the person you know, and you wave to get that person's attention. The person sees you but turns and walks away.

Now open your eyes and write down all of your thoughts and feelings about the story in the circles at the top of the page.

Discuss adolescents' responses:

What were some thoughts you wrote in the circle? What were some feelings? Are they pleasant, unpleasant, or neutral?

Now I'm going to read the story again, and I want you to close your eyes and imagine yourself in the story. When I've finished, please write your thoughts and feelings in the second set of circles.

Imagine that your school is sponsoring a big social event. It could be a dance, a party, or something like that. Lots of people your age will be there from many different schools. You asked some friends to go with you, but they had something else to do and didn't want to change their plans to go with you. You feel excited about going and a little nervous because you are going alone. When you get there, you enter the hall and see someone you know across the way. You look at the person you know, and you wave to get that person's attention. This person sees you but turns and walks away. Now you notice that your friend is not wearing his or her glasses.

Now open your eyes and write down all of your thoughts and feelings about the story in the circles in the lower part of the page.

What were some thoughts you wrote in the circle? What were some feelings? Were they pleasant, unpleasant, or neutral? What were the differences between the first and the second sets of examples? Why were they different?

R Discuss responses. Compare and contrast the two, and identify the thoughts and feelings as pleasant, unpleasant, or neutral. Note the impact of thoughts on feelings. Point out that everyone has different perceptions of pleasant, unpleasant, and neutral. The stories we tell ourselves change the way we continue to think about things and the way we feel.

· ·

As suggested in an earlier chapter, instructors may wish to do some background reading in the extensive research and clinical literature about the interrelatedness of thoughts, feelings, and behaviors. A core element from this body of work is that our perceptions or interpretations (thoughts) of events cause the emotional reactions we experience. In and of themselves, events lack emotional content, whereas cognitive interpretations are highly significant for eliciting emotional responses. For background, see the work of Aaron Beck (1979), David Burns (1999), and Albert Ellis and Robert Harper (1975) in the references.

Our brains come with some built-in features, like the way they help us make sense of things. So often, we get ourselves stressed out about things in our lives because our minds create stories about people and events.

These stories or thoughts get connected to feelings. Sometimes our thoughts and feelings are pleasant, unpleasant, or neutral. Sometimes our minds replay these stories over and over and keep us thinking about the events for a long time, even after the actual event is over.

Students may wish to share examples of this from their own experiences. You, as the teacher, may also choose to provide an appropriate example.

Understanding that this is the way the mind typically works can be helpful in learning how to manage our "mental storytelling" when it happens. Sometimes we have lots of thoughts or stories going on in the mind all at the same time. Since paying attention to one thing precludes paying attention to something else, what we choose to pay attention to is important. Let's see how this works.

ACTIVITY: My Mind Is a Cast of Characters

MATERIALS: Name tags, index cards, and a math worksheet or something similar

This is an activity used to demonstrate inner speech (chattering mind). Ask for one student volunteer (number 1) to sit in the front or middle of the class. Ask for several other student volunteers to be that student's "thoughts." After student volunteer 1 is seated in the center, have the other students stand in a circle around the seated student.

Let's try an exercise that shows how the mind's chatter can affect us.

This student, _____ (name), is a stand-in for all of us. I am going to ask her/him to do something in a minute. The other students (use their names) *stand in for her/his "thoughts." I'm going to give each of them a name tag and a "thought" to read.*

Give each of the other volunteers a name tag with the name of a role (parent, teacher, friend, self) and an index card with an appropriate message written on it. See suggested messages for the various roles belows.

Put the name tag on each student. Using name tags on a cord that can be placed around the student's neck makes this easy. Allow each actor to read the message quietly before the activity begins.

Now I am going to give _____ (name of the seated student) a math worksheet to do. While she/he is filling out the worksheet, all the "thoughts" need to walk around her/him in a circle and keep repeating the sentence on your index card. You don't need to yell or walk too close to the student in the middle. Just remember that you are the thoughts in her/his head.

The first "thought" reads the message aloud and begins circling the seated volunteer as that person works on the math sheet. One by one, each "thought" enters the circle. Students in the "roles" walk in a circle around the working student and repeat their scripted message over and over. If teachers use more than four volunteers and space permits, make the circles concentric. This may be done for three to four minutes while the student volunteer works on the problems. At the end, all roles might speak their "thoughts" at the same time.

After the demonstration, discuss the following questions with the actors and with the whole class:

How did this experience affect your concentration?

Were the messages (thoughts) helpful or unhelpful? Pleasant, unpleasant, or neutral?

How did listening to this affect your mood?

How difficult was it to stay focused?

What other kinds of messages or thoughts did you find in your mind at times?

R Suggested Roles and Messages

Teachers may develop additional roles if they wish.

Parent 1: "Did you do your homework?"

Parent 2: "Hurry up and finish, or you'll be late."

Teacher 1: "This test is worth 40 percent of your grade."

Teacher 2: "This material will be on your final exam."

Friend 1: "Why are you always studying so much?"

Friend 2: "Did you hear what she said about you today?"

Self 1: "I'm no good at math. I'm afraid I'm not doing well."

Self 2: "I hate math. It's so boring."

For a variation, include some positive thoughts like *This is easy because I'm good at math.*

• •

Call attention to several elements demonstrated in the activity: the repetitive nature and automaticity of self-talk, the positive and negative tone of self-statements, the impact of mind chatter on attention and concentration, and the universality of this "wandering mind" experience. Some discussion from personal experience may be useful.

Potential questions include *Have you ever been lost in thought? Have you ever been unable to sleep or study for a test because your mind was racing?*

Sometimes we have thoughts that bother us over and over again. They're a little like Velcro: they seem to stick in our minds, and we have trouble getting rid of them.

Demonstrating these "sticky thoughts" using a toy ball that sticks to a Velcro board can be useful.

Sometimes we try to stop them. What happens when you try to do this?

Is there a way we can stop our thinking?

How helpful has this been for you in your experience?

If time permits, teachers may use the "White Polar Bear" activity in chapter 12 to illustrate the ineffectiveness of thought suppression.

A set of famous experiments in the 1980s demonstrated that attempts to suppress thoughts (for example, *Don't think of a white polar bear*) actually had a paradoxical rebound effect. Deliberately trying to suppress unwanted thoughts resulted in more unwanted thoughts than would have occurred if thoughts were not suppressed at the outset. Subsequent studies have generally supported this finding. For background, see the work of Wegner (1989) in the references.

Moving to Practice

1. Emphasize that mindfulness of thoughts is like mindfulness of the body.

2. Paying attention "without judgment" involves noticing or observing thoughts without giving them too much attention unless we choose to do so.

3. Note that we can watch thoughts and let them go gently, instead of grabbing on to them or suppressing them.

4. Practice mindfulness of thoughts.

The essential message for the theme is: We all experience the wandering, chattering mind. You are not the only one! The stories we tell ourselves can change the way we think and feel. However, you can pay attention to your thoughts and get better at knowing where your mind is going. You can disengage and learn to become an observer of your thoughts. This is often difficult to do in the beginning, so practice is important.

Instructors should not expect adolescents to reveal the content of their thoughts or the reasons for their feelings. The lesson is not to engage group members in self-disclosure but to illustrate the processes by which thoughts and emotions affect us all. You may use a prop (for example, a snow globe) to illustrate that thoughts can settle and the mind can become clear if we are patient and focused.

If we want to experience balance and inner strength, we need to be aware of the nature of our thoughts and what our mind stories are. We can try to stop our thinking, but that's not really possible or helpful. We can become mindful of the thoughts that circle around in our heads and just observe them, like clouds that pass by in the sky or like water that flows in front of us as we stand behind a waterfall. We can also use the image of thoughts circling around, as was done in the class activity just now. Remember that thoughts are just thoughts. We don't have to believe everything we think.

PRACTICE: Mindfulness of Thoughts

Take some time to prepare the group for this practice. Allow for some stretching or other movement before sitting if the group is restless. Then, invite members to find a comfortable sitting position, with some room between each participant. Instruct them to put down anything they are holding. Lead them in a few deep breaths, breathing through the nose and letting the breath come out through the mouth like a soft sigh. Make the out-breath slow and long. Repeat this process two or three times to help everyone relax. Then allow students to close their eyes if they feel comfortable with that. If not, suggest that they allow their gaze to fall softly on the ground in front of them.

Now, we're going to spend the next part of the class doing a short practice to cultivate present-moment attention.

We'll be paying attention to our breath as we did in the "Body Scan." We'll also be practicing noticing and letting go of thoughts as we repeatedly bring our attention back to the breath.

Remember not to be too hard on yourself if your attention wanders. Remember that the practice simply involves paying attention to the breath. Cultivating your attention will take practice.

When you find that your attention has wandered from the breath, gently but firmly escort it back to the breath, no matter how often this happens.

We are practicing steadiness and balance.

(pause)

So put down anything you might be holding, including any thoughts, worries, plans, or images that are in your mind right now,

…and sit back in your chair

…with your head, back, and neck straight but not too stiff,

…with your shoulders relaxed and your hands comfortably placed in your lap,

…gently closing your eyes when you feel ready.

(pause)

Now become aware of the breath moving into and out of your body.

Just notice it, wherever you can feel it in your body:

…perhaps the sensations of breath moving past the nostrils,

…perhaps the rising and falling of your chest,

…perhaps the feeling of your belly expanding gently on each in-breath and deflating on each out-breath.

(pause)

Just feel the breath as it comes in and as it goes out, without trying to control it in any way,

…just letting the breath be as it is,

…trying to maintain awareness of the full breath from the beginning of the in-breath to the end of the out-breath,

…being fully present and aware of each new breath.

(pause)

As you sit here watching your breath,

…you may find yourself thinking about something you did or something you need to do,

…something that happened to you,

…or something that is going to happen.

These are the kinds of thoughts that occur spontaneously in our minds all the time.

(pause)

See if you can notice when a thought arises in the space of your mind.

Just becoming aware that you are thinking,

(pause)

…notice the thought without trying to push it away.

Just let it go gently on its own,

…and then direct your attention back to the breath.

Focus your attention on the sensations in your abdomen or at the nostrils or the chest,

…just paying attention to the actual sensations of breathing.

(pause)

R *Your mind is like a revolving door,*

…with thoughts moving in and thoughts moving out while you just sit observing them as they come and go,

…bringing your attention back to the breath.

(pause)

As you sit here feeling your breath and observing the thoughts that arise in your mind, you may make a very soft mental note about what you notice;

…as you notice a thought, inwardly say to yourself,

Just thinking,

Just remembering,

Just planning.

(pause)

And then, without giving the thought any more attention, let it go and come back to the sensations of the breath,

…reminding yourself that for this period of time, your intention is to be fully present, fully awake,

…simply watching the breath as it enters and leaves the body,

…staying awake and alert in each moment until the sound of the bell.

(bell)

At the end of the lesson, remind adolescents about the workbook page ("Dealing with Troubling Thoughts") to help them with their day-to-day practice.

Invitation to Home Practice

1. *Practice mindful breathing for at least three breaths at a time, three times per day.*

2. *Practice a short period of mindfulness of thoughts (once a day, ideally; see audio downloads at www.newharbinger.com/27831).*

3. *Log your practice in the student workbook ("My Home Practice: Theme R").*

4. *Continue practicing mindfulness in your day-to-day life, especially in your personal area of practice (see theme B, "Mindfulness in My Life").*

R

Chapter 7

Theme E: Emotions

Key Point: **Surf the waves of your emotions.**

Essential Message of Theme E:

Emotions are like energy surges. We can handle them by paying attention to them and watching them come and go.

Class Objectives:

- To understand the role our feelings play in our sense of wellness, balance, and inner strength

- To understand and experience the rising and fading away of emotions

- To learn to work with emotions mindfully

Review of Previous Themes and Introduction of Theme E

1. Begin with the "Opening Mindfulness Practice" (see chapter 4).

2. Review previous themes: B and R.

3. Add the letter "E" to "B," "R," and the final "E."

4. Reinforce the intention to shift out of automatic pilot by paying attention to the inside and the outside.

5. Emphasize that understanding and working with emotions (especially strong, uncomfortable emotions) is critical to inner strength and balance; this complements awareness of thoughts and physical sensations.

So far we have been learning how to be mindful of what we experience in our bodies and in our thoughts. This means bringing attention to what is happening right now. To the best of our ability right now, we try to notice what's happening without judging it or immediately needing to change anything. The ability to look at our experiences mindfully can help us shift out of automatic pilot. We gain a little bit of space between our thoughts and actions. We learn to "take a breath" so that we're more relaxed and clear about what we want to do or say. We become better able to let go of thoughts that distract us and affect our work.

Students may wish to ask questions or share experiences of practicing mindfulness. Some connections may be made from previous lessons.

In this program, we're learning to pay attention to the inside and the outside. Today we'll pay particular attention to feelings or emotions on the inside. Often, the words "feelings" and "emotions" are used to mean the same thing, so that's how we'll be using them here.

Activities to Develop Theme E

1. Use "The Lineup" to demonstrate that emotions are a part of everyone's experience and are necessary for survival. Some discussion of helpful and unhelpful emotions might be included.

2. Experience emotions in the body and their connectedness to thoughts and sensations using "Emotion in Three Acts."

3. Note that emotions we often call "positive" and "negative" can be called "pleasant," "unpleasant," or "neutral."

4. People try to seek out pleasant feelings and avoid unpleasant ones. Discuss the impossibility of avoiding unpleasant feelings using "The Great Cover-Up."

5. Experience a way of working mindfully with uncomfortable feelings using "Surfing the Waves."

We all have emotions, even though we might not talk about them. They're part of being human, and they help us communicate with others and adapt to circumstances. For example, smiles communicate happiness to others. Feeling afraid can be a very useful emotion to feel if it helps us escape from a dangerous situation.

Open the discussion by asking for some examples of emotions and what they communicate. You might address how other nonverbal behaviors (such as gestures or body movements) also communicate feelings. If time permits, demonstrate the universal nature of emotions using "The Lineup."

. . . .

ACTIVITY: The Lineup

MATERIALS: None, but some open floor space is necessary. A rope or tape measure is optional.

The purpose of this activity is to normalize the experience of emotions. As students approach adolescence, they often feel as if their emotional experiences are unique to them. This can result in feelings of isolation and unwillingness to recognize and admit feelings.

Students line up in single file (side to side) across the length of a room with enough space to take steps forward. The teacher points out an "imaginary" line about eight inches in front of the line of students, spanning the whole group. If a tape measure or rope is available, you could lay it down in front of the group to mark the line.

Let's do a little experiment to explore our emotions. I'm going to ask several questions, and if the answer is yes for you, then step over the line. If the answer is no, then just stay where you are.

Have you ever felt happy? (Students take a step ahead, over the line. The line is moved ahead.) *Have you ever felt angry?*

Continue with other emotions from the list:

> adventurous, afraid, alert, amazed, amused, annoyed, anxious, appreciative, apprehensive, ashamed, astonished, compassionate, concerned, confident, contemptuous, content, curious, disgraced, disrespected, downhearted, eager, embarrassed, encouraged, excited, fearful, flirtatious, giggly, glad, grateful, guilty, hopeful, humiliated, interested, irritated, joyful, lonely, loving, nervous, optimistic, peaceful, proud, resentful, sad, scared, scornful, self-assured, self-conscious, serene, shy, silly, stressed, surprised, sympathetic, tense, trusting, unhappy, worked up, worried.

Use other feelings if desired.

At various times, invite students to look around and see how many other people have felt the same thing.

What do you notice about the experience of emotions?

Discuss the fact that feeling a range of emotions is a universal experience:

Emotions can be perceived as pleasant, unpleasant, or neutral. Can you give some examples? Does everyone feel the same way about all the emotions?

. . . .

Emotional experiences can be pleasant for some people and distressing for others. For example, anxious feelings can be perceived as a thrill or a threat.

We feel our emotional experience in the body and the mind, even though we might not be aware of it. If we want to be more balanced, we can try to cultivate mindfulness of feelings as well as awareness of thoughts and body sensations. So far, we've been practicing becoming aware of our breath, our bodies, and our thoughts. Let's add the experience of emotions to that list. We'll explore the variety of emotions that exist, how we communicate them, and how we experience them.

. . . .

ACTIVITY: Emotion in Three Acts

MATERIALS: None, except some open floor space, bell (optional)

This activity has three parts, or "acts," so instructors may adjust the activity for their groups according to available time. The parts provide a gradual experience of connecting emotions to their felt sense in the body and to thoughts.

Act 1

First, divide the group into two or three smaller groups depending on size and floor space. Ask the members to line up along two or three walls in the room. Remove as much furniture as possible to create open space for each group member to walk from the starting wall to the opposite wall, and then back to the original spot.

When I ring the bell, I'd like for each of you to make your way slowly, mindfully, and in silence from where you're standing now to the opposite wall, and then turn around and come back to the spot where you began. As you walk across the room, try to be aware of your body's movements, your thoughts, and your feelings. Be aware of the people and the space around you. Try not to bump into anyone else, and do not make eye contact during this exercise.

Ring the bell.

Once the groups have returned to their starting points, discuss the activity, allowing volunteers to share experiences.

What did you notice in your body? In your thoughts? What feelings were you aware of? What was is like to do this in silence? What was it like to do this without making eye contact?

Act 2

Repeat the activity in silence but, this time, with eye contact. Remind the group members to try to be aware of their bodies, thoughts, and feelings as they move around.

When I ring the bell, I'd like for you, once again, to make your way slowly, mindfully, and in silence from your spot to the opposite wall, and then turn around and come back to where you began. As you walk across the room, try to be aware of your body's movements, your thoughts, and your feelings. Be aware of the people and the space around you, but this time you are invited to make eye contact with people around you.

Ring the bell.

Once the groups have returned to their starting points, discuss the activity with the whole group, allowing volunteers to share experiences.

What did you notice in your body? In your thoughts? What feelings were you aware of? What was is like to do this with eye contact? What differences did you notice in your body, thoughts, and feelings this time, compared to the last time?

Act 3

This part ("Emotion Charade") may be done on its own, if time is limited. Group members are asked to choose an emotion (perhaps one they became aware of during the previous acts) and to demonstrate it through facial expression and body movement. Invite adolescents to mill around the room in silence, looking for others who are also demonstrating the same feeling. Once they find a person or group with the same emotions, they should stand together until you ring the bell to begin the discussion. An alternative way to prime this activity is to use the list of emotion faces in the eighteen-session version of the student workbook as a way for students to choose a feeling.

We have had some practice with feeling the emotions in our bodies and noticing the thoughts that arise with the emotion. Let's see if we can explore the range of emotions and the ways they are communicated in this part of the activity. Each of us will choose an emotion and demonstrate it using some movement or facial expression, or both. When I ring the bell, walk around the room in silence while continuing to act out the feeling. Try to find someone with the same feeling. When you think you've found someone or a group of people showing the same feeling, stand next to them. As you do this activity, pay attention to the way the emotion feels in your body.

Ring a bell after all of the members are standing in dyads or groups. Some may be alone because they have not found an emotion partner. Teachers should allow a short period of time for students to check in with their groups about their emotional assessments to see if they were correct in their selection. Then, go around the room and invite dyads or groups to report:

What was the emotion you were expressing?

How did it feel in your body?

Did you notice any thoughts that arose as you demonstrated the feeling?

How could you tell that others were feeling the same thing?

If you were the only one expressing a certain emotion, what was your experience like? Did not finding a partner change your experience?

Was the emotion you chose to demonstrate pleasant, unpleasant, or neutral? Describe this experience.

You may also offer an optional activity, "How Does It Feel?" from the eighteen-session version of the program, chapter 13.

· ·

Sometimes we think of emotions as positive and negative. (Ask students for examples.)

This distinction depends on the circumstances. Sometimes feelings of anger can make you feel strong and empowered to take action or to stand up for yourself. But we also recognize that we can be "bullied" by certain emotions or we can "bully" others as well. Feeling angry a lot can make us more irritable with others and result in hurting our friends. Emotions of sadness, jealousy, and anxiety can make us isolate ourselves from others.

Instead of using the terms "positive" and "negative" to describe different emotions, some have suggested using "destructive" emotions (Goleman, 2003). The primary objection to the use of "negative" is its implication that some emotions are bad and should be avoided. This is an impossibility, for we obviously feel what we feel. A large body of research documents the pitfalls of trying to avoid distress or discomfort (often called *experiential avoidance*). Opportunities to become more skilled at handling uncomfortable emotions are essentially reduced through avoidance patterns. Ultimately, it's not which emotions we feel, but what we do with emotions that matters. The work of Daniel Goleman (2003); Steven Hayes, Kirk Strosahl, and Kelly Wilson (1999); and Marsha Linehan (1993) in the references provides useful background material on emotions.

Remember that we all have all these feelings to deal with as humans. Instead of thinking about emotions as positive or negative, we can think about them as pleasant, unpleasant, or neutral.

It's not that the emotions are bad in themselves; it's how we handle them that matters. When people experience uncomfortable or unpleasant feelings, they often call it "stress" or "distress." When we experience these feelings, we often want to get rid of them right away. We want our stress to go away. Sometimes we're not very successful at this, and some feelings are hard to get rid of. If they go on for a long period of time, we can call them "moods." Sometimes we feel stuck in bad or irritable moods. We might want to get rid of the bad mood, but we often can't figure out how.

What are some ways that people deal with uncomfortable emotions or bad moods?

Perhaps elaborate by asking for student responses that describe the human tendency to avoid or cover up uncomfortable feelings. You can demonstrate this point by using "The Great Cover-Up" activity.

. . . .

ACTIVITY: The Great Cover-Up

MATERIALS: Paper or index cards, and pencils or pens. This activity can be done with the whole group or in small groups of two to four.

The objective of this activity is to illustrate how people tend to avoid unpleasant or uncomfortable feelings. Avoiding can take many forms, so this activity invites students to consider the behaviors people use to block out or avoid distress. Begin the discussion by identifying some uncomfortable or unpleasant feelings. Note that these feelings can be given the generic name "distress" and that they can stress us out.

1. Invite each group to come up with a typical situation that produces distress or stress (such as a problem with friends, teachers, or parents; the inability to do something well; dissatisfaction with appearance; too much pressure; unrealistic expectations; and so on).

2. Once each group agrees on a good hypothetical situation, the members should identify the underlying uncomfortable feelings (such as anger, fear, worry, sadness, rejection, resentment, shame, loneliness, boredom, restlessness, and so on). Select one or two of the main uncomfortable feelings and print them on large index cards. Put the cards face up in the middle of a circle. If possible, try to select feelings that are not similar (for example, anger and worry, rather than worry and anxiety).

3. Now ask students to use the rest of the paper or index cards to list ways that people avoid or try to cover up the uncomfortable feelings that occur in the hypothetical situation. These cover-ups should be specific behaviors. Write one "cover-up" per page.

   For example, students might choose "problems with schoolwork" as a situation that provokes distress or stress. Uncomfortable feelings related to this situation might be anxiety, fear, worry, frustration, boredom, shame, guilt, anger, and so on. The common "cover-ups" might be sleeping, watching TV, playing video games, spending time online, drinking, going out with friends, procrastinating, taking drugs (illegal and prescription medications, like performance-enhancing drugs), daydreaming, blaming teachers, complaining, and so on.

4. Each group reports on its "problem situation," and the related uncomfortable feelings and cover-ups. The index cards with the cover-ups can be put on top of the problem cards in the center, *covering them up*. If appropriate for certain groups, students can role-play the problem and the cover-ups.

Discuss:

Does the cover-up work? Why or why not?

Is there a cost attached to the cover-up?

What are the problems that can arise from covering up these feelings?

Negative or uncomfortable feelings seem to come automatically. They can be triggered by outside events, but they can also arise from our thoughts (as we discussed in the last session). Just thinking the thought can bring to life a feeling that wasn't there before.

. . . .

Sometimes we get really good at avoiding things that are unpleasant. But you can miss out on a lot too. You miss out on the opportunity to become stronger and more empowered. You miss out on practicing strength for the times when the uncomfortable situations surprise you. We can work with feelings with the same kind of mindful attention we brought to the body and to thoughts. Paying attention "without judgment" involves noticing emotions without giving them too much attention unless we choose to do so. We can practice kindness to ourselves by letting go of judgments about what we're feeling, like not being good enough or feeling upset about something.

When we become aware of a feeling, we can notice it, locate it in the body, and let it go gently. We can observe that we don't need to act on it right away or cover it up.

Emotions are like energy surges in the body. We can watch the energy rise and fall. We can learn to surf the waves of our emotions while keeping our balance.

The following ideas and examples may be useful to supplement the message of this lesson:

Feelings are just feelings. What does it feel like when you say to yourself It's just worrying *rather than* Stop worrying, *or* That's just some anger *instead of* I shouldn't feel angry? *With practice, we can sit still and become aware of when our feelings start and when they fade away, like waves. We can just let them do their thing. Just by noticing, we take away some of the power of bad moods to overwhelm us.*

. . . .

ACTIVITY: Surfing the Waves

MATERIALS: None (optional bell or chime)

Invite members to take a position for mindfulness practice. This could be sitting on chairs or cushions with the head, neck, and back straight but not too stiff, and with the feet on the floor. Remind group members that at any time they wish, they can find a comfortable place in the body to which they can return their attention (like using the breath as an anchor).

The goal of this activity is to help adolescents experience feelings in the body and mind, watch the feelings rise and fall, and ultimately help them understand that they can just observe the energy of their feelings without acting on them. They have a safe space (like the breath at the belly or the soles of the feet) that they can return to, if needed.

Ask adolescents to observe their reactions and to practice not reacting to (not covering up) mild discomfort. The activity is short and may be followed by discussion and a pleasant-feeling (gratitude) practice (introduced toward the end of this activity).

The "unpleasant" experience in this activity is that of the boredom, restlessness, or mild frustration involved in sitting still. The choice of restlessness and boredom may be most appropriate for settings like classrooms. Dealing with restlessness and boredom is related to sustaining focus in the classroom, following up on boring tasks, or being attentive when you prefer to do something else. The example of mild frustration that can be present when something (like an assignment) is difficult to do or when it's not possible to do something you want to do immediately (like responding to a text message) might also be used.

During the subsequent discussion of the experience, instructors can make the connection between the experience of mild discomfort and stronger emotions that can be handled mindfully. The mindful way of dealing with uncomfortable feelings is applicable to many unpleasant feelings, including anger, sadness, jealousy, or pain and physical discomfort. This important point might be brought out in discussion. Point out that you can work with the full range of uncomfortable feelings in the same mindful way, with curiosity and openness. An example of how to work mindfully with stronger emotions like anger or sadness is included in the student workbook ("Tips to Take Away"), and the parallels might be discussed during the lesson. Keep in mind that discussion should center on the experience of emotion as a shifting energy rather than on details specific to past situations. It's the generic experience of emotion that's important, not individuals' specific stories about feelings.

The directions clearly invite adolescents to notice a mildly uncomfortable feeling and the discomfort of boredom or restlessness that is common. Instructors and clinicians should be aware that in certain situations (for example, when a student is clearly depressed, when working with traumatized individuals, when a crisis has occurred in the adolescent's family or in the school, and so on), some adolescents might bring to mind more distressing memories and feelings. Good clinical judgment is needed in these cases. It may be useful to shorten the activity, replace it with a pleasant-feeling (gratitude) practice (introduced toward the end of this activity), or simply discuss the points of the lesson.

If we want to experience balance and inner strength, we need to be aware of our emotions. We can try to stop or hide our emotions, but that's not really effective. We can become mindful of emotions as they arise and pass away. We can notice how they shift and change in our bodies. We can think of emotions as ever-changing waves that we can learn to surf, or as energies in the body that well up and then disappear. Through it all, we can remain balanced and centered. Noticing emotions and learning how to manage them effectively is a skill that can be developed with practice. This skill can help us to act more effectively in order to accomplish our goals in life. We learn to recognize the thoughts and emotions that work against our best interests, practice kindness toward ourselves by gently letting them go, and cultivate skill in surfing the waves.

As we begin this activity, find a comfortable position, sitting in your chair or on a cushion. Your back should be straight but not too rigid, your feet making contact with the floor, your hands resting in your lap, and your eyes closed if that's comfortable for you.

Let's take a few full breaths. (Include the relaxing deep breaths from the "Opening Mindfulness Practice" in chapter 4, if desired.)

Allow your mind to get as quiet as possible.

Let your attention come to rest on the breath.

When you notice that your mind has wandered, just bring your attention back to the breath.

As you do this activity, try to notice what's happening inside you. Notice your thoughts, your feelings, and any sensations that you experience in your body. We'll be sitting for a brief period in silence.

Pause for two to three full minutes. The point here is to have enough silent sitting to allow the presence of some discomfort in the form of boredom or restlessness in the mind or body. You should use your judgment about the best timing.

As you sit quietly for this period of time, just notice if any feelings of discomfort arise.

Perhaps there is some restlessness in the body and mind as you sit in silence.

(pause)

Can you pay attention to the restlessness?

Where is it in your body?

(pause)

What does the experience of restlessness feel like for you?

Is it loud and intense, or soft and gentle?

Is it moving around or in one place?

(longer pause)

Perhaps there is some boredom that you notice.

Pay attention to the boredom.

Where is the feeling in your body?

(pause)

Is it loud and intense, or soft and gentle?

Is it moving around or in one place?

Does it change as you pay attention to it?

(longer pause)

Let the feelings of restlessness or boredom be like waves coming and going.

Don't try to block them or get rid of them.

Don't try to hold on to them or keep them.

See if you can approach them with curiosity.

(pause)

Notice that you don't need to act on them. They are just a kind of energy in the body and the mind that you can be curious about.

(longer pause)

Just focus on the breath. See if you can ride the waves of the restlessness or boredom, and notice whether they change.

Say to yourself inwardly, "I can feel these feelings without covering them up."

(bell)

You may choose to discuss this activity before moving into the gratitude practice. If so, allow time for members to describe their experiences. Focus on the experience of thoughts, emotions, and feelings in the body. Make a list on the blackboard.

What was the experience like for you? What did you notice in your body, thoughts, and feelings?

What might it be like to surf the waves of more-difficult feelings?

A second part of this practice invites group members to experience a different emotion: gratitude. The practice of gratitude is a way to cultivate wholesome emotions. Invite group members to notice any changes in body, thoughts, and feelings. Remind them that they can cultivate helpful emotions through this practice at any time.

Pleasant Feeling (Gratitude) Practice

Next let's practice noticing a different kind of feeling.

Once again, use your breath to calm yourself as you simply observe your feelings, thoughts, and sensations.

(longer pause)

So, to the best of your ability right now, bring to mind something in your life that you are very grateful for, something that comes to mind for you to complete this sentence:

"I am really lucky to have _____ in my life."

It may be somebody you love, something you love to do, a pet that makes you happy, something in nature, or anything at all.

"I am really grateful to have _____."

(pause)

Bring the image of this person or thing to mind as vividly as you can.

Hold it in your mind's eye right before you.

(pause)

See if you can notice the feeling of gratefulness.

Notice where it is in your body; perhaps you can sense some warmth in the area around your heart, perhaps a sense of lightness.

(pause)

Just stay with this memory of gratefulness, and really observe your experience.

Notice whether it is pleasant, unpleasant, or neutral.

(pause)

Allow the sense of gratefulness to get bigger and bigger, if you can, and feel it expanding in your body.

(pause)

Now, as I read some statements, experience each one as if it were written for you (read the statements about fifteen seconds apart):

I feel grateful for the good things in my life.

I'm pleased that many people have been good to me.

I feel peaceful, confident, and balanced.

(pause)

Notice that emotions, both pleasant and unpleasant, are like energy surges. You can witness them in your body.

We can learn to be strong and balanced as we simply observe their coming and going, without reacting to them and without judging ourselves.

(pause)

Let's conclude with a few mindful breaths.

(bell)

. . . .

Moving to Practice

1. Review the idea that feelings come and go like energy surges.

2. Practice mindfulness of feelings by observing the energy of feelings (noticing them and then letting them go).

3. For this E lesson, the previous activities might be used as practice if time is limited. The following mindfulness practice provides additional practice in mindful awareness of thoughts and feelings. Lead this guided mindfulness practice slowly and reflectively. Allow time for silent periods between the instructions.

. . . .

PRACTICE: Mindfulness of Feelings

MATERIALS: None except a bell or chime (optional)

Now, we're going to spend the next part of the class doing a short mindfulness practice to cultivate present-moment attention. We'll be paying attention to our breath as we did in the "Body Scan."

We'll also be practicing noticing and letting go of thoughts and feelings as we repeatedly bring our attention back to the breath.

Remember that cultivating your attention will take practice. When you find that your attention has wandered from the breath, gently but firmly escort it back to the breath, no matter how often this happens.

We are practicing steadiness and balance.

So putting down anything you might be holding—including any thoughts, worries, plans, or images that are in your mind right now—sit back in your chair with your head, back, and neck straight but not too stiff,

…with your shoulders relaxed and your hands comfortably placed in your lap,

…gently closing your eyes when you feel ready.

(pause)

Now becoming aware of the breath moving into and out of your body,

…just notice it wherever you can feel it in your body:

perhaps the sensations of breath moving past your nostrils,

…perhaps the rising and falling of your chest,

…perhaps the feeling of your belly expanding gently on each in-breath and deflating on each out-breath;

…just feeling the breath as it comes in and as it goes out,

…without trying to control the breath in any way,

…just letting the breath be as it is.

(pause)

Try to maintain awareness of the full breath from the beginning of the in-breath to the end of the out-breath,

…and if your mind wanders, as it will, just bring your attention back to your nostrils or your belly,

…being fully present and aware of each new breath.

(pause)

As you sit here watching your breath, you may notice thoughts coming into your mind.

You may also notice feelings arising.

See if you can notice when a feeling arises, perhaps a feeling related to an earlier activity.

See if you can notice the feeling in some part of your body,

…perhaps your stomach, your chest, your shoulders, your throat. Wherever it is, just be aware of it.

(longer pause)

Watch how it arises, is present for a while, and then passes away.

Be aware of how the feelings shift and change as you pay attention to them in your body.

(longer pause)

You might think of feelings as surges of energy in your body,

…sometimes soft and quiet,

…sometimes strong and intense,

…sometimes sharp and fast,

…sometimes slow.

Just see if you can observe all of these energies without getting too caught up in them.

As best you can right now, try not to react to or judge any of your thoughts or feelings, but just observe whatever comes into the space of your mind.

(longer pause)

Just sit here watching the show as thoughts and feelings arise, are present for a while, and then fade away.

Feelings coming and going,

…feelings arising and passing away like clouds in the sky, moving across the field of your awareness,

…just observe what arises, and come back to the breath,

…staying open and awake in the present moment until the sound of the bell.

(bell)

Encourage adolescents to review the workbook page "Tips to Take Away: Working with Anger" as a way to help them to practice mindfulness when difficult feelings arise.

Invitation to Home Practice

1. *Practice mindful breathing for at least three breaths at a time, three times per day.*

2. *Do a short mindfulness practice on feelings (once a day, ideally; see audio downloads at www .newharbinger.com/27831).*

3. *Begin to notice thoughts, feelings, and physical sensations as they arise throughout the day.*

4. *Practice being kind to yourself when uncomfortable feelings arise. Don't try to push them away. Just notice them and where they show up as sensations in your body.*

5. *Continue practicing mindfulness in your day-to-day life, especially in the practice of your choice (from theme B, "Mindfulness in My Life"). Write about your practice on the "My Home Practice: Theme E" page of the workbook).*

Chapter 8

Theme A: Attention

Key Point: **Attention to body, thoughts, and feelings is good stress reduction.**

Essential Message of Theme A:

Stress comes from external and internal events. Paying attention to how the body feels, what we think, and what emotions we experience prevents the buildup of problems that can harm the mind and body.

Class Objectives:

- To understand key concepts about stress and the body's stress response

- To integrate knowledge about thoughts, feelings, and sensations with the understanding of stress processes

- To bring mindful awareness to the stressors in our lives

- To practice mindful movement

Review of Previous Themes and Introduction of Theme A

1. Begin with the "Opening Mindfulness Practice" (see chapter 4).

2. Review previous themes: B, R, and E.

3. Add the letter "A" to "BRE" and the final "E."

4. Introduce the idea that balance depends on mindfulness of what's happening inside and outside of us. Note that distress or stress can be minimized through mindfulness.

Inner strength is the foundation of personal wellness and power. We need to be mindful of what our bodies are telling us and the nature of thoughts and feelings. To the extent that we can become aware of these events as they are occurring, we can maintain greater balance, make more conscious decisions about how to respond, and take more control of our stressors because we can see some of them coming.

Wellness depends on awareness of the internal and external landscape. That is, we need to pay attention to the outside and the inside.

To begin, we'll take a look at what stress is and how it affects us. Then we'll consider how mindfulness can help us reduce stress and become more balanced.

Activities to Develop Theme A

A

1. Explain that the experience of stress or distress depends on perceptions of your situation. Examine the stressors in the life of the hypothetical student in the "Case Study."

2. Discuss key points about stress, such as its definition, acute and chronic stress, allostatic load, and so on. Use the "Case Study" and "Memo from the Body-Mind" (in the workbook), if desired.

3. Note the universality of stress or distress, as in previous lessons. Use the "Cross the Line (Stressors)" activity, if desired.

4. Examine and discuss the effects of chronic stress on physical and mental systems. Useful activities include "How Much Can You Handle?" and figures in the student workbook: "What's the Best Balance?" and "What's My Limit?"

5. If appropriate, this material may be used as the basis for a more academic project on the physiology of stress, the brain, and so on (see "Memo from the Body-Mind" in workbook).

In this lesson, we'll be spending some time talking about stress and its relationship to the body and the mind. Let's start by considering the stressors in the life of a hypothetical student named Dan.

ACTIVITY: Case Study

MATERIALS: Paper, and pencils or pens

Read the case study aloud while the students write down as many stressors as they can identify. Alternatively, the case study can be copied for students to read as they work in teams to identify stressors. The gender, name, and circumstances of the character in the case study can be changed at your discretion.

Discussion may include issues of chronic stress, awareness of chronic stress, and ways of coping.

I'm going to read you a case study of a student about your age. As I read the description, jot down as many stressors as you can detect that are in this person's life. After I finish reading, I'll give you a few minutes to compare your list to that of your partner. Then we'll share the list of stressors with the whole class.

> *Dan attends South Valley High School. He is the second-oldest child in his family and has one older sister and younger twin brothers. His parents got divorced two years ago, and his mother remarried last year. He and his brothers live with their mother and stepfather in a suburb near the high school. One of his twin brothers was born with a serious illness that makes him unable to do a lot of things for himself. He needs regular medical attention, and his mother is highly involved with his care.*
>
> *Dan was always a good student who got mostly A's and B's when he was younger. In middle school, his grades started to slip. He took an interest in playing video games with his friends and often stayed up late playing games on the computer in his bedroom. From his point of view, homework was a lot more boring than playing video games, so he put it off until the last minute. Often he'd rush out of the house without breakfast to catch the bus after oversleeping, a pattern that has persisted into high school. Sometimes, he tried to do his homework on the bus, but his friends teased him, and he just put it away.*
>
> *Dan's father moved far away after the divorce and is unable to have regular contact with Dan and his siblings. Dan's stepfather, on the other hand, has tried to crack down on Dan's poor school performance. He has insisted that Dan get a "real" job to teach him responsibility, instead of wasting hours on the computer. Dan works about eighteen hours a week in a restaurant near his home. The other kids who work there are older than Dan. They encourage him to party with them after work. This usually includes drinking, and he is experiencing a lot of pressure to use drugs.*
>
> *Meanwhile, Dan is failing a few subjects and is still in trouble at home. His stepfather thinks Dan should have a career plan in place and that he should be working toward it. Dan has no idea what he wants to do when he graduates. Some of the kids at his school*

seem to have a much better idea about their future plans. This fact makes Dan feel even more upset than he usually does. When he starts to think about this or when his stepfather nags him, he typically plays video games or resorts to drinking to get a break from the stress. He feels that his teachers don't understand or take into account all the hours he's working in the restaurant and that they are unreasonable in their demands.

Dan has had a girlfriend for the last six months. He has been able to talk to her about what's going on in his life, but recently he's been a little worried about their relationship. A friend of Dan's mentioned to him that he noticed her picture posted online showing her with another boy at a party. Now Dan is worried that she might leave him, but he doesn't think he can discuss this with her.

Have the group split into smaller groups and discuss the following questions:

What are the stressors in Dan's life?

Which ones are chronic? Which ones can be changed, and which ones are harder to change?

How might other people view the stressors in Dan's life?

Would everyone perceive the same things as stressful?

Are differences in perception coming up in your group discussion?

What support does Dan have to help him?

How is Dan coping with his stressors?

What suggestions would you make to him?

Using the "Case Study" as a springboard, introduce some basic concepts about stress, such as types of stress (acute versus chronic), the nature of various stressors, individual differences in perception of what is stressful, the body's stress response, the effects of chronic stress on the body-mind, stress and illness, and so on. "A Primer on Stress" (chapter 18) provides instructors with some background. Although this level of detail is not intended to be part of the student lesson per se, you may choose to use whatever material helps to explain basic concepts. The references might also be helpful to teachers who want more background in this area.

It's really important and even surprising to realize that our bodies' stress response is triggered by exposure to actual external events (like problems with friends) and internal events (like thoughts). The very same physiological changes are activated in response to external and internal stressors, because the body doesn't recognize the difference between "real" events and "mental" events.

Sometimes we feel that we're the only ones who have a lot of stressors in our lives. Let's see if that's accurate.

. . . .

ACTIVITY: Cross the Line (Stressors)

MATERIALS: Rope or tape (optional), the results of a previous poll

An alternative to the "Case Study" (or one additional activity) is based on the "The Lineup" exercise described in theme E (chapter 7).

This activity is best done with some advance preparation from the instructor, so it may be part of a previous lesson.

At some point prior to this theme (A), give students a sheet of paper with numbers from 1 to 10. Ask them to write down their list of stressors (things that stress them out in their lives) in no particular order. Lists should be anonymous. Collect the list and tally the items so that the most frequently mentioned stressors become the prompts for the second part of this activity.

Using the method employed in theme E (chapter 7), put a line on the floor using string or a tape measure. Explain to the students that the object of the exercise is to step over the line if they have ever experienced the stress. Students are told that the list of stressors comes from the class. Choose to read aloud the stressors that are common to at least three or four people in the group so that no one feels singled out.

Cross the line if you've ever felt stressed about _____.

Encourage the students to notice that many people feel the same things. This reduces the sense of isolation and normalizes the experience of stress.

It's clear that we all experience stress. We're not alone in this, because it's part of being human. Therefore, it's important to learn ways to be kind to ourselves and others so that we don't add to the problem. Remember from lesson E that covering things up is not the most helpful way to deal with unpleasant experiences or stress. Practicing mindfulness of our experiences can help us be more at ease and balanced.

An alternative way of doing this is to use the adolescents' lists to create a tally of the top five or ten stressors in the whole group. Ask the group to guess what stressors are on the list before providing the results.

. . . .

Let's take another look at some reasons for Dan's stress. It may not be the particular things that are going on in his life. Maybe it's something else.

. . . .

ACTIVITY: How Much Can You Handle?

MATERIALS: tennis balls (one for each volunteer)

This activity illustrates how difficult it is to do many things at the same time. As a metaphor for chronic stress, teachers may use this activity to demonstrate what happens if a person's resources are drained. Ask for a volunteer or have a small group of volunteers do this activity. Ask the volunteers to come to the front on the room and stand facing the class.

I will ask you to start this activity by giving you one thing to handle; then I will add another and another, and so on. See how long you can keep all the activities going at the same time.

A

1. *Tap your right foot; keep it going.*

2. (Throw a tennis ball to each volunteer.) *Using your left hand, keep throwing the ball up in the air and catching it as you tap your right foot.*

3. *Start bending to the front and to the back, as you tap your right foot and throw the ball in the air with your left hand. Keep everything going.*

4. *Swing your right arm in circles next to you. Keep bending to the front and to the back, as you tap your right foot and throw the ball in the air with your left hand. Keep everything going.*

5. *Now begin to count backward from one hundred by twos as you swing your right arm in circles next to you, bend to the front and to the back, tap your right foot, and throw the ball in the air with your left hand. Keep everything going.*

Discuss:

What was that experience like for you, volunteers?

What did you observers notice about the volunteers as they did this?

How might this exercise apply to the stress in your life?

What happens when too many things pile up or when they go on for a long time? How might this apply to the character in the case study?

. . . .

Supplementary Materials in the Student Workbook

The figures in the workbook can be used here to facilitate discussion about the effects of stress on schoolwork, athletics, performance, mood, and so on. "What's the Best Balance?" (in the six-session workbook) is a graphic demonstration of the mental capacity that mindfulness cultivates: *relaxed and alert attention*. Physiological arousal is related to performance as a function of task difficulty. This relationship, defined by the Yerkes-Dodson law, indicates that performance on easy (boring) tasks is improved when there is a higher level of physiological arousal, whereas performance on challenging tasks is impaired when arousal (stress or anxiety) is high. Relaxed, alert attention is correlated with peak performance in athletics and other areas.

In the student workbook, "What's My Limit?" illustrates the body's "normal" response to short-term stress, and the "Long-Term Chronic Stress" page shows the problematic effects of unchecked chronic stress. Although our bodies and minds are well designed to cope with emergencies, they need to return to a nonstressed state after an emergency in order to maintain a healthy condition. Too many ongoing stressors (chronic stress) lead to a breakdown in the overall system that can have serious repercussions on the health and wellness of mind and body. Some of these consequences include reduced effectiveness of the immune system, increased blood pressure, bone deterioration, irritable bowel syndrome, ulcers, sleep disturbances, problems with memory and attention, mood disturbances such as anxiety and depression, reproductive-system problems, weight gain, and premature aging. At your discretion, you may explain the mechanisms of a chronically activated stress response (for example, action of stress hormones).

"Memo from the Body-Mind" (six-session workbook) is a tongue-in-cheek overview of the stress system for students and may be discussed in this lesson or used as a basis for student research.

Moving to Practice

1. Stress management depends on paying attention to body, thoughts, and feelings.

2. Practice movement while paying attention to all three areas: body, thoughts, and feelings.

3. Practice *not changing* our experience, but letting ourselves have it "just as it is."

4. In order to expand mindful attention to movement and breath, consider using the activity "Waterlines" from the 18-session version (chapter 14). This is a brushstroke practice that can be a supplement or an alternative practice. "Waterlines" requires some art materials.

The first step in stress management is becoming aware of the stress.

What might be a sign from the body that we're under stress? A sign from our thoughts? A sign from our emotions? (Discuss.)

A

These messages function as an interconnected early-warning system. We might be attentive to one of them, in particular, and simply noticing it allows us to "breathe" a bit, reducing the intensity of the stress. Bodily feelings, thoughts, and emotions are interconnected, like a mobile with three parts. If we pay attention to one part, we can affect the whole.

Today we'll practice mindful movement. You're invited to pay attention to your present experience, regardless of what it is. This is different from some of the activities we typically do. We're not trying to get anywhere or compete with anyone. We're just practicing becoming aware of experience in the body, thoughts, and feelings. So find a confortable position seated in your chair. Put down anything you're holding. Take three full breaths to relax yourself before we begin.

Mindful-movement practice may be done seated or standing as space and time permit. As with other practices, remind adolescents about guidelines (posture, using the breath as an anchor, and so on).

Images of the specific postures are in the student workbook ("Sitting Postures" and "Standing Postures").

The following sequence is done first from a seated position and then from a standing position. Instructors should introduce the movements in the same way as the other practices. If desired, use some parts of the "Opening Mindfulness Practice" (chapter 4). A quick "Body Scan" might also be used before moving to the postures. (*Use your attention to scan your body, looking for any places that are tense or tight, and breathing into those areas.*) Instructors can choose the postures depending on time and space availability.

Note that the point of mindful movement practice is not to have any special experience, but to experience fully whatever you are experiencing. Care should be taken to clarify the intention of the mindful movement practice. That is, it is important to distinguish this practice from exercise typically done with the intention to lose weight or tone the body. Although regular mindful movement practices can increase physical health, strength, and tone, they are fundamentally mindfulness practices. Therefore, there is no standard for performance other than trying to be aware of all that is happening within you moment by moment. Remember to practice nonjudgment yourself, and remind students to do so.

PRACTICE: Mindful Movements

Seated Position: Palm-Press Pose

Sit in your chair with your back straight and your feet flat on the floor. Bring your palms together and hold them against your chest, with your forearms parallel to the floor. Inhale and twist to the right, and look over your right shoulder, keeping your palms pressed in the same position. Notice how that feels in your body. On the next out-breath, twist to the left and look over your left shoulder. Notice sensations in your body, as well as your thoughts and feelings, as you hold this pose for a few seconds. Now return to center and inhale. Notice your experience.

Now reverse and start with the left side.

Repeat twice on each side.

Seated Position: Upward Stretch

Lift your arms up and bend your elbows, clasping your hands behind your head. Push your elbows back, and feel your shoulder muscles contracting and your chest expanding. Just spend a few seconds in this position, noticing your breath, any sensations in your body, any thoughts, or any feelings.

On the next in-breath, raise your arms as you clasp the fingers of both hands together, palms up. Hold for several seconds. Notice what this feels like in your arms and hands. On the next out-breath, release and return your hands back behind your head.

Repeat two or three times.

Seated Position: Seated Tree

Sit with your feet flat on the floor and your hands in your lap. Feel your neck and head balanced on your spine. Your back is straight but not rigid. Inhale and raise both arms above your head, interlacing your fingers together. Exhale slowly as you bend to the right without moving your hips. Breathe deeply while holding the posture as you notice sensations in your body, the movement of the breath, and any thoughts or feelings that might arise.

On the next out-breath, return to center.

Repeat on the left side. Then repeat the entire sequence.

Seated Position: Seated Twist

From the seated position, with your back straight, hips facing forward, and feet on the floor, grab the left side of the chair with the right hand, putting your left hand on the upper back of the chair. Keeping your shoulders as level as possible, twist your upper body as far to the left as possible, using your hands to pull on the chair for support.

As you hold this position, breathe for three or four breaths, and notice sensations, thoughts, feelings. On the next out-breath, slowly allow your body to rotate back to the center and your hands to come back to your lap. Tune in to your breathing and notice sensations in your body.

Repeat on the right side. Then repeat the entire sequence.

Standing Position: Mountain Pose

Begin by standing in mountain pose, with your feet about hip-width apart, your knees not locked, your hands either by your sides or palms together. Adjust your posture so that your weight is evenly distributed on each foot. Imagine that there is an invisible piece of thread pulling your head toward the ceiling. As you hold this position, notice the breath moving through your body. Perhaps you can notice the breath moving freely from the crown of your head to the soles of your feet. Become aware of your complete experience, including any physical sensations, thoughts, and feelings, without trying to change anything.

Standing Position: Reaching-Up Stretch

Starting from mountain pose, with your hands along your sides, gently adjust your weight to come to rest on the right side (and foot). Extend your right hand up to the ceiling as far as you can, while keeping your left hand at your side, feeling the stretch along your right side. You might wish to lift your left heel to lengthen the stretch. As you hold this position, feel the sensations in your body, notice your breath, and observe any thoughts or feelings you are having.

Repeat on the left side. Do the sequence twice on each side.

Standing Position: Rag-Doll Stretch

This is not recommended for anyone with back problems.

On your next in-breath, in one sweeping movement, raise your arms up overhead, and gently arch back as far as feels comfortable and safe. Then as you exhale, slowly bend forward (arms outstretched if space allows), bending your knees if necessary, and allow your head, arms, and hands to drop down so that you are bending from the waist. Use your hands to grasp the opposite elbow, and let your head hang down, getting a little closer to the floor with each breath. As you stay in this position for a few breaths, notice sensations in your body. Then gently come up, very slowly, one vertebra at a time, into a standing position. Notice the way your body feels right now.

Back to Seated Position: Taking Your Seat

Mindfully sit down, keeping your back straight, take a deep breath in, and tuck your chin into your chest. Place your feet flat on the floor about hip-width apart. On the next out-breath, slowing drop your upper body forward, bending at the waist. Let your head and arms slide down between your knees. Notice your breath and any sensations in the body as you remain in this position. With each breath, release a little bit more. Then, on the next in-breath, gently and very slowly, come back to a seated position.

At the conclusion of the movement practice, use some time to reflect on these questions:

How is your body feeling right now?

What did you notice about your body during this practice?

What thoughts and feelings did you notice?

Can you practice accepting whatever your experience happens to be?

Invitation to Home Practice

1. *Practice mindful breathing for at least three breaths at a time, three times per day.*

2. *Do a short mindful-movement practice, ideally, once a day (use the illustrations in the student workbook, "Sitting Postures" and "Standing Postures"). Write about your practice ("My Home Practice: Theme A").*

3. *Continue to notice thoughts, feelings, and physical sensations as they arise throughout the day.*

4. *Continue practicing mindfulness in your day-to-day life, especially in your chosen area (from theme B, "Mindfulness in My Life"). Add the practice of kindness to yourself and others.*

5. *Use the workbook pages "Tips to Take Away: More Ways to Practice Mindfulness in Action" and "Eating Awareness Calendar" to help with mindful-walking and mindful-eating practices.*

Chapter 9

Theme T: Tenderness

Key Point: **Learn to be kind to yourself.**

Essential Message of Theme T:

 We can not only reduce distress by learning to be mindful, but also train our attention and practice healthy habits of mind, such as kindness and compassion, to improve inner strength.

Class Objectives:

- To understand that the mind is a trainable organ

- To learn ways to train the mind to support well-being and happiness

- To connect mindfulness practice to self-care and care for others

- To practice cultivating the mind in ways that support health, wellness, and inner strength

Review of Previous Themes and Introduction of Theme T

1. Begin with an "Opening Mindfulness Practice" (see chapter 4).

2. Review previous themes: B, R, E, and A.

3. Add the letter "T" to "BREA" and the final "E."

4. Note the tendency to judge our experience as a way of introducing the alternate possibility of nonjudgment.

It's clear that stress is a part of life, that we don't always get what we want, and that we must do things that we don't want to do. All of this can lead us to feel "stressed out." When we are stressed out for too long, we lose some of our balance and personal power, and we can get sick. This describes the problem of chronic stress that we have been learning about.

Some of the things that stress us come from within ourselves. Recall from the last lesson that the body's stress response is triggered by thoughts as well as actual events. (Review if necessary and give examples.) When we are not aware of this, we are practicing mental habits that work against our best interests. Sometimes these habits of mind include being very judgmental of ourselves, our experiences, and other people. Let's examine whether these tendencies of mind help or hurt us.

Activities to Develop Theme T

1. Introduce the idea of "practicing meanness" and "practicing kindness." Discuss what "practice" means in this context and whether or not this is conscious. (Use the "Ways We Take Care of Ourselves" and "Ways We Don't Take Care of Ourselves" pages in the student workbook.)

2. Emphasize that habits of mind can be trained and that we can practice kindness to ourselves (self-compassion).

3. Note that we can increase well-being through the practice of wholesome emotions. Loving-kindness and gratitude are emotions that amplify our well-being and inner strength.

4. Extend the discussion (and possible expression) of self-compassion to others as well. Self-care starts with ourselves and extends to others. Self-compassion is the foundation for kindness and compassion to others.

I'm going to read you a brief excerpt from a book that describes how we often practice unhelpful mental habits. The author calls this "practicing meanness" to ourselves.

ACTIVITY: Practicing Mental Habits

This excerpt is from Brantley, 2003, page 140:

Since kindness can be practiced, it is important to understand that its opposite attitude, meanness, can also be practiced. In fact, meanness is practiced quite a lot. Most often, we aim it at ourselves. We usually don't fully recognize how mean we are to ourselves. This meanness is a habit of thinking and feeling that arises often and is felt deeply in the body.

Read this twice if appropriate. Discuss it with the group.

Have you ever thought about "practicing" meanness? What's new about this idea?

Is this kind of practice conscious or unconscious?

Of course, there are ways that we practice kindness toward ourselves, too.

Let's think of some ways that we practice kindness or taking care of ourselves, and ways that we practice meanness. Examples can include things that we do consciously and things that we do unconsciously.

ACTIVITY: Ways We Care for Ourselves, or Not

MATERIALS: Student workbook, pencil or pen, and blackboard or flip chart

This activity allows adolescents to think about all the ways they practice kindness and meanness toward themselves. The intention is to raise awareness of habitual patterns of thought or behavior that support or detract from well-being. The group can engage in this activity in a number of ways. The following suggestion involves small groups of three to four, but group members may work in dyads or individually at the discretion of the instructor.

Use these pages from the student workbook: "Ways We Take Care of Ourselves" and "Ways We Don't Take Care of Ourselves."

Divide the class into small groups of three or four students. Ask groups to begin by brainstorming to think of examples of how we generally practice kindness toward ourselves.

For this exercise, you should come up with as many examples as you can, even if they are things that you don't do yourselves but have seen other people do.

If desired, each small group can be assigned a certain category (thoughts, emotions, behaviors) to brainstorm for examples of practicing kindness in these domains. After sufficient time, the result can be are shared with the large group and may be recorded on the blackboard or flip chart.

The same instructions apply for ways in which we practice meanness toward ourselves (for example, sabotage ourselves or don't take care of ourselves). One group identifies destructive behaviors; another, destructive thoughts; and the other, destructive emotions. Depending on the size of the class, some groups may have the same task.

Some examples of practicing kindness to yourself are:

- **Behaviors (Acting):** getting enough sleep, eating properly, exercising, taking breaks when needed; cultivating hobbies and leisure interests; acting responsibly with regard to school and other work; spending money wisely (to avoid later debt); speaking kindly and truthfully (to strengthen relationships with others); expressing love and appreciation.

- **Feelings (Feeling):** feeling gratitude for life, others, circumstances, and so on; feeling a sense of interest in things; feeling appreciation; feeling love and affection for others; feeling pride in accomplishments.

- **Thoughts (Thinking):** thinking about your own strengths accurately; thinking that you can accomplish things you set your mind to; recognizing the support that you get from others; thinking about the personal qualities that you like in yourself; thinking about the good things in your life.

Some examples of practicing meanness to yourself are:

- **Behaviors (Acting):** not eating enough; eating too much; eating an unhealthy diet; taking drugs (illegal and prescription); not getting enough sleep; self-injury; drinking alcohol, smoking; riding a bike without a helmet; not exercising; being mean to others or gossiping so that social relationships are harmed; procrastinating with schoolwork so that grades go down, or missing school.

- **Feelings (Feeling):** being chronically angry or impatient with yourself or others; being chronically intolerant of yourself; being chronically embarrassed about the way you look or talk; feeling inadequate (as if you don't do things well); feeling superior to others; feeling deprived (as if you don't have enough of something); feeling entitled (as if you should always get your way).

- **Thoughts (Thinking):** thinking about yourself as a loser; always thinking that others are better than you are; always thinking that you are better than others; thinking that no one pays attention to you; thinking that nobody cares about you; thinking that you are unattractive; thinking that you are too fat; thinking that you are too skinny; thinking that you are not smart; thinking that you can't be successful.

Discuss the results in the large group. Draw the group's attention to the importance of self-care.

. . . .

So we've been talking about what we do automatically, like mindlessly practicing certain behaviors that ultimately hurt us in some way. Learning something new involves paying attention and making new choices.

How many of you have ever learned something new that you thought was going to be hard to learn? Can you give some examples?

What attitude did you have to adopt to learn this new thing? How did your usual way of thinking or behaving need to change?

Allow students time to respond to each question. Note that in order to learn something new, you have to believe that it is *possible* to learn the new skill or concept.

What do you think about the possibility of changing some of the mean mind habits you listed on the worksheet?

Allow time for some discussion.

Emerging research shows that the brain is a trainable organ (see Davidson et al., 2003; Begley, 2007). Barbara Fredrickson and colleagues (2008) demonstrated improvements in positive emotions after practicing daily loving-kindness practice. In a follow-up study (Cohn & Fredrickson, 2010) after one year, positive emotions in the daily loving-kindness group (such as love, joy, gratitude, contentment, hope, pride, interest, amusement, and awe) were three times as great as they were during the first week. Furthermore, these changes were associated with increased resources like self-acceptance, mindfulness, better health, and improved social relationships. The authors conclude that the path to improved life satisfaction was heavily influenced by positive emotions that build inner resources. This follow-up study of these participants showed that the gains persisted, but mainly for those individuals who continued to practice.

Here's some very good news. We know from scientific studies that it's possible to change the brain through mental training like the mindfulness practices we've been learning. We've learned how to bring ourselves back to feeling more balanced when we're stressed by letting go of thoughts and feelings that are not helpful. We can also do something more. We can actually practice making our minds healthier and more compassionate in the first place.

We can use mindfulness to practice kindness toward ourselves. This may seem a little strange to some of us at first, because we're not used to doing this. But the fact is that we can change our habits of mind and heart with practice, and this practice can give us an inner edge. We can practice habits of tenderness or self-compassion so that we learn to take ourselves and others as we are and as they are, without getting too stressed out about things. We can practice taking life as it is.

Adolescents may be asked to consider the extent to which the ways they treat themselves are conscious (mindful) or automatic (mindless).

Practicing tenderness does not mean letting ourselves get away with things, being lazy, or slacking off. Instead, it reminds us to relax and use basic good intentions as the foundation for our actions. It reduces the tendency to perceive ourselves judgmentally and unrealistically, which can undermine our capacity to be compassionate to ourselves and others.

. . . .

ACTIVITY: Additional Options
What I Wish for Myself

MATERIALS: Letter paper, envelopes, pen or pencil

Invite group members to write a letter to themselves that they will seal and address. The letters should be mailed to them after the program is over. In the letter, they should reflect on what good wishes they extend to themselves, and write them down or draw images of these wishes.

What do you wish for yourself?

What do you want to take away from this program?

What thing in your life would you most wish to change after having taken this program?

If you don't make changes in your life, how might you feel?

How do you wish to change a habit of meanness toward yourself?

Which habits of self-care do you wish to strengthen?

Message in a Bottle

MATERIALS: Slips of paper; a container, such as a large wide-mouth bottle or basket; pens or pencils

This activity is intended to provide students an opportunity to extend positive wishes to others in the group. It can be used as an adjunct to the "What I Wish for Myself" activity.

Ask group members to write a positive wish for another member on a small piece of paper. Wishes should be general rather than specific to any individual. Fold the papers and place them in a container. As group members leave the room, each one takes a message.

. . . .

Moving to Practice

1. Note that in addition to removing obstacles (stress reduction), we can also practice wholesome qualities of mind. We are training ourselves to have healthy habits of mind and heart. Practicing self-compassion is the essence of practicing kindness to ourselves.

2. We can expand the practice of compassion to others.

3. Introduce the loving-kindness practice and note that the phrases can be adapted to suit the individual.

Throughout all of the classes, we have been noticing thoughts, emotions, and feelings in the body without judgment. In this activity, we will be practicing a way to strengthen these healthy habits of thinking and feeling. We will be learning a way to be more compassionate toward ourselves and less judgmental. We will practice kindness instead of meanness. This is a skill that can be trained. Don't be upset if this seems awkward at first, because we're not used to doing this. However, if we start wherever we feel comfortable and give it a try, we will get better and better with time. In the long run, this can become a comfortable habit.

This practice includes short statements that you practice saying to yourself. If at any time, you wish to change the words to suit yourself better, go ahead and do so.

Sometimes it feels easier to offer kindness to others instead of to ourselves, but here we start with ourselves and then move outward to others.

Loving-kindness practice is a form of self-care and self-compassion, which should be distinguished from self-esteem. Frequently, self-esteem becomes associated with expectations for achievement or striving to excel in order to be "better than" others on some dimension. Inadvertently, this message can become an opportunity for self-criticism. Self-compassion, in comparison, offers the alternative practice of true self-acceptance and self-regard (see Neff, 2003).

Encourage group members to change the words of the practice to suit themselves. Emphasize that it is a form of mental self-care. Remind them of how unsettling it was to think hurtful thoughts and dwell on hurtful feelings by practicing them unconsciously. This is a way to cultivate positive emotions that are initially directed to the self and then can be extended to others.

As with other practices, remind adolescents about guidelines (posture, using the breath as an anchor, and so on). If there is time after the practice, provide the opportunity to share experiences or ask questions.

. . . .

PRACTICE: Loving-Kindness

MATERIALS: None. Instructors may wish to use the audio version for this practice (see audio downloads at www.newharbinger.com/27831).

Loving-kindness practice involves the use of phrases and images to evoke and cultivate friendliness toward yourself and others. Generally the practice starts by evoking a time when you felt truly loved by someone (a parent, friend, peer, teacher, or even a stranger or a favorite animal).

Students are invited to hold the image of the scene in mind, pay attention to the details of the scene, and allow it to evoke the felt sense of being loved and treated with kindness. Then, taking that felt experience of loving-kindness, they direct it to themselves using phrases in the script. Other statements may be used based on the individual's preference.

The idea is to practice directing feelings of love, kindness, and acceptance toward yourself in whatever way feels right to you. This is the antidote to practicing meanness. An antidote is a remedy that counteracts the effects of something harmful. As the practice progresses, you may wish to repeat one phrase or repeat them all inwardly over and over. The next step is to extend loving-kindness to a loved one. The practice leads, eventually, to directing loving-kindness to all people, even those who may have caused you difficulty in your life.

This can take a lot of practice, so it's best to start with the basics for adolescents.

Some people experience the recollection of loving memories as mildly awkward or difficult. Some may resist doing this because they can't recall such memories easily. It is important for instructors to be aware of this. It may make it easier for some to ask them to begin by thinking about some people to whom they feel or have felt close (see Kok and Fredrickson, 2010). Loving-kindness could be introduced as a way of training yourself to be kinder to yourself. Or, instructors may replace loving-kindness with a longer gratitude practice, which may be more accessible to some adolescents. The practice of cultivating gratitude may serve as a bridge to the practice of loving-kindness. You may want to discuss the experience afterward, if time permits.

Now for this short period of time, let's do an exercise that will help us cultivate feelings of loving-kindness to ourselves and others.

Loving-kindness practice is simply the wish that we enjoy peace, happiness, and well-being.

The important thing to recognize is that we can cultivate these attitudes if we practice.

In so many ways, we practice meanness to ourselves. So why not practice some kindness?

This can help our minds and bodies be healthier and more at ease.

Remember that loving-kindness has nothing to do with self-centeredness and everything to do with healthy self-acceptance and self-compassion.

By helping ourselves in this way, we can become stronger and better able to extend kindness to others.

During the course of this practice, you will be invited to repeat inwardly certain phrases or wishes.

Once you get used to this, you can use one or two—or even change the phrases to suit yourself.

It's helpful not to try too hard to feel something, especially at first.

Just do the best you can, planting the seeds of self-compassion that will support your inner strength.

It's also a good idea to be patient, because it will often take several weeks or perhaps months of daily practice to freely express and accept these feelings.

So now, sitting quietly or lying on a mat, just begin by tuning in to the breath.

Notice that you are breathing.

(pause)

And now bring to mind someone whom you have felt close to in your life.

This may be a person, like a parent, a relative, a friend, a teacher, a coach, or a stranger, or it might even be a favorite pet.

Accept whatever memory comes.

Recall a time when you felt especially close to this person or pet.

Make the memory as vivid as possible.

Visualize the event, and see if you can experience the feelings of being close.

Notice what this feels like in your body right now.

Perhaps feeling an opening or a lightening in the area of your chest, around your heart,

...really tune in to the experience of being treated kindly.

And now take the feeling of being loved and cared for, and direct this feeling toward yourself, offering the gift of loving-kindness to yourself while you inwardly repeat the phrases:

> *May I be strong,*
>
> *May I be balanced,*
>
> *May I be happy,*
>
> *May I be peaceful,*

...inwardly repeating the phrases as you practice, directing the feelings of kindness and caring toward yourself.

> *May I be strong,*
>
> *May I be balanced,*
>
> *May I be happy,*
>
> *May I be peaceful.*

Now recalling the person, such as a relative, friend, teacher, coach, stranger, or the pet that you remembered before, and calling to mind the special qualities of this person or favorite pet,

...with this person or pet in mind, direct feelings of kindness to him or her:

Just as I wish to be strong, may you also be strong.

Just as I wish to be balanced, may you also be balanced.

Just as I wish to be happy, may you also be happy.

Just as I wish to be peaceful, may you also be peaceful.

Now, for the rest of this practice time, choose to continue to extend loving-kindness to yourself or to the person you feel close to, or if you wish, bring to mind someone in your life who has caused you difficulty.

Just as with the friend or loved one, you can practice extending loving-kindness with the same intention to the difficult person,...

(pause)

...remembering that it's best not to try too hard to feel something.

We are practicing to be strong, balanced, and happy, and undoing the meanness that we sometimes practice toward ourselves.

(pause)

Just do the best you can, planting the seeds of self-compassion that support your inner strength.

(bell)

....

Invitation to Home Practice

1. *Practice mindful breathing for at least three breaths at a time, three times per day.*

2. *Try to do a short loving-kindness practice (once a day, ideally; see audio downloads at www .newharbinger.com/27831). Change the language to suit yourself.*

3. *Begin to notice thoughts, feelings, and physical sensations as they arise throughout the day. Pay particular attention to thoughts and feelings that are related to self-criticism or criticism of others. Try offering yourself and others kindness instead.*

4. *Continue practicing mindfulness in your day-to-day life, especially in your practice area. Write about your practice (see the student workbook, "My Home Practice: Theme T").*

T

Chapter 10

Theme H: Habits

Key Point: Practice healthy mind habits to reduce stress and increase inner strength.

Essential Message of Theme H:

Take these mindfulness tools and use them in your life.

Class Objectives:

- To identify ways to apply mindfulness in daily living

- To discuss ways of developing a personal mindfulness practice

- To review the major points of the course

Review of Previous Themes and Introduction of Theme H

1. Begin with a short period of practice.

2. Review previous themes: B, R, E, A, and T.

3. Complete the word by adding "H" to "BREAT" and the final "E."

4. Reinforce the intention to do "inner strength training" by restating the meaning of the last letter "E" (empowerment/gaining an inner edge).

5. Emphasize that the skills learned in this program can be applied to everyday life.

Over the course of the last five themes, we've been learning to pay attention in a new way. By practicing mindfulness, we've been training our attention to see what's happening right now in our bodies, in our thoughts, and in our feelings. We've learned that we have some mindless habits, both in what we do and how we think about things.

The news is that we can shed the light of mindfulness on our lives, use the breath as an anchor, and approach every moment with more ease and less judgment.

We also talked about practicing new mental habits. You might have noticed that you have tendencies in your mind and heart, perhaps toward chronic worry, anger, jealousy, and so on. You can view these tendencies as unhelpful mind habits. These habits or patterns can be changed. We can choose to be mindful—to be more aware and empowered.

Activities to Develop Theme H

1. Lead the group in practices that were learned in past themes: awareness of breath, body, thoughts, and feelings.

2. Include loving-kindness meditation at the end if desired.

3. Have the students reflect on what they've learned and what they want to take away, using the "Mindful Quilt" activity.

Over the course of this program, we have seen that we're not always really here for our lives. We're moving around, doing work, having fun, and getting things accomplished, but our minds and hearts may be someplace else. We also learned that the strongest place to operate from is "right here." We are steadier and more empowered when we are fully aware of the present moment. We are less likely to get pushed around by our unconscious thoughts and feelings. We can make better choices and take better care of ourselves.

So now, we'll practice being mindful of our bodies, thoughts, and feelings in order to strengthen our ability to be right here for whatever is happening today in our lives.

After the period of practice, introduce the "Mindful Quilt" activity.

ACTIVITY: Mindful Quilt

MATERIALS: large index cards, art paper, markers, crayons, colored pencils

The "Mindful Quilt" activity produces a montage ("quilt") of group members' sentiments that can be arrayed on a bulletin board or in another place in the room. Have materials ready and distribute them to group members at the beginning of the session. Invite them to work quietly and mindfully, perhaps with music in the background.

Read a few questions several times each. Invite group members to listen very deeply and consider each question. Then, invite members to choose one question and respond to it by creating a drawing, an image, or a symbol, or by writing a word or a longer response on the index card or paper.

Allow about five to ten minutes for students to work.

Read the questions at least three times:

What did I learn in this program?

What is the most important message for me?

How will I use what I learned in my life?

Moving to Practice

1. Close with a circle activity.

2. Have students share what they learned and consider how they can apply mindfulness on a regular basis in their daily lives (and in the group). Invite adolescents to review the workbook pages from theme T, "Tips to Take Away: Dial Up the Gratitude," and the final theme E, "Mindfulness Cues," to help them continue mindfulness practice after the end of the program.

3. Use the last page of the student workbook as a starting point for this discussion.

4. Distribute wallet cards (downloadable at www.newharbinger.com/27831) or another small remembrance of the program if desired.

A large portion of the last session involves practice. The final activity provides an opportunity for participants to share what they have learned and what they plan to take away from the program to use in their daily lives. As with all of the activities, this is an opportunity for mindful listening (to the bell and to others' comments) and mindful speaking. Allow sufficient time so that this closing practice is not rushed.

PRACTICE: Closing—Mindful Listening and Mindful Speaking

MATERIALS: Bell or chime, wallet cards, or small gifts (optional)

For the closing activity, invite students to share something about their experience of the program with the group. They may share anything they choose (what they learned, liked, did not like, noticed about themselves, wrote on the card for the quilt, and so on).

Bring the group into a circle.

The first student to speak takes the bell from the instructor, rings the bell, shares a comment, rings the bell to finish, and passes it to the next group member, who does the same. Invite participants to practice mindful listening by waiting for the end of the bell sound before speaking or moving. The instructor thanks each group member for sharing and participating. Depending on the size of the group, this can take up most of the time for the session.

You may wish to give group members a token gift at the completion of the course. Some suggested gifts include a small bell, a stone, a certificate, or a card with a relevant message. Small wallet cards may be printed (see downloads at www.newharbinger.com/27831) with the acronym BREATHE and the key messages of each letter. You may also wish to prepare a list of readings or websites that are suitable to the age of the students, for future reference.

H

Invitation to Continuing Practice

Before concluding the program, the group should discuss how they plan to continue practicing mindfulness in their lives, classrooms, and other settings. The group may decide on a regular practice session together, take turns leading the group in practice, or both. Whatever the decision, the point is that Learning to BREATHE only represents a starting point. Mindfulness is an everyday practice. Use the student workbook page for the final theme E, "Mindfulness Cues," as a starting point for this discussion.

Part 3

Eighteen-Session Program

Part 3 presents an eighteen-session version of Learning to BREATHE. This version may be appropriate for use with younger adolescents or in situations when there is less time available per session. The themes, essential messages, and key objectives are the same for both versions, so I will not repeat them here. The same holds true for activities that are used in the six-session version. Some activities (for example, "Between Session Mindfulness Boosters") are included in this version, but may be useful in any L2B implementation. These boosters provide suggested activities for teachers or clinicians who see adolescents between sessions for reinforcing the practices students are learning. The duration of the booster practices can be short or long depending on the circumstances. In some situations, consistent short practices (like five mindful breaths or three silent minutes spent in awareness of breath) may be done every day rather than varying the between-session practices. The important thing is to practice regularly. Home-practice suggestions for the eighteen-session version may be adapted from the six-session version.

Chapter 11

Theme B: Body

Theme B, for body, is taught over three sessions, numbered 1 through 3.

Session 1

1. Introduce the program (the aim or intention for the class).

2. Discuss what mindfulness is.

3. Discuss the mindfulness-of-sound activity.

4. Introduce mindful-breathing practice.

Introduction to Theme B

This course is called Learning to BREATHE, and it is about using mindfulness to help us in our day-to-day lives. This class is different from other kinds of classes you have in school. There are no written tests or projects. You don't have assigned reading to do. Instead we're going to learn a special way of paying attention, called mindfulness. We'll be paying attention to what's outside of us and what's inside of us. Then we'll be taking what we learn in class and using it in our lives, both in school and at home. Each time we meet, we'll have some time to talk about mindfulness, and we'll have time to practice our skills.

Mindfulness is a way of using our minds to be aware of what's going on inside and outside of us at the moment that it is happening.

Being mindful can help us be strong and balanced. Just as we exercise our bodies in gym class, in athletic events, and just for fun, we can also exercise our minds: training them to be stronger, more focused, and more balanced. Every one of us, no matter who we are or how old we are, gets upset from time to time and feels stressed out. We'll be learning how to use our minds to help us deal with stress, too. It's kind of like "inner-strength training." Another way to say this is that we'll learn to be "empowered" and to gain an "inner edge."

We'll keep a list of key words to remind us of the new things we're learning to practice.

Put "E" poster on the blackboard or wall. Define and discuss "empowered" if needed.

Sometimes when people are asked to do something new or unusual, they may feel awkward or a little uncomfortable. Sometimes people have reactions that make them want to act silly or laugh. It's okay if you feel these things. See if you can just notice these feelings without acting on them and distracting others. See if you can be kind to yourself by accepting whatever your feelings happen to be. It's important for you to try to participate fully in order to gain the benefits of the program. If at some time you do not wish to practice some of the mindfulness activities, remember to respect others who might want to participate, by remaining still and quiet.

Group Guidelines

Instructors may wish to develop a group statement about aims and intentions for the program. This statement would reflect an agreement shared by members of the group, for example, to work together, to respect what others say, to listen, and so on. This is most effective when students generate the list together. The finished statement may be posted as a reminder. Teachers may also choose to repeat the group guidelines from time to time as needed.

When we are mindful, we use our attention to notice what's happening. What are some things you are noticing right now? They can be things happening inside of you or outside of you, in this room. (Allow students to respond.)

How were you able to notice these things? What did you use? (Identify the senses: hearing, seeing, tasting, touching, smelling; and discuss the role of senses in perceiving.)

These experiences are called sensations.

Activity to Develop Theme B

Lead the group in a short mindful-listening pratice.

BELL-SOUND PRACTICE

When we are mindful, we use all our senses and our attention to help us. In other words, our attention is really awake and is focused on what's going on right at this moment. Now let's try an experiment. Sit quietly and close your eyes if you're comfortable with that. Use your attention to follow the sound of the bell. Raise your hand when you can't hear the sound of the bell any longer.

Wait until the students are settled and quiet. Ring the bell or chime.

How was that way of paying attention different from the ways we normally pay attention? (Allow students to respond.)

Are there other times you can remember when you were very aware of what was happening in that moment? (Allow students to respond.)

This kind of paying attention is called mindfulness. Now we'll try it again by practicing paying attention to the breath.

Moving to Practice

Do a short breath-awareness practice.

General Guidelines

You should transition into practice with some activity like a little stretching, mindful movements, or both, especially if the class is restless. Then guide the class in taking some deep breaths, allowing the breath to move into the nose and out through the mouth like a soft sigh. Do this a few times to relax everyone (see chapter 4 for the "Opening Mindfulness Practice").

B SHORT BREATH-AWARENESS PRACTICE

All mindfulness practice periods should be led slowly and reflectively. Allow time for silent periods between instructions. Invite students to sit or lie down and get quiet. Ring a soft bell or chime to start (if desired).

So, please find a comfortable position.

> **(If seated)** *put both feet flat on the floor. Your back should be straight but not too stiff, and both hands are in your lap or placed, palms down, on your upper legs.*

> **(If lying down)** *lie on your back with your feet falling away and your arms at your sides.*

(short pause)

Now, let's start by paying attention to the inside.

See if you can become aware of your breathing.

Notice your breath wherever it's easiest for you: going in and out at the nose, perhaps at the chest, or maybe at the belly.

Just see if you can notice your breath and follow it from the beginning of the in-breath to the end of the out-breath.

If you wish, place your hand on your belly and feel the rhythm of your breath.

We're just focusing on one thing right now: follow the whole breath with your full attention from the beginning of the in-breath to the end of the out-breath.

We're mindfully paying attention to what's inside.

Ring the bell at the end. Briefly summarize as time permits.

You can make some mention of the key words at the end of the session by asking what words were new to group members.

Let students know that they can record their experiences outside of class in the log in the student workbook, "My Home Practice: Theme B."

Key Words: mindfulness, present moment, attention, five senses, sensations, inner-strength training, "inner edge," empowered

Between-Session Mindfulness Booster: *Practice belly breathing, holding your hands on your belly for five to ten full breaths.*

Session 2

1. Introduce a short mindfulness practice.

2. Ask, "What do you remember about mindfulness?"

3. Discuss what mindlessness is.

4. Do a mindful-eating activity (or the "Sense Doors" activity, in chapter 5).

5. Do a mindfulness practice: awareness of feet on the floor (or hands in lap).

Reintroduction to Theme B

Guide the students in a short mindfulness practice. This may include a few breaths or listening to a sound to provide a short practice opportunity.

Welcome students and remind them of the overall goal of empowerment and about class guidelines if needed. (The last letter "E" should be displayed.)

What do you remember about mindfulness? (Allow students to respond.)

Mindfulness is using our attention to be very aware of what's happening both inside and outside of us. Being aware can help us feel more balanced and strong. Remember how we talked about doing inner-strength training? That's what we're learning in this program when we learn about and practice mindfulness. We already know how to be mindless because we practice mindlessness all the time. One way to think about mindlessness is that our attention is on "automatic pilot."

What does this mean? (Allow students to respond. Some answers might include being zoned out, thoughtless, spaced out, and so on.)

Are there times when your mind is on automatic pilot? (Students can write examples as an activity, using the "My Mindful/Mindless Life" page of the workbook.)

When this happens, can you hurt yourself? Can you hurt others? (Discuss some examples.)

Is it better for athletes to be in a mindful zone or a mindless zone when they are competing?

So it's a good idea to try to be more mindful in our lives. And, like most things, practice makes us better at it.

Activity to Develop Theme B

One way we can develop mindfulness is by doing a simple thing in a certain way, as if it were the most important thing that we could possibly pay attention to. Let's try this now.

....

ACTIVITY: Mindful Eating

MATERIALS: raisins, napkins or small paper plates, bell (optional)

Jon Kabat-Zinn (1990) introduced this awareness activity in his groundbreaking book, *Full Catastrophe Living.* The "raisin exercise" is a simple eating practice that illustrates how mindfulness involves doing something ordinary with great awareness. Students are given three raisins that they eat as directed. Directions are given slowly with pauses in between. Some teachers may prefer to vary the food item and use other types of fruit, candies, and so on, or even a bag of various food items with different tastes. Make sure that students are not allergic to the sample foods provided. The point is to fully experience the richness of eating, using all the senses.

Let's practice developing our mindfulness muscle by eating mindfully.

Sit comfortably, and I will come around the room and hand a few objects to each of you.

I'd like you to focus on one of the objects as if you've never seen it before. Imagine that you've arrived here from another planet and the object is completely new.

Now take the object in your hand and turn it around.

Become aware of what you see: shape, texture, color, size, temperature, hardness, or softness.

Now, being aware of the movement of your arm, bring the object to your nose and smell it.

Place the object in your mouth, without chewing or swallowing. Become aware of all the sensations you are experiencing.

Then when you're ready, consciously take a bite and notice the taste. Notice the texture. Notice the rest of your mouth and the sensations there.

Now slowly, consciously, chew the object and, when you're ready, allow yourself to swallow.

Students may choose to eat the other raisins mindfully. Or they may choose not to do so. Note the process of making this choice. After the exercise, process the activity with questions such as the following:

What are some textures? Some colors? Some tastes? Some movements? (Add other dimensions if desired.)

Is this the way we normally eat? What was different?

What made this activity mindful eating?

. . . .

Moving to Practice

We can also learn to notice physical sensations in the body, just as we did with eating. Much of the time we don't pay much attention to our bodies. But by paying close attention, we can learn a lot about mindfulness. Let's start by bringing mindful attention to the body in the same way that we did in eating the raisin.

(Put the letter "B" on the blackboard with enough space before the final "E" to suggest missing letters.)

. . . .

SHORT BODY SCAN (FEET)

Guide the class in a bit of stretching, some mindful movements, or both before having them sit down (see the "General Guidelines" box in session 1).

Invite students to find a place to sit and become quiet and still. Ring a soft bell or chime to start.

So, please find a comfortable position, putting both feet flat on the floor.

Your back should be straight but not too stiff, and both hands are relaxed in your lap or placed, palms down, on your upper legs.

Now, become aware of your breathing. Find your breath in your body.

On the next in-breath, see if you can move your attention along with the breath all the way down your body to the soles of your feet.

See if you can focus your attention on the contact that your shoes make with the floor.

Maybe you can notice the sensations of your socks or shoes. Perhaps you can notice sensations of warmth or coolness in your feet, feelings of lightness or heaviness, pulsations of circulation.

Become aware of the toes of both feet, the soles of the feet, the heels.

Now let your attention rest on the whole right foot making contact with the floor,

(pause)

…and now the whole left foot making contact with the floor;

(pause)

…now both feet.

Now move your attention away from your feet and back to your belly,

…focusing once again on the in-breath and the out-breath until the sound of the bell.

(bell)

Mention that this is a practice in mindfulness because we're using attention in a special way. Invite group members to practice mindfulness (perhaps of eating) outside of class.

. . . .

Key Words: mindlessness, automatic pilot, mindful zone, mindless zone

Between-Session Mindfulness Booster: *Practice tuning in to the breath at your belly. Move your attention to your feet. Experience the connection of your feet with the floor. Move your attention back to the breath at your belly. A variation of this is to focus your attention on your back, shoulders, or head.*

Session 3

1. Lead the students in a short mindfulness practice.

2. Review mindfulness. Review previous sessions on theme B and the last letter "E."

3. Discuss how it will help to be mindful. An optional activity to do during this session is "Mindful Walkabout" (see chapter 5).

4. Guide students in the "Body Scan" mindfulness practice.

5. Have students pick a mindfulness practice of their own ("Mindfulness in My Life").

Reintroduction to Theme B

Do a short mindfulness practice. This may include taking a few breaths, listening to a sound, or doing a short "Body Scan" (awareness of the soles of the feet).

Welcome students and remind them of the overall goal of empowerment and class guidelines if needed. Put the letter "B" and the last letter "E" on the blackboard. Most of the class session should be used for the "Body Scan" practice. Take time to prepare the students for this.

Mindfulness is "really meaning" to pay attention. What's another way of saying that we really mean to do something (intention or intending)? We intend to pay attention to what's happening "right now" inside and outside of us. We do this with an attitude of curiosity, interest, and kindness.

Activities to Develop Theme B

Using the first page of the student workbook, review the three key features of mindfulness, using the images on the page.

How can you be kind to yourself? You can treat your "self" like a friend. You can try to look at what's happening both inside and outside with interest instead of judgment.

Now that we've learned more about mindfulness, what do you think are some of the advantages of being mindful?

Mindfulness offers a means of experiencing our lives more fully.

Remind the students of what they noticed while eating the raisin that they ordinarily fail to notice. If students practiced mindful eating outside of the session, some examples from volunteers might be useful.

If time permits, do the optional activity, "Mindful Walkabout" (see chapter 5).

Moving to Practice

Guide students in a bit of stretching, some mindful movements, or both before having them lie down (see the "General Guidelines" box in session 1 of this chapter).

Today we're going to be mindful of the body as a whole. We'll be doing the "Body Scan," so we should find a place to lie down on the floor, on a mat or a blanket.

Group members should have mats (for carpeted floors) or mats and blankets (for hard floors) as well as throws or blankets for warmth. Encourage them to find a separate space, not right next to other group members. The following script provides a scan of feet, belly, shoulders, head, and face. The scan may be shortened to just one or two of these areas depending on circumstances.

This activity should be led slowly and reflectively. Allow time for silent periods between instructions. Answer questions if time permits and hand out the web address for the audio downloads (www.newharbinger.com/27831) at the end of this class if desired.

. . . .

PRACTICE: Body Scan

MATERIALS: Mats, blankets, or both for lying on the floor, throws for warmth

Ring the bell.

This "Body Scan" practice is designed to help you relax and pay attention to how your body feels and what it might be telling you. It's a time to listen to your body and to be in your body as fully as possible.

(If lying down) *lie on your back on the mat or blanket, with your feet about hip-width apart and falling away from one another, and your arms at your sides.*

(If sitting) *sit with your back erect but not stiff, with both your feet on the floor and your hands comfortably in your lap.*

Close your eyes if that's comfortable for you. Listen to and follow my instructions, as best you can.

Try to stay awake and alert.

Remember to breathe completely and let the breath flow freely into and out of the body.

When you notice that your mind is wandering, as it will, gently bring it back to focus on the instructions.

Now become aware of your belly rising as the breath moves into your body, and falling as the breath moves out of your body—not controlling the breath in any way, just letting it find its own rhythm.

Feel your body sink more deeply into the mat or your chair on each out-breath.

(pause)

And now on the next in-breath, direct your attention all the way down through your body to the soles of both feet.

Become aware of your toes, the arches of your feet, the place where the heels meet the floor. Notice any sensations in your feet, sensations of warmth or coolness, sensations of pressure, tingling, or tightness.

(pause)

Letting your breath move down to both feet, imagine that you can breathe right into your feet, first into your right foot, and on the out-breath, letting go of any tiredness, any tension, right from the sole of the right foot.

And now breathe into your left foot, and on the out-breath, let go of any tiredness, any tension, from the sole of the left foot.

(pause)

Moving your attention away from your feet and now to your belly, feel the movement of your abdomen as it rises and falls with each breath.

Taking a deep breath in, allow the abdomen to really expand on the in-breath, and then releasing, breathe out, noticing the feeling of the abdomen deflating.

Be aware of the rhythm of the breath without trying to change it.

(pause)

See if you can keep your attention on the breath at the belly from the beginning of the in-breath all the way to the end of the out-breath.

And if your attention wanders, remember not to judge yourself, but just gently bring your attention back.

(pause)

Now move your attention up your body and allow it to settle on your shoulders.

Notice the muscles here, exploring any sensations in the shoulders: perhaps burning, tightness, tension, heaviness, or lightness.

Whatever is there, we can observe it with interest.

Just breathing deeply into the shoulders, release any concerns, and allow your shoulders to relax.

(pause)

Remember that if your mind wanders, you can always bring it back to your breath.

You can use your breath at any time as an anchor for your attention.

(pause)

Next we'll draw the attention to the head.

Notice the contact that your head makes with the floor.

Is it heavy or light?

Notice sensations at the top of your head, your forehead, your eyes, your nose, your cheeks and mouth, your jaw.

As best you can, notice any and all sensations in this area of your face and head.

Then, let the next breath fill your entire head area, breathing in new energy and relaxation, breathing out any tightness, any tension, any fatigue.

(pause)

Now see if you can feel your breath moving easily through your whole body as you lie here, noticing the movement of the breath from your head to your feet.

(pause)

As we conclude this practice, be fully aware of your body as a whole, lying here,

…aware of the breath moving in and out at its own pace,

…feeling relaxed, strong, at ease.

(bell)

Review "Tips to Take Away: Three-Minute Body Scan" in the student workbook to help students practice throughout the day.

. . . .

PRACTICE: Personal Mindfulness—Mindfulness in My Life

At the conclusion of the session, invite group members to turn to the student workbook page, "Mindfulness in My Life," for the list of possibilities for practicing mindfulness. Suggest that they choose one activity as their personal opportunity to practice mindfulness outside of class. Teachers might choose to copy the activities on paper slips and let students select their practices randomly.

This is a way to illustrate that mindfulness can be helpful in daily life. If time permits, students can write or draw how they plan to do their activities on the student workbook page, "Mindfulness in My Life Activity."

. . . .

Key Words: intention, curiosity, interest, body scan, practice

Between-Session Mindfulness Booster: Lead the group in a short "Body Scan" focusing on the feet, belly, shoulders, or head.

Chapter 12

Theme R: Reflections

Theme R, for reflections, is taught over three sessions, numbered 4 through 6.

Session 4

1. Guide students in a short mindfulness practice.

2. Review the letter "B" and the final letter "E" in the BREATHE acronym.

3. Discuss the nature of the busy mind.

4. Guide students in "The Big Event" and "Fill in the Blanks" activities to demonstrate the way the mind creates meaning based on perception of events.

5. Guide students in a mindfulness-of-thoughts practice.

Review of Previous Theme and Introduction to Theme R

Guide students in a short mindfulness practice. This may include taking a few breaths, listening to a sound, doing a mindful-movement activity, and so on.

Recall that mindfulness is strengthening your attention in order to become more aware of what's happening. Attention can be narrow and focused, as we experienced it when we paid attention to the sound of the bell and the breath. Attention can also be broad, so we can be aware of many things going on inside and outside us. Our attention is a little like a zoom lens on a camera. You can get a close-up of one thing or expand it to show the whole scene.

What did you notice about your mind when you tried to pay attention to one thing, like your breath?

Discuss distractions, how there are lots of things going on in the mind and it takes time to settle. Instructors can use a snow globe to illustrate the busy mind. A recipe for making a simple kind of snow globe called a "mind jar" can be found in the book *Moody Cow Meditates*, by Kerry Lee MacLean (Wisdom Publications, 2009).

We talked about mindfulness as paying attention to the inside and the outside. On the inside, the mind is filled with thoughts. It's always chattering and constantly busy. Some of the things that fill the mind are words, ideas, fragments of sentences, pictures, and so on. To be able to find inner balance and strength, we need to be able to see what's going on in our minds.

Why do you think knowing what's in your mind is important?

One of the reasons this is important is because our thoughts affect how we feel and how we act. Let's try an activity to illustrate this.

Activities to Develop Theme R

Let's try this experiment; find the "Big Event Circles" page in your student workbook. Note the different ways in which individuals interpret situations.

. . . .

ACITIVITY: The Big Event

MATERIALS: Student workbook, pencils or pens

Be ready to write down your thoughts and feelings in the circles. In a moment I'm going to ask you to close your eyes and listen carefully as I read you a story.

I want you to imagine yourself as the character in the scene I will describe. As best you can, try to notice what thoughts and feelings are occurring for you as you imagine what's happening in the story.

Imagine that your new friend at school has asked you to go to a big game. It's on a weeknight after school. You are very excited about this because lots of people from your school will be there. Your parents are working late tonight, so you rushed home and got your homework done in time. Now you're all ready and waiting by the door for your friend to come so that you can go together. You wait for a long time. It gets really dark, and your new friend never shows up.

Now write down all of your thoughts and feelings about the story in the two circles at the top of the page. Write thoughts in the first circle and feelings in the second circle.

Discuss students' responses.

Now I'm going to read the story again, and I want you to imagine yourself in the story. When I've finished, please write your thoughts and feelings in the second set of circles.

Imagine that your new friend at school has asked you to go to a big game. It's on a weeknight after school. You are very excited about this because lots of people from your school will be there. Your parents are working late tonight, so you rushed home and got your homework done in time. Now you're all ready and waiting by the door for your friend to come so that you can go together. You wait for a long time. It gets really dark, and your new friend never shows up. Just then, your mom walks in and sees you waiting. She asks, "Did you forget that it's Wednesday? That game is on Thursday night."

Discuss students' responses. Compare and contrast the two different scenarios. Ask students to note the effects of thoughts on feelings.

The stories we tell ourselves change the way we continue to think and feel about things. The same situation produces many different responses. Each one of us has different perceptions of events, but we all experience a connection between the way we think (or perceive things) and how we feel. These thoughts and feelings affect our behaviors, too.

. . . .

ACTIVITY: Fill in the Blanks

Let's try another activity to show how this works.

Ask students to number a page from 1 to 5. Read the sentence prompts and ask students to write their first responses to each statement on a piece of paper, numbering the responses from 1 to 5.

1. *I get a B on a test. I feel _____ because _____.*

2. *During lunch in the cafeteria, I see my best friend talking to the new student in class. I feel _____ because _____.*

3. *The coach comes into the gym to tell us who made the team. I feel* _____ *because* _____ .

4. *My brother has a surprise party for his birthday. I feel* _____ *because* _____ .

5. *I get a notice that the tickets for the school field trip cost fifty dollars each. I feel* _____ *because* _____ .

Allow students to read some examples of their responses. Note the differences among responses. Emphasize how ideas (or perceptions) about a situation affect feelings about the situation.

So what good does it do to know this about ourselves? It's important to notice that everyone has thoughts in their minds. The thoughts we have can affect our feelings and actions. We can be curious about what's going on in our minds, but this is just the first step. Once we recognize the thoughts in our minds, we can simply observe them, without giving them too much attention, especially when they're upsetting. We can let the thoughts settle like the glitter in a snow globe. We can use our breath to calm ourselves. The main idea is that thoughts (reflections) are just thoughts.

· ·

Add the letter "R" to "B" and final "E."

Let's practice doing this.

Moving to Practice

Guide students in a bit of stretching, some mindful movements, or both before asking them to sit down. (Review the "General Guidelines" box in chapter 11, session 1).

Encourage students to come back to the awareness of their breath when they notice that they are distracted. They can use the breath as an anchor whenever they lose focus. Allow time for pauses between instructions. Using a bell or chime is an optional way to start and conclude. If there is time after the practice period, provide the opportunity to share experiences.

SHORT MINDFULNESS PRACTICE

Ring the bell.

So, please find a comfortable position.

(If seated) *put both feet flat on the floor. Your back is straight but not too stiff, and both hands are in your lap or placed, palms down, on your thighs.*

(If lying down) *lie on your back with your feet falling away and your arms at your sides.*

(pause)

Now, let's start by paying attention to the inside.

See if you can become aware of your breathing.

Notice your breath wherever it's easiest for you: going in and out at your nose, perhaps at your chest, or maybe at your belly.

Just see if you can notice your breath and follow it from the beginning of the in-breath to the end of the out-breath.

We're mindfully paying attention to what's inside.

(pause)

If you notice that your mind is thinking or if there is a lot of chatter going on, see if you can notice thoughts and let them go, watching your mind settle to the best of your ability.

(pause)

We can simply notice our thoughts and let them go

…and bring our attention back to the breath.

(bell)

You may help students process this mindfulness practice by asking them if they noticed any thoughts and how they dealt with them. There should be no expectation to reveal the content of any thoughts.

Let students know that they can record their experiences outside of class on the "My Home Practice: Theme R" page of the student workbook.

Key Words: chattering mind, focused attention, broad attention, zoom lens, perception

Between-Session Mindfulness Booster: *Practice tuning in to your breath at the belly. Move your attention to your thoughts. Practice becoming aware of the thoughts in your mind. At the end of your session, return your attention to focusing on the breath at your belly.*

R

Session 5

1. Guide students in a short mindfulness practice.

2. Review themes B, R, and the final E.

3. Guide students in the "Name That Thought" activity to illustrate how people have different thoughts about the same event.

4. Guide students in "The White Polar Bear" activity to show how hard it is to get rid of thoughts.

5. Guide students in a mindfulness practice on thoughts.

Review of Previous Theme and Reintroduction of Theme R

Guide students in a short mindfulness practice. This may include taking a few breaths, listening to a sound, doing a mindful-movement activity, and so on.

We've been practicing mindfulness of the body and also mindfulness of thoughts. What do you remember about being mindful of sensations and thoughts? Have you noticed that you have lots of thoughts in your mind? (Discuss.)

Activities to Develop Theme R

Let's try to identify some of the thoughts in our minds. What might someone be thinking in these situations?

R ACTIVITY: Name That Thought

Read the following vignettes and invite discussion. The message is that there are always thoughts in the mind, and that they differ depending on our interpretation or perception of circumstances (pleasant, unpleasant, or neutral).

1. *It's the last three minutes of the basketball game. Jake is standing at the foul line, ready to make a foul shot. His team needs the points to win the game. He is holding the ball in his hands and looking at the basket. He hears the crowd around him yelling. He shoots and misses. What's in his mind?* (Discuss.)

2. *Jen sits down in her science class and watches her teacher take a stack of papers from the big desk in the front of the room. The teacher announces a surprise quiz on the science homework. The papers get passed down the aisle. What is Jen thinking?* (Discuss.)

3. *It's the first day of middle school and Darryl is standing at the end of a long hallway full of noisy students at their lockers. Everywhere he looks, he sees students talking, laughing, and rushing around. What is he thinking?* (Discuss.)

4. *Maria is getting ready for a big dance that is being held at her school. She has carefully selected what to wear and has spent a long time working on her hair and makeup. She takes a last look at herself in the mirror. What is she thinking?* (Discuss.)

Notice how many different kinds of thoughts people can have about the same situation. That's because we're all different.

Are you aware that your thoughts can be pleasant, unpleasant, or neutral? We usually like to think about things that are pleasant. We usually don't like to think about things that are unpleasant. Neutral thoughts are neither very pleasant nor very unpleasant. Can you identify which of the thoughts from the previous examples were pleasant, unpleasant, or neutral?

Ask students to use the student workbook page, "All Kinds of Thoughts," to write examples of pleasant, unpleasant, and neutral thoughts.

Discuss.

Can you really get rid of unpleasant thoughts? Did you ever try to not think about something? Then what happens?

· ·

ACTIVITY: The White Polar Bear

Let's see if we can not think about something.

Take a moment for the class to settle. Ask students to sit quietly and put down anything they might be holding.

Just take a few deep breaths and let your mind settle. Now bring to mind an image of a white polar bear, this large animal with its white fur and dark eyes, standing very still. Keep the image in mind in as much detail as possible.

Pause for about thirty seconds.

Now clear your mind and do not think of a white polar bear.

Just sit for a few moments, but do not think of a polar bear.

(brief pause)

If the image does enter your mind, raise your hand.

(Allow about one or two minutes.)

What happened? (Allow students to discuss the experience of trying to block out thoughts.)

It's hard not to think of things. Sometimes the thoughts in our minds seem to get stuck there. They're "sticky thoughts" that sometimes don't go away very easily. If they're unpleasant, we might call these kinds of thoughts "worries."

We might try to get rid of them, but this doesn't really work very well. There's another way to work with thoughts that come into the mind. We can learn to be mindful of thoughts and say to ourselves: "It's just my mind thinking." "It's just my mind thinking pleasant thoughts." "It's just my mind thinking unpleasant thoughts."

In other words, we can notice the thought and choose to think about it or, to the best of our ability, let it go. Let's practice this.

. . . .

Moving to Practice

Guide students in a bit of stretching, some mindful movements, or both before asking them to sit down. (Review the "General Guidelines" box from chapter 11, session 1).

. . . .

PRACTICE: Mindfulness of Thoughts

So, please find a comfortable position.

(If seated) *put both feet flat on the floor. Your back is straight but not too stiff, and both hands are in your lap or placed, palms down, on your thighs.*

(If lying down) *lie on your back with your feet falling away and your arms at your sides.*

(pause)

Now, let's start by paying attention to the inside.

See if you can become aware of your breathing.

Notice your breath wherever it's easiest for you: going in and out at your nose, perhaps at your chest, or maybe at your belly.

Just see if you can notice your breath and follow it from the beginning of the in-breath to the end of the out-breath.

We're mindfully paying attention to what's inside.

If you find your mind wandering, just notice that your mind has wandered; let go of the thoughts, the stories, the plans, or whatever is there right now; and bring your attention back to the breath.

(pause)

We can simply notice our thoughts and let them go.

(pause)

We're practicing noticing our thoughts,

…maybe noting if they are pleasant, unpleasant, or neutral

…but without giving them too much attention.

And then returning the attention to the breath.

(pause)

Thoughts can be like clouds in the sky, moving across the field of awareness.

We can just imagine that we're lying in the grass, very still and calm, watching the thoughts come and go like clouds until the sound of the bell.

(bell)

Teachers may process this mindfulness activity by asking if students noticed any thoughts and how they dealt with them.

· ·

Use the student workbook page, "Dealing with Troubling Thoughts," to review how to practice outside of class.

Key Words: pleasant, unpleasant, neutral, "sticky thoughts"

Between-Session Mindfulness Booster: *Practice tuning in to the breath at your belly. Move your attention to your thoughts. Practice becoming aware of the thoughts in your mind. At the end of the session, return your attention to focusing on the breath at your belly.*

Session 6

1. Guide students in a short period of mindfulness practice.

2. Review themes B, R, and the final E in the BREATHE acronym.

3. Discuss how thoughts affect attention and performance.

4. Guide students in the "My Mind Is a Cast of Characters" activity to illustrate how thoughts can overwhelm us and affect how we feel and perform.

5. Guide students in the awareness-of-thoughts practice: "Notice and Let Go."

Review of Previous Themes and Reintroduction to Theme R

Guide students in a short mindfulness practice. This may include taking a few breaths, listening to a sound, doing a mindful-movement activity, and so on.

Recall that mindfulness is a special way of paying attention. It's paying attention, on purpose, to whatever is happening right now, without judging it or immediately needing to change anything. Once we stop and pay attention, we realize that our minds are full of activity, filled with thoughts coming and going. Remember the story of the person who was waiting to go to the game with a new friend? The way we think about things can affect the ways we think and feel, especially if we hold on to thoughts too tightly when they are hurtful.

Our brains are amazing. They help us think, solve problems, plan ahead, remember information, communicate with others, feel certain things, and do what we want to do. Most of the time, our brains are generating thoughts. Usually we're not aware of the brain's constant chatter, but we can become more aware. This lesson is about learning to pay attention to thoughts in a mindful way, and we'll discuss how this can help us develop inner balance.

Activity to Develop Theme R

Lead the group in an activity that demonstrates the mental chatter of the mind and its effects on emotions and performance.

ACTIVITY: My Mind Is a Cast of Characters

Let's try an exercise that shows how the mind's chatter can affect us. (See the instructions for conducting this activity in chapter 6.)

Moving to Practice

Guide students in a bit of stretching, some mindful movements, or both before asking them to sit down. (Review the "General Guidelines" box in chapter 11, session 1).

Introduce a short period of mindfulness practice. Begin with focus on the breath and add guidance about thoughts.

If we want to be strong and balanced, we need to be aware of the nature of our thoughts and what our sticky thoughts are. We can try to stop our thinking, but that's not really possible. We can become mindful of the thoughts that circle around in our heads and just observe them, like clouds that pass by in the sky or like water that flows in front of us as we stand behind a waterfall. We can also use the image of thoughts floating around us in a circle, like in the class activity we just did. That way we can have more choices about what we pay attention to. We won't waste a lot of energy fighting with our thoughts. Remember that thoughts are just thoughts. We don't have to believe everything we think.

PRACTICE: Mindfulness of Thoughts

Now, we're going to spend the next part of the class doing a short mindfulness practice to cultivate present-moment attention. We'll be paying attention to our breath, as we did in the "Body Scan." We'll also be practicing noticing and letting go of thoughts as we repeatedly bring our attention back to the breath.

Remember not to be too hard on yourself if your attention wanders. Cultivating your attention will take practice. When you find that it has wandered from the breath, gently but firmly escort your attention back to the breath, no matter how often this happens. We are practicing steadiness and balance.

Just sitting back in your chair, with your head, back, and neck straight but not rigid, with your shoulders relaxed and your hands comfortably placed in your lap, your feet on the floor, gently close your eyes if you are comfortable with this.

Now become aware of the breath moving into and out of your body,

…noticing the breath at the nostrils,

…feeling the rising and falling of the belly expanding gently on each in-breath and deflating on each out-breath,

…just feeling the breath as it comes in and as it goes out, without trying to control it in any way,

…seeing if you can be aware of the breath from the beginning of the in-breath to the end of the out-breath.

(pause)

As you sit here watching your breath,

…you may notice sensations in your body;

(pause)

…just let them come and go.

(pause)

You may notice thoughts that arise in your mind.

Thoughts arise in our minds all the time.

See if you can notice the thoughts in your mind,

…noticing that you are thinking,

…then just let thoughts go on their own and gently direct your attention back to the breath.

(pause)

Your mind is like a revolving door,

…thoughts moving in and thoughts moving out while you just observe them coming and going, bringing your attention back to the breath,

...staying awake and alert in each moment until the sound of the bell.

(bell)

Key Words: concentration, "notice and let go"

Between-Session Mindfulness Booster: *Practice tuning in to the breath at your belly. Move your attention to your thoughts. Practice becoming aware of the thoughts in your mind. At the end of your session, return your attention to focusing on the breath at your belly.*

Chapter 13

Theme E: Emotions

Theme E, for emotions, is taught over three sessions, numbered 7 through 9.

Session 7

1. Guide students in a short period of mindfulness practice.

2. Review themes B, R, and last E.

3. Define and discuss emotions.

4. Introduce "The Lineup" activity to illustrate the universality of emotional experience.

5. Guide students in the "Emotion in Three Acts" and "How Does It Feel?" activities to help them identify the different emotions.

6. Conduct a mindfulness-of-feelings practice.

Review of Previous Themes and Introduction to Theme E

Guide students in a short mindfulness practice. This may include taking a few breaths, listening to a sound, doing a mindful-movement activity, and so on.

We are practicing training our minds to be more mindful and less mindless so that we can feel more balanced and strong. We started by learning what mindfulness is. We did this by focusing our attention on our breath, on our bodies, and on the thoughts in our minds. We're learning to pay attention to the inside and the outside. Today we're going to add the next letter in the BREATHE acronym: "E," which stands for emotions.

Emotions (or feelings) happen on the inside. Events that happen on the outside can lead us to feel certain emotions as well. Very often we have feelings that we're not aware of or don't want to pay attention to. Feelings can be present even when we don't acknowledge them.

Why is it important to know how we are feeling?

A few examples might be helpful to use. Basically, emotional awareness is implicated in decision making and effective action. Emotions are important motivators of behavior. Unacknowledged feelings can work behind the scenes to influence behavior in problematic ways. Unacknowledged resentment, for example, can lead to bullying.

We wouldn't want to be a passenger on a plane that's on automatic pilot when it's time to land. To land an airplane safely, a pilot needs to be aware of all the air traffic. The pilot needs to be completely awake. Awareness of our internal experience gives us information we need to be on top of things, to feel more balanced, and to make good decisions. Otherwise we can act without awareness of what's really happening to us on the inside. We can act in ways that hurt ourselves and others.

Today we'll experiment with being aware of our emotions and rating them as pleasant, unpleasant, or neutral. Let's start by naming some emotions.

Use the "emotion faces" page in the student workbook to help with this.

Activities to Develop Theme E

From the activities "The Lineup," "Emotion in Three Acts," and "How Does It Feel?" choose the activity or activities that best suit the group and the available time.

. . . .

ACTIVITY: Emotion in Three Acts

Refer to the description in chapter 7.

. . . .

ACTIVITY: How Does It Feel?

The purpose of this activity is to name some emotions and show that there are levels of intensity as well as pleasant, unpleasant, and neutral valence to emotions. This activity can be useful, because it allows students the opportunity to name some feelings that are commonly experienced in various situations. The goal is to develop some skill in emotion identification and in awareness of the universality of emotional experience. At their stage of development, adolescents often feel that their emotional experience is unique. This perception can result in feelings of isolation and unwillingness to recognize and accept feelings.

Ask group members to suggest feelings that fit the following situations. Try to name as many feelings for each situation as possible. Discuss whether the feelings are pleasant, unpleasant, or neutral to group members. Perceptions will differ.

How does it feel…

…when I get the grade I want on a project?

…when my brother or sister fights with me?

…when I get a compliment?

…when someone teases me?

…when I don't understand what my teacher or parents want me to do?

…when I get a stomachache?

…when my team wins?

…when I don't make the team?

…when I am with my friends?

…when my friends try to talk me into doing something that I don't want to do?

These are examples of emotions that we all experience. Let's see if this is true for all of us in this class.

ACTIVITY: The Lineup

Refer to the description of this activity in chapter 7.

Moving to Practice

Guide students in a bit of stretching, some mindful movements, or both before asking them to sit down (review the "General Guidelines" box in chapter 11, session 1).

So we have seen that there are many different feelings or emotions that we can experience. We also see that everyone has these feelings. Sometimes these feelings can be a little overwhelming, and they can upset our inner balance. We can bring mindful awareness to our emotions, just as we did with our bodies and our thoughts. Let's start by putting nonjudgment into practice, by becoming aware of what we are feeling, and noticing the tendency to like or dislike the feeling without needing to feel a certain way. And, after we notice that feeling, just play detective: be curious about the feeling, such as where it shows up in the body. Then after watching it with curiosity, let it go and guide your attention back to the breath.

Let's practice this.

E

. . . .

PRACTICE: Mindfulness of Emotions

So, please find a comfortable position. Sit with both feet flat on the floor. Your back is straight but not too stiff, and both hands are in your lap or placed, palms down, on your thighs.

(pause)

Now, let's start by paying attention to the inside,

seeing if you can become aware of your breathing.

Notice your breath wherever it's easiest for you,

just letting the breath be as it is,

trying to maintain awareness of the full breath from the beginning of the in-breath…

…to the end of the out-breath,

…fully present and aware of each new breath.

(pause)

As you sit here watching your breath,

you may notice sensations in your body;

(pause)

just let them come and go.
You may notice thoughts that arise in your mind;

(pause)

just let them come and go.
You may also notice feelings or emotions.

(pause)

Notice where they are in your body, maybe at your chest, stomach, forehead, throat, shoulders.
Just notice and become aware of any emotions.
Notice if you rate them as pleasant or unpleasant.

(pause)

Try to be kind to yourself as you practice.
You might be feeling some frustration because it's hard to pay attention.
You may be feeling some restlessness.
See if you can be okay with these feelings and just become aware of them, allowing them to be without trying to change anything.
Then gently move your attention back to the breath to calm and balance yourself.

(bell)

Discuss this practice if desired.

· ·

Inform students that they can record their practice experiences outside of class on the "My Home Practice: Theme E" page of the student workbook.

Key Words: emotions, feelings

Between-Session Mindfulness Booster: *Tune in to the breath. Now see if you can be aware of any feelings or emotions. Notice them in your body, maybe at your chest, stomach, forehead, throat, or shoulders. Just notice. As you notice feelings, become aware of the way that you judge them. Then gently move your attention back to the breath to calm and balance yourself.*

Session 8

1. Guide students in a short mindfulness practice.

2. Review themes B, R, E, and the last E.

3. Guide students in "The Great Cover-Up" activity to illustrate the tendency to avoid unpleasant feelings.

4. Guide students in the mindfulness practice "Finding the Feeling."

Review of Previous Themes and Reintroduction to Theme E

Guide students in a short mindfulness practice. This may include taking a few breaths, listening to a sound, doing a mindful movement activity, and so on.

In the last class, we talked about feelings or emotions. Emotions are part of being human, and they help us communicate with others and deal with what happens to us. For example, smiles communicate happiness to others. Fear can be a very useful emotion to feel if it helps us escape from a dangerous situation. Remember that we talked about how we tend to rate our thoughts as pleasant or unpleasant. This seems to be especially true of emotions. We even call some emotions good and some bad. We say, "I'm feeling good," or "I'm feeling bad."

Can you name some emotions that we say are good? Some that we identify as bad? The reality is that we can't avoid feeling bad sometimes. It's just part of life.

Activity to Develop Theme E

What do people do when they experience an uncomfortable emotion (when they're feeling bad)? Let's try an activity to explore this question.

. . . .

ACTIVITY: The Great Cover-Up

Refer to the description of this activity in chapter 7.

. . . .

E

Moving to Practice

Guide students in a bit of stretching, some mindful movements, or both before asking them to sit down (review the "General Guidelines" box in chapter 11, session 1).

Now we'll try a short mindfulness practice to see if we can find the feelings and simply observe them without covering anything up.

The goal of the following practice is to help students experience feelings in the body and mind, watch the feelings rise and fall, and ultimately help them understand that they can just observe the energy of their feelings without acting on them. Students are asked to observe their reactions and to practice not reacting to (covering up) any part of the experience. In general, this means not avoiding the feeling by distracting yourself. Instead, the practice involves turning toward all feelings, including uncomfortable ones, with curiosity and attention.

This practice invites students to find feelings in the body so that they become more aware of the connections between emotions and physical sensations. The emotions are happiness, mild worry or anger, and peacefulness. Because of the practice needed to access a feeling, it might be best to choose one feeling and work with it, rather than include all three in one practice period. Sometimes it is difficult to shift, and it can take time to get in touch with the felt sense of the emotions. Other parts of this practice can be done in other sessions or between classes. Use the same introductory and closing instructions for each part.

PRACTICE: Finding the Feeling

Guide students in a few stretches or mindfulness movements before asking them to sit down.

Introduction

As we begin this activity, find a comfortable position, closing your eyes, if that's comfortable for you, and getting as quiet as possible.

Find your breath in your body and just feel its movement for three breaths.

(Pause for a few breaths.)

We'll be practicing paying attention to feelings on the inside.

We'll be paying special attention to where the feelings show up in the body.

Remember that we're just observing the sensations of the body as they reflect the energy of the feelings. We're not trying to change or cover up anything.

Just remember that feelings are like waves that come and go. We can surf their waves.

Remember, too, that at any time you can bring your mind back to focus on your breath, using your breath as an anchor to calm yourself.

(pause)

Happiness

Let' s start with happiness.

See if you can experience what happiness feels like in your body.

To help you do this, you might remember a time when you felt happy.

(pause)

Notice the sensations in your body,

perhaps in the area of the heart.

What are the sensations like?

Are they ...warm, ...light, ...bright, ...loud, or ...soft like a whisper?

As you sit here feeling happiness, be curious about this feeling.

Notice if it gets stronger or if it fades away.

(pause)

Worry or Anger

Now choose to investigate a mild but uncomfortable feeling, maybe worry or anger.

See if you can begin to experience worry or anger in your body.

Notice any sensations,

perhaps in your belly, in your shoulders or back, in your forehead or jaw.

(pause)

What are the sensations like?

Are they ...hot, ...tight, ...burning, ...cold, ...sharp?

Do they move around, or are they fixed?

(pause)

As you sit here, be curious about this feeling.

Notice if it gets stronger or if it fades away.

See if you can just observe it without covering it up.

(pause)

Peacefulness

Now bring to mind the feeling of peacefulness.

See if you can experience what peacefulness feels like in your body.

To help you do this, you might remember a time when you felt peaceful.

Notice the sensations in your body.

What are the sensations like?

Are they in one place or throughout your body?

(pause)

Be curious about this feeling.

Notice if it gets stronger or if it fades away.

(pause)

Closing

Notice the connections between your feelings and the sensations in your body.

Perhaps different feelings are connected to different sensations.

We can learn to notice the feelings and sensations, and watch them move and change.

We can also return our attention to a safe place, like the breath, when we want to feel more balanced and secure.

Now return your attention to your breath, and focus on the movements of the breath at your belly until the sound of the bell.

(bell)

Discuss the experience. Do not ask or expect adolescents to disclose the content of any memories. Focus on the experience of emotions and bodily feelings. Ask the students to recall if the emotion changed over the course of the practice or if they noticed different sensations for different emotions.

. . . .

Use the student workbook page "Tips to Take Away: About Anger and Other Uncomfortable Emotions" to help students understand how to practice outside of sessions.

Key Words: Uncomfortable emotions

Between-Session Mindfulness Booster: *Tune in to the breath. (Pause.) Now see if you can be aware of any feelings or emotions. Notice them in your body, maybe at your chest, stomach, forehead, throat, shoulders, and so on. Just notice. As you notice feelings, become aware of the way that you judge them. Then gently move your attention back to the breath to calm and balance yourself.*

Session 9

1. Guide students in a short mindfulness practice.

2. Review themes B, R, E, and the final E.

3. Guide students in the "Surfing the Waves" activity.

Review of Previous Themes and Reintroduction to Theme E

E

Guide students in a short mindfulness practice. This may include taking a few breaths, listening to a sound, doing a mindful movement activity, and so on.

Review themes B, R, E, and the final E, and the experiences of mindfulness thus far. Allow group members time to report on their personal mindfulness practices outside of the group, either at the beginning of the class or at the end. Students might wish to make a change in their choice of activity for the remaining sessions.

We've talked about comfortable emotions, like happiness, and uncomfortable ones, like worry. Remember that we discussed how people often try to avoid feeling emotions that they don't like to feel. We try to block out the uncomfortable feelings, as we did with unpleasant thoughts. But this strategy can backfire. If we don't recognize what we're feeling, the energy of the feeling can make us behave in ways that hurt ourselves and others.

Sometimes we hang on to the uncomfortable feelings and keep dwelling on them. This approach can make us feel really bad. It brings us down and takes away some of the energy we need for doing other things.

Now we're learning a new way to behave with our emotional ups and downs. We're practicing mindfulness of emotions—which means that we notice what we're feeling as we feel it, recognize it, face up to it, and maybe even call it by its name. It's like saying to ourselves, Hey, this is just anger. And then we use the breath to calm ourselves and watch the feeling rise and pass away. We don't try to force the feeling to go away. We let it pass in its own time. It's a little like watching the air go out of a balloon.

We'll spend more time during this session being mindful of our emotions. This time we'll practice just observing them, really being curious about them, and noticing where they show up as sensations in our bodies.

Let's notice if we register the emotions we feel as pleasant, unpleasant, or neutral. Instead of avoiding the feelings, let's practice watching them come and go as we stay strong and balanced.

Activity to Develop Theme E

Guide students in a bit of stretching, some mindful movements, or both before asking them to sit down (review the "General Guidelines" box in chapter 11, session 1).

Most of the session time for this theme should be spent on the practice of recognizing emotions and learning how to handle them mindfully. For the sake of time, since these are shorter sessions, this is accomplished using the "Surfing the Waves" activity, which will also serve as the practice portion of this session.

E

ACTIVITY: Surfing the Waves

Allow students to sit or lie down comfortably. Ring the bell to start if desired.

Find your breath in your body and just feel its movement for three breaths. We'll be practicing paying attention to feelings on the inside. We'll be paying special attention to where the feelings show up in the body. Remember that we're just observing the sensations of the body as they reflect the energy of the feelings. We're not trying to change or cover up anything. Just remember that feelings are like waves that come and go. We can surf the waves. Remember that at any time, you can bring your attention back to focus on your breath or to another safe space in your body, using the breath like an anchor.

Continue with the "Surfing the Waves" activity in chapter 7.

Key Words: mindfulness of feelings

Between-Session Mindfulness Booster: *Tune in to the breath.* (Pause.) *Now see if you can be aware of any feelings or emotions. Notice them in your body, maybe at your chest, stomach, forehead, throat, shoulders, and so on. Just notice. As you notice feelings, become aware of the way that you judge them. Then gently move your attention back to the breath to calm and balance yourself.*

Chapter 14

Theme A: Attention

Theme A, for attention, is taught over three sessions, numbered 10 through 12.

Session 10

1. Guide students in a short mindfulness practice.

2. Review themes B, R, E, and the final E; and introduce theme A.

3. Discuss what stress is.

4. Go over "A Stressed-Out Case" to provide an opportunity to identify stressors in a hypothetical case study.

5. Guide students in the "Cross the Line" activity to illustrate the commonality of stress in everyone's life.

6. Guide students in a mindful movement practice.

Review of Previous Themes and Introduction to Theme A

Guide students in a short mindfulness practice. This may include taking a few breaths, listening to a sound, doing a mindful movement activity, and so on.

Review themes B, R, E, and the final E. Introduce theme A.

If time permits, ask for examples of how students are being more mindful.

What have you been noticing about your thoughts, feelings, and physical sensations? What has been happening in the way that you do the activity you chose (from theme B, "Mindfulness in My Life," in student workbook)?

When we are paying attention to what's going on in the present moment in our thoughts, our feelings, and our bodies, and when we are treating ourselves kindly, we can be stronger and more balanced. This is really important in helping us deal with day-to-day stress. That's what theme A is all about. "A" stands for attention, the kind of mindful attention we've been practicing. We're paying attention to the inside and the outside.

Let's imagine that your computer is operating more and more slowly. Strange messages are popping up on the screen. You can't open certain files, and a big, flashing warning message says, "Your computer is at risk!" But you keep ignoring this, because you're too busy with other things.

What is likely to happen? (Discuss.)

In a similar way, if we're not mindful of the signs of stress and don't try to manage them, we can have big problems after a while.

What is stress?

"Stress" is a general term used to mean distress, discomfort, fear, and anxiety that we can experience when we perceive ourselves to be unable or unwilling to cope with events.

What are some things that stress people out? Let's try some activities to explore this question.

Activities to Develop Theme A

Two activities can be used for this lesson: "A Stressed-Out Case (Middle School)" and "Cross the Line (Stressors)." Instructors may use both or select the one that is best for the group.

. . . .

A STRESSED-OUT CASE (MIDDLE SCHOOL)

MATERIALS: "A Stressed-Out Case" page in the student workbook, a pen or pencil

Read the case study of an adolescent with many life stressors. Group members can work individually and write on the workbook page, "A Stressed-Out Case," as many stressors as they can identify from the story. Ask them to write each stressor in one of the bubbles. Alternatively, the case study can be copied for group members to read as they work in teams to identify stressors.

The gender, name, and circumstances of the student can be changed at the teacher's discretion. Sharing of responses can be done in small groups or pairs before sharing with the whole group.

Sam is a _____ grade student in Main Street School (use the same grade as students). He (or she, if gender is changed) has one older sister and younger twin brothers. His parents got divorced two years ago, and his mother remarried last year. He and his brothers live with their mom and stepdad. He usually sees his dad every other Saturday. Sometimes Sam and his dad go to the movies or a game, but usually his dad is too busy with work to take him anywhere. When this happens, Sam plays video games in his dad's apartment while waiting for his dad to get home from work. Sam was always a good student who got mostly A's and B's when he was younger.

Now that he's in middle school, his grades are not as good. He has so many projects and tests for his classes that he can't figure out how to get everything done. He doesn't know where to start.

When his mom tells him to start his homework, he usually goes to his room and gets out his books. Then his mind wanders to something he wants to see on the computer or to a text message from a friend. Hours can go by, and he doesn't get much done. He's got a big class presentation coming up in social studies, and Sam feels that he is really bad at public speaking. Not only that, but he's convinced that his social studies teacher doesn't like him. He's worried that he's going to forget the information, so he's trying not to think about it right now.

Often, Sam gets so caught up in playing games on the computer that he stays up way past the bedtime his mom set for him. From his point of view, homework is a lot more boring than playing video games, so he puts it off until the last minute and then is too sleepy to finish it.

Usually he rushes out of the house without breakfast to catch the bus because he has overslept. When he tries to do his homework on the bus, his friends tease him, so he just puts it away.

Sam's stepfather is very upset with him about his grades. It seems that every day, they have a fight about homework. Sam can't stand it when his stepfather talks to him as if he were a baby. Sometimes he gets so angry about it, he'll yell at his younger brothers, and then he really gets in trouble. One of the things Sam likes to do is hang out with his friends on the weekends and play ball. He used to have a lot of fun doing this, especially with his best friend, Dave. Now Dave has a girlfriend, and Sam feels left out. He'd like to have a girlfriend, but it hasn't worked out for him. Sam is starting to think that he's a loser and that no girl would like him. He worries about this a lot. Lately he's been having a lot of stomachaches before school, especially when he has a test in class and because his friends don't call him to hang out as much as before.

Discuss student responses. Describe and discuss "chronic" stressors. Use questions from chapter 8.

Sometimes things pile up, and we don't even notice them. What are some signs from Sam's case that he (or she) should pay attention to his bodily symptoms, the way he's thinking, how he's feeling, and so on?

If we notice the stresses when they start, then we can do something about them before they get too big. Remember that noticing things—really being aware—is what being mindful is all about. We can notice our thoughts, feelings, and bodily sensations with interest and kindness, and this can help us relax more and not add to the problem.

Cross the Line (Stressors)

Refer to the instructions for this activity in chapter 8.

It's clear that we all experience stress. We're not alone in this because it's part of being human. Therefore, it's important to learn ways to be kind to ourselves and others so that we don't add to the problem. Remember from theme E that covering things up is not the most helpful way to deal with unpleasant experiences or stress. Practicing mindfulness of our experiences can help us be more at ease and balanced.

Use the workbook pages "What's My Limit?" and "Long-Term, Chronic Stress" to reinforce the messages of the lesson.

Moving to Practice

Guide students in a bit of stretching, some mindful movements, or both before beginning, if desired (review the "General Guidelines" box in chapter 11, session 1).

Today we'll practice mindfulness in motion by walking mindfully. Every time we practice moving our attention to the present moment—and whatever is happening in that moment—we are strengthening our attention muscle, helping ourselves to be more balanced and strong.

Have you ever thought of your attention as being like a muscle? In what ways might this be true?

We can strengthen this "muscle" through practice. When we don't practice, it gets weak. We can direct it to do something, such as when we focus on a video game, just as we can direct the muscles in our hands to play the game.

We can practice mindfulness in every moment of the day. Whether we're sitting, working, walking, or playing, we can be aware of what's happening inside us and outside us.

···

PRACTICE: Mindful Walking

Group members may line up single file, in a circle, or in shorter lines, depending on the physical space available. Invite them to stand in a balanced posture, take some deep breaths, and bring their attention to the breath moving in and out of the body. Before asking them to walk, guide them to bring their attention to their feet and take one step for practice.

This is a mindfulness activity that can be practiced anytime, without any special equipment, whenever you are walking somewhere. Try it while walking to class, up or down stairs, to the bus stop, and so on. It can help you center yourself, using your breath and the movement of walking to help you be more aware of the present moment, more relaxed, and more balanced.

Notice how your right foot feels as it lifts off the floor, how it feels as it is poised in space, and how it feels as it is placed down again. Repeat with your left foot. Be conscious of your foot as it lifts, moves in space, and connects with the floor. Try to be aware of the coordination of your body as it moves and how your body allows you to walk without falling. Try to keep your focus on the experience of walking. When your mind wanders, bring your attention back to the experience of walking. Practice noticing the experience of walking.

···

Let students know that they can also record their experiences outside of class on the "My Home Practice: Theme A" page of the student workbook.

Key Words: stress, mindful walking, attention muscle

Between-Session Mindfulness Booster: Guide students in practicing mindful walking for three minutes.

Session 11

1. Guide students in a short mindfulness practice.

2. Review themes B, R, E, and the final E. Reintroduce theme A.

3. Discuss the basic facts about the stress system.

4. Guide students through the "How Much Can You Handle?" and "What's My Limit?" activities to illustrate the effects of chronic stress.

5. Guide students in a mindful-movement practice.

Review of Previous Themes and Reintroduction of Theme A

Guide students in a short mindfulness practice. This may include taking a few breaths, listening to a sound, doing a mindful-movement activity, and so on.

Last time, we talked about stress. We can't avoid all stress. Some stress is helpful, like when we're really working hard to win a game or meet some challenge. But sometimes things happen that we don't like. We might not think that we can cope with some challenging situation, and this can make us feel stressed out.

What happens to us physically when we're under stress?

Discuss the stress response and what the body does to respond (fight, flee, or freeze).

What happens in our minds? (Review how we have uncomfortable thoughts, and we often can't let go of them. Things bother us for a long time or keep coming back to mind.)

What kinds of feelings or moods do we experience? (Review uncomfortable emotions.)

Sometimes a big thing happens that upsets us. (Ask for examples or provide a few, like being in an accident, failing a class, having someone you care about break up with you.)

This kind of stress is called "acute stress," because it's usually not expected, and it can make you feel pretty bad. Sometimes we have a lot of smaller stressors, but they go on for a long time. This is called "chronic stress."

Activities to Develop Theme A

Let's take a look at chronic stress by doing an experiment. Use the activities "How Much Can You Handle?" and "What's My Limit?"

....

ACTIVITY: How Much Can You Handle?

Refer to the instructions for this activity in chapter 8. Afterwards, use the following questions for discussion.

What happened? How does this apply to the stress in your life? (Discuss the problem of having stress or strain go on for too long.)

Although our bodies and minds are well designed to cope with emergencies, they need to return to a more relaxed state after an emergency in order to be healthy. Too many ongoing stressors or chronic stress can lead to physical, mental, and emotional problems. For example, we can have problems sleeping if we have too much ongoing stress, we can eat too much or eat too little, or we can get headaches or stomachaches. We have difficulty concentrating and remembering things. We can also start to think in ways that are pretty negative.

Remember when we did that activity ("My Mind Is a Cast of Characters" from theme R, session 6) with the student in the middle of the circle trying to do the math problems? Having a lot of stress is like being in the middle of that circle.

....

ACTIVITY: What's My Limit?

Use the student workbook page "What's My Limit?" If time allows, use the workbook to show the trajectory of chronic stress. Adolescents can identify things that they are dealing with at the present time and list them.

The problem is that we often are unaware of the stress piling up until it gets really, really bad. So, if we are more mindful of what's happening both inside and outside of us, we can help ourselves let go of a lot of stress that we'd be carrying around otherwise.

....

Moving to Practice

Guide students in a bit of stretching, some mindful movements, or both before beginning if desired (review the "General Guidelines" box in chapter 11, session 1).

Today we'll practice mindfulness by doing mindful movement. Let's practice paying attention to the breath in the body.

Guide students in doing several of the mindful movements from chapter 8, using the workbook pages "Sitting Postures" and "Standing Postures."

Key Words: acute stress, chronic stress

Between-Session Mindfulness Booster: Guide students in practicing mindful movement ("Sitting Postures," "Standing Postures," or "Mindful Walking") or in practicing some routine classroom or group-session activity (like packing up books, leaving the room, and so on) with mindfulness.

Session 12

1. Guide students in a short mindfulness practice.

2. Review themes B, R, E, and A.

3. Guide students through the "Mindfulness 360" activity to connect sensations of movement, thoughts, and feeling.

4. Guide students in a mindful-movement or "Waterlines" practice.

Review of Previous Themes and Reintroduction to Theme A

Guide students in a short mindfulness practice. This may include taking a few breaths, listening to a sound, doing a mindful-movement activity, and so on.

The first step in gaining inner strength and dealing with our stress is becoming aware of the stress (paying attention).

Today we'll practice more mindful movement. When moving mindfully, we try to pay attention to our present experience, regardless of what it is. Some days we can move easily; some days it's harder. Some days we have a lot of energy; other days we might be feeling tired or sick. Whatever it is for you today, let's pay attention to it without judging it.

This is different from some of the movement we typically do. We're not trying to get anywhere, get something done, or compete with anyone. We're just practicing becoming aware of experiences in the body, thoughts, and feelings.

Let's try an activity that shows this difference.

Activity to Develop Theme A

The following activity may be used as a precursor to the mindful-movement practice. It enables students to experience the difference between mindless and mindful movements.

. . . .

A ACTIVITY: Mindfulness 360

MATERIALS: Depends on choice of activity

Mindful movement is being fully present to the complete experience of movement in the body. It means knowing with full awareness that you are moving, whatever form that movement takes. It also promotes awareness of all the dimensions of that experience: thoughts, feelings, sensations.

Allow group members to select a movement that they usually do without awareness. Examples might be standing up from a chair and moving the chair under a desk or table; opening or closing a door; picking up a coat and putting it on; getting a drink of water; tying or untying shoelaces; packing or unpacking a book bag; sending a text message or an e-mail.

Allow the students to perform the activity at a normal pace. Then, invite them to repeat the activity very slowly and mindfully while being aware of the full range (360 degrees) of the action.

As you do the action, can you be aware of all the tiny movements in your body?

Can you be aware of the space around you?

Can you be aware of thoughts and feelings?

Can you be aware of when the action begins and when it ends?

Can you be aware of any changes in physical sensations or movements, thoughts, and feelings from the beginning to the end of the activity?

Discuss.

How were the experiences different? What movements, thoughts, and feelings were you aware of in the first part of the activity? In the second part?

There's a lot going on in every activity: walking, eating, talking, and so on. Each activity is an opportunity to develop more mindfulness.

Repeat if desired. Group members may practice with another activity.

. . . .

Moving to Practice

Move directly into the mindful movement practice. Use pictures in the student workbook, if helpful. The mindful movement practice may be done seated or standing as space and time permit. As with other practices, remind students about guidelines (posture, using the breath as an anchor, and so on). If there is time after the practice, provide the opportunity to share experiences or ask questions.

See the "Mindful Movement" practice in chapter 8.

. . . .

ALTERNATE PRACTICE: Waterlines

MATERIALS: art paper, round watercolor brushes, paper cup filled about one-quarter to halfway full with water, cloth to cover the desk or table

This activity is adapted with the permission of Richard Brown. Prepare the work space in advance, providing cloth backing, paper, brush, and water for each participant.

Guide students in a bit of stretching, some mindful movements, or both before asking them to sit down (review the "General Guidelines" box in chapter 11, session 1).

This practice involves mindful brushstrokes. Each movement of this practice should be done mindfully so that you are aware of your body sitting in the chair, your hand holding the brush, the contact

of the brush with the water, and the movement of the brush across the page in "waterlines." The steady movement of the brush across the page is mirrored by the movement of the breath.

First, let's take our seats. Notice the contact your body makes with the chair. Feel your feet flat on the floor. Just observe the materials in front of you without touching anything. Notice your thoughts and feelings.

When you are ready, pick up the brush and examine it carefully. Notice the shape and the textures, the color, and the weight of the brush.

Then, pick up the brush and hold the tip directly above the table at a 90-degree angle. Keep your fingers straight. Let your thumb hold the front of the brush and the other four fingers touch the back of the brush, keeping them straight but not too stiff. Don't hold it too tightly, just enough to be able to move it lightly across the page when I tell you do so. Feel the weight of the brush in your hand.

When you're ready, bring the tip of the brush above the cup of water. Be aware of the movements of your arm and hand. Move the brush down, slowly and mindfully, to the surface of the water. Notice the point when the brush touches the water. Notice how the brush drinks in the water as you move it around.

Then, lift the brush to the edge of the cup and allow the water to drain a bit. Smooth the edges of the brush along the sides of the cup.

Slowly and mindfully, move the brush to the left side of the paper. Notice the weight of the brush as you move the tip closer to meet the page. Notice the point of contact, and then make a waterline from one side to the other.

Repeat the process, making lines all the way down the page, slowly and mindfully.

You can also experiment with drawing lines more quickly or more slowly.

Find your own rhythm.

Notice your breath as you do this.

Feel the rhythm of your breath and the rhythm of the lines.

You could ring a chime to end the work. Invite the students to share their experiences of this activity.

. . . .

Let students know that they can use the workbook pages, "Tips to Take Away: Mindful Eating," "Eating-Awareness Experiment," and "Tips to Take Away: Mindful Walking" as between-session booster activities or home practice.

Key Words: mindful movement

Between-Session Mindfulness Booster: Using the student workbook page, "Tips to Take Away: Mindful Eating," guide students in practicing mindfulness of eating.

Chapter 15

Theme T: Tenderness

Theme T, for tenderness, is taught over three sessions, numbered 13 through 15.

Session 13

1. Guide students in a short mindfulness practice.

2. Review themes B, R, E, and A, and introduce theme T.

3. Guide students in the "Ways We Take Care of Ourselves/Ways We Don't Take Care of Ourselves" workbook pages and the "Practicing Meanness or Kindness Card Sort" activity.

4. Guide students in practicing loving-kindness toward the self.

Review of Previous Themes and Introduction to Theme T

Guide students in a short mindfulness practice. This may include taking a few breaths, listening to a sound, doing a mindful-movement activity, and so on.

We've been practicing a lot over the course of the last few weeks. Let's think about the idea of "practicing." What kind of people practice (athletes, musicians, actors, and so on)?

Why do they practice (to improve and get better at something)?

Is it always easy to practice something? (Give examples.)

What has your experience been like when you've practiced something? Why do you do it? (Discuss)

What's actually happening when someone practices something? (Discuss)

Practice changes the part of you that's in control of how you think, how you act, and how you feel: your brain! The brain is an amazing organ. It allows you to work, learn, sleep, play, read, talk, feel, and dream. It's what makes you who you are!

Today we're in class; it's really like boot camp for your brain. You're in brain training. Every day, you learn new things, and your brain changes a little. It registers new information and changes the way you think about things. If you play sports, the parts of the brain that are responsible for coordination, speed, agility, muscle control, and so on get better.

From scientists who can see inside the living brain, we now know that the brain can change with practice. We can practice healthy mind habits. In other words, the more we practice healthy ways of thinking and feeling, just as we practice sports or musical instruments, we can get better at being balanced, strong, and happy.

Throughout all these lessons, we have been practicing mindfulness as a way of becoming more empowered. This means getting strong and balanced on the inside as well as on the outside. It's easy to feel empowered when things are going well for us. It's harder to do when things are not going well. But we can still do it!

We can help ourselves a lot by remembering to be kind to ourselves, especially when things don't go our way. (Discuss why.)

We'll use theme T as another way of saying, "Be kind to yourself." "T" stands for tenderness or "Take it as it is." Instead of being really hurtful to ourselves, we can practice being tender, as you would act if you were taking care of someone who was important to you.

Practicing tenderness doesn't mean letting ourselves off the hook or not expecting very much of ourselves. It's recognizing that we don't help ourselves when we don't take care of our insides and our outsides. We can take ourselves as we are and be compassionate to ourselves when we need to be.

Sometimes we practice kindness, but sometimes we practice meanness, too. When we practice meanness, we're not taking it as it is. We're usually trying to cover up or get rid of something we don't like. Let's investigate some of the ways in which people treat themselves.

Activities to Develop Theme T

Use the activity "Ways We Care for Ourselves, or Not" or use the alternate activity, "Practicing Meanness or Kindness Card Sort."

ACTIVITY: Ways We Care for Ourselves, or Not.

Use the student-workbook page "Ways We Take Care of Ourselves/Ways We Don't Take Care of Ourselves." Refer to the instructions in chapter 9 for this activity.

ALTERNATIVE ACTIVITY: Practicing Meanness or Kindness Card Sort

Card sorting is a technique that allows for grouping into categories examples that are printed on index cards. In this activity, the students get some practice in identifying hurtful or helpful thoughts, feelings, and behaviors. Prepare a set of index cards with examples of unhelpful thinking, persistent destructive emotions, and unhealthy behaviors. Use one example per index card. Depending on the number of card sets, this can be done independently, in groups, or in a large group setting.

Another way to do this with the whole group is to designate three areas of the room as "thinking," "feeling," and "acting" sections, using large sheets of paper taped to the wall or words on a blackboard. Prepare the index cards and ask one group member at a time to select a card from the deck of index cards, read the example, and move to the appropriate section of the room to write the example on the appropriate list. Once all the cards have been recorded, allow for discussion and other additions to the lists by group members.

Then provide new sheets of paper and ask students to list ways to practice kindness in each respective area. Repeat the process of sharing with the whole class.

The following examples of practicing meanness to the self may need some explanation from the instructor.

Behaviors (Acting): not eating enough or eating too much, having an unhealthy diet, taking drugs, not getting enough sleep, self-injury, drinking alcohol, smoking, riding a bike without a helmet, not exercising, being mean to others or gossiping so that social relationships are harmed, procrastinating with schoolwork so that grades go down, missing school, and so on.

Feelings (Feeling): being chronically angry or impatient with ourselves, being chronically impatient with others, being chronically intolerant of ourselves, being chronically embarrassed about the way we look or talk, thinking that we can't do anything well, feeling superior to others, having feelings of inadequacy.

Thoughts (Thinking): thinking about ourselves as losers, always thinking that others are better than we are, always thinking that we are better than others are, thinking that no one pays attention to us, thinking that nobody cares about us, thinking that we are unattractive, thinking that we are too fat, thinking that we are too skinny, thinking that we are not smart, thinking that we can't be successful. Examples of practicing kindness can be found in chapter 9.

. . . .

Moving to Practice

Guide students in a bit of stretching, some mindful movements, or both before asking them to sit down (review the "General Guidelines" box in chapter 11, session 1).

. . . .

PRACTICE: Loving-Kindness

Refer to the general description and instructions for this activity in chapter 9. This practice is a shorter version.

Let's practice a way of strengthening helpful emotions through loving-kindness. We often cultivate unhelpful thoughts and feelings by practicing them unconsciously. This is a way to cultivate feelings that can help us and that we can also extend to others.

So sit quietly, and tune in to the breath.

(pause)

Notice the in-breath and the out-breath as you take five deep, full breaths.

(Pause for five breaths.)

We'll be bringing to mind something we've experienced before and letting that help us practice kindness right now.

Bring to mind a time when someone was kind to you.

It doesn't have to be something very big. It could be a small act of kindness from a friend, a relative, a teacher, a coach, or even a stranger.

Maybe it happened today; maybe it happened a long time ago.

Just do your best to recall this experience, remembering how you felt.

And as you recall this experience of kindness,

…see if you can locate it in your body, perhaps noticing sensations of warmth, of lightness, of movement, of calmness, or whatever it is you are experiencing right now.

If you can't remember anything or if you can't locate it in your body, that's okay.

Just pay attention to your breath.

Whatever you are experiencing right now is fine.

(pause)

So stay with this memory.

Notice that someone wanted to show kindness to you.

(pause)

Now see if you can take this sense of kindness and tenderness, and offer it to yourself,

(pause)

…sending this wish to yourself:

"I wish to treat myself with tenderness."

"I wish that others be treated with kindness."

Take a few full breaths as you repeat the wishes until the sound of the bell.

(bell)

Discuss participant experiences if desired.

. . . .

Let the students know that they can record their experiences outside of class on the "My Home Practice: Theme T" page of the student workbook.

Session 14

1. Guide students in a short mindfulness practice.

2. Review themes B, R, E, A, and T.

3. Discuss practicing unhealthy mental habits.

4. Guide students in practicing loving-kindness to self and others.

Review of Previous Themes and Reintroduction to Theme T

Guide students in a short mindfulness practice. This may include taking a few breaths, listening to a sound, doing a mindful-movement activity, and so on.

We've learned that the brain can change with practice. We've also learned that we often operate on automatic pilot—without mindfulness—so that we can actually be practicing mindlessness without knowing it.

Sometimes this mindlessness shows itself as unhealthy ways of thinking, feeling, and acting. Sometimes we can get into a mindless mental rut and practice unkindness to ourselves because we don't accept ourselves as we are.

When we don't accept ourselves, we don't treat ourselves with compassion. And if we treat ourselves very judgmentally, then we are likely to treat others this way too.

Sometimes athletes can't improve even if they practice a lot because they don't realize that they are practicing in the wrong way. They are training themselves using habits that won't help them and that can actually hurt their game.

Can you think of some examples? (Some examples might be a tennis serve, golf swing, swimming stroke, or football pass.) *Athletes can benefit when coaches call their attention to the unskillful patterns so that they can practice more skillful ones.*

This applies to mind habits as well. We can become aware of our unwholesome habits, like the hurtful thoughts and emotions we discussed earlier, and we can practice more wholesome habits of mind.

Activity to Develop Theme T

In this session, instead of going into activities next, follow the introduction with the loving-kindness practice so that there is sufficient time to complete it. If there is more time, the "Message in a Bottle" activity may be done after the mindfulness practice.

Moving to Practice

Use the "Loving-Kindness" practice or the optional activity "Message in a Bottle."

· ·

PRACTICE: Loving-Kindness

Refer to the instructions for the "Loving-Kindness" practice, above.

· ·

OPTIONAL ACTIVITY: Message in a Bottle

An alternate practice is to use the "Message in a Bottle" activity from chapter 9. Group members can write messages of kindness either to themselves or others (or both).

· ·

Key Words: loving-kindness

Between-Session Mindfulness Booster: Guide students in the loving-kindness practice directed to themselves. Allow students to change the phrases to suit themselves, or let them pick a favorite.

Session 15

1. Guide students in a short gratitude practice.

2. Review themes B, R, E, A, and T.

3. Guide students in the "Stream of Gratitude" activity.

4. Guide students in a loving-kindness practice to self and others.

Review of Previous Themes and Reintroduction to Theme T

Guide students in a short gratitude practice.

SHORT GRATITUDE PRACTICE

Ring the bell to start, if desired. Allow for pauses in-between sentences.

Close your eyes and find the breath in your body.

Now think of something good that happened to you today or yesterday.

If you need to go back further in time, that's fine.

It can be big or little. Just bring it to mind. Breathe slowly and notice your gratefulness for this thing that you remember.

Ring the bell to finish if you wish.

We started this session today by becoming mindful of something we're grateful for and by cultivating that sense of gratitude. This is one way to practice healthy habits of mind and heart. Remember that we learned that the brain changes depending on what we're thinking about and practicing. So we can start practicing healthy habits of mind and heart, like gratitude, that can make us stronger and more balanced.

Activity to Develop Theme T

The following activity involves a period of mindful writing. This writing should be done in a specific way: without editing or changing anything, and without stopping or lifting the pencil from the page until the end. Ask students to keep rewriting the same thing if they get stuck, until something else comes to mind. The activity involves listing things that evoke gratefulness. Bringing to mind these people, objects, activities, and so forth, and writing them down helps cultivate the experience of this wholesome emotion. This exercise also gives the students a tool to use to cultivate gratitude on their own.

STREAM OF GRATITUDE (MINDFUL WRITING)

MATERIALS: Paper and pencil

Today I will guide you through a mindfulness practice that involves some writing about gratitude. Just take out a pencil and a piece of paper, and listen to my instructions. Put everything else away.

When I ring the bell, I'm going to ask you to start writing—but in a special way. Once you put your pen or pencil on the paper, you shouldn't take it off the page until I ring the bell again. So just keep writing.

Don't worry about spelling or about putting things in sentences, because no one will see this but you.

If you get stuck and can't think of anything to write, just keep writing the same thing over and over again until something new comes to you.

If you wish, you can draw instead of write, or even draw for only part of it. The activity is to write or draw all the things you're grateful for in your life. They can be big things or very small things. They can be people, places, things like activities, food, nature, or anything, until you hear the bell.

Just write as many as you can.

Allow about five minutes. Ring the bell to conclude, allowing the students to finish the last entry.

What was it like to write in this way (without pausing or correcting)?

What feelings did you notice as you were writing?

What thoughts did you have?

Were you aware of any sensations in the body?

Do you notice any difference between how you felt when you started this session and how you feel now?

How can we practice gratitude in our daily lives to support ourselves?

Refer students to the "A Recipe for Positive Emotions: Daily Doses of Gratitude" page in the student workbook.

. . . .

Moving to Practice

Guide students in a bit of stretching, some mindful movements, or both before asking them to sit down (refer to the "General Guidelines" box in chapter 11, session 1).

You may have included in your gratefulness list some people who are in your life. Even if we don't always think about it, let's now recognize how many good things others have done for us.

. . . .

PRACTICE: "A Person Just Like Me"

We'll do a practice that can help us cultivate appreciation and compassion for others.

Students can move their chairs so that they are seated in pairs facing each other. Alternatively, students can sit in their regular configuration or in a circle. This activity is reproduced here with permission of the author, Chade-Meng Tan. A few words have been changed to make it appropriate for adolescents.

Pause after each statement.

Sit comfortably and close your eyes if you wish.

Take a few deep breaths to calm yourself.

Now, become aware that there is a person in front of you. (Or, think of a person in this room and bring that person's image into your mind.)

Let's consider a few things about this person:

"This person is a human being, just like me."

"This person has a body and a mind, just like me."

"This person has feelings, emotions, and thoughts, just like me."

"This person has, at some point, been sad, disappointed, angry, hurt, or confused, just like me."

"This person wishes to be free from pain and unhappiness, just like me."

"This person wishes to be safe, healthy, and loved, just like me."

"This person wishes to be happy, just like me."

Now, let's allow some wishes to arise:

"I wish for this person to have the strength, resources, and support to help him or her through the difficult times in life."

"I wish for this person to be free from pain and unhappiness."

"I wish for this person to be strong and balanced."

"I wish for this person to be peaceful,

…because this person is a fellow human being,

…just like me."

(bell)

· ·

T

Key Words: gratitude, appreciation

Between-Session Mindfulness Booster: Guide students in the "A Person Just Like Me" practice. Perhaps have students bring to mind a person whom they don't know or don't know well.

Chapter 16

Theme H: Habits

Theme H, for habits, is taught over three sessions, numbered 16 through 18.

Session 16

1. Guide students in a short mindfulness practice.

2. Review themes B, R, E, A, T, and the final E. Introduce theme H to complete the BREATHE acronym.

3. Provide a review of the main themes.

4. Guide students in the "Designed to 'Re-Mind'" activity to help them develop creative reminders to practice mindfulness.

5. Guide students in the "Body Scan" practice.

Review of Previous Themes and Introduction to Theme H

Over the course of the last few weeks of practice, we've been learning to pay attention in a new way. By practicing mindfulness, we've been training our attention to see what's really going on in our bodies, in our thoughts, and in our feelings. The news is that we can bring mindful attention to every moment of our lives.

Every time we stop, check in, and really pay attention, we can find our inner balance. But because we get distracted easily, it helps to find ways to be mindful. Let's look at the word "remind." What does the prefix "re-" mean in a word?

Use the following examples if it's helpful: rewrite, reheat, replay, reintroduce, return, and so on.

All of these words share an idea of going back and doing something again. So now let's consider the word "remind." What does this mean from this perspective? What do we come back and do again?

We return our attention again and again to the present moment. We "come back" to our minds.

This is what we need to practice, because we're often so distracted. We can help ourselves by thinking of ways to "re-mind" ourselves to be mindful. Remember that it's normal to get distracted. You can always bring your attention back, no matter how many times you need to do this. Remembering to pay attention is the important thing.

Activity to Develop Theme H

This is a small-group activity that allows the students to consider ways to use what they have learned in class or in their lives after the L2B classes have ended. Sometimes groups have chosen to start the day with a bell and a few minutes of mindfulness. Older students have decided to teach younger students about mindful breathing. A random bell sound can be downloaded to computers or phones, posters may be drawn and hung in the room, and so forth.

....

DESIGNED TO "RE-MIND"

H Divide the class into small groups. The object of the activity is to develop a reminder to be mindful. "Re-minders" can include cues, prompts, strategies, rituals, props, signs, or other ideas. The working question is "What can I do to remind myself to be more mindful?" One example is to design a mindfulness desktop background for a computer, to search for and evaluate mindfulness applications for phones, to use low-tech reminders like sticky notes, to make it a ritual to practice three mindful breaths before opening a book, and so on. Small groups can choose personal or whole-group reminders. The goal is to be creative and practical. Each group should illustrate or write about their ideas in the workbook. The projects can be shared or posted in the room.

Today we're going to work in small groups (or pairs) to think about ways to remind ourselves to be more mindful. You might have noticed that the sound of the bell has helped you to be mindful. Now let's think about what we can use or do after this program is over to remind us be more mindful. You can decide to talk about ways that work for you individually or ways that can work for all of us in the group (or classroom).

Each group can write or draw their ideas in the workbook on the "Designed to 'Re-mind'" page, and then we'll share the ideas with the rest of the group.

Here are some steps to do this:

1. *First, think about what might really help you remember to be mindful. Each person should come up with ideas.*

2. *Then, choose one idea and talk about how it could work. Write about it or draw an image of it in your workbook.*

3. *Finally, share it with the whole group.*

A class or group may decide to adopt an idea or try a new "re-minder" every few weeks.

Moving to Practice

Guide students in a bit of stretching, some mindful movements, or both before asking them to sit down (review the "General Guidelines" box in chapter 11, session 1).

PRACTICE: Short Body Scan

As a review of what the class has practiced before, lead the group in a short "Body Scan" (refer back to the instructions for the "Body Scan" practice in chapter 11).

Let participants know that they can record their experiences outside of class on the "My Home Practice: Theme H" page in the student workbook.

H

Session 17

1. Guide students in a short mindfulness practice.

2. Guide students through the "Mindful Quilt" activity to reflect on personally important messages from the program.

3. Guide students in the "BREATHE Beading" activity to create a program keepsake.

4. Guide students through the "What I Wish for Myself" activity to allow them to reflect on their intentions.

5. Lead students through a loving-kindness practice.

Review of Previous Themes and Reintroduction to Theme H

Begin with a short period of mindfulness practice that includes practices learned over the course of the program.

As the program comes to an end, an important objective is to help students reflect on what they have learned and consider how to use it in their day-to-day lives.

Activities to Develop Theme H

H

Among "Mindful Quilt," "BREATHE Beading," and "What I Wish for Myself," instructors should choose which of the activities best suits the group.

MINDFUL QUILT

Refer back to the instructions for the "Mindful Quilt" activity in chapter 10.

BREATHE BEADING

MATERIALS: Seven beads for each member with the letters B, R, E, A, T, H, and E; plastic craft string; beading thread; bracelet clasps; metal key rings; and so on.

This activity involves making bracelets or key chains (by choice of each group member) using beads that spell "BREATHE." There are many craft websites that provide specific instructions for making this type of bracelet and key ring (see, for example, www.craftprojectideas.com/index.php/how-to/seasonal-projects/valentines-day/475-love-words-bracelet and www.ehow.com/how_4671919_make-beaded-key-chain.html). The result is a tangible reminder of the program themes for students to take away.

WHAT I WISH FOR MYSELF

Refer back to the instructions for the "What I Wish for Myself" activity in chapter 9.

Moving to Practice

As a reminder of what the class has practiced before, lead the group in a short loving-kindness practice.

PRACTICE: Loving-Kindness

Refer back to the instructions for the "Loving-Kindness" practice in chapter 9).

Between-Session Mindfulness Booster: Allow group members or the whole class to choose a practice.

Session 18

1. Guide students in a short mindfulness practice.

2. Lead students in the "Closing Circle" activity.

3. Guide students through a mindfulness practice.

Review of Previous Themes and Reintroduction to Theme H

Start with a short practice of the group's choice (awareness of breath, body, thoughts, and so on).

Activities to Develop Theme H

Guide students through the "Closing Circle" activity and, if time permits, the optional activity "Message in a Bottle."

· ·

ACTIVITY: Closing Circle

Close with an activity in which all members of the group sit in a circle and take turns sharing something about their experiences during the course of the program. They may share anything they choose (what they learned, what they liked or didn't like, what they noticed about themselves, what they wrote for the "Mindful Quilt" activity, what they want to take away, and so on). This practice is an exercise in mindful listening and mindful speaking, so it's important for group members to be mindful of others' comments and to refrain from speaking until their turn comes. Practice mindful listening to the bell each time. Invite the students to notice what they are thinking and feeling as they engage in this circle practice.

You may use the following process:

The teacher rings a bell or chime.

The first group member to speak takes the bell or chime from the teacher, rings the bell, shares a comment, rings the bells to finish, and passes the bell to the next member to speak.

The sequence continues until everyone has had a chance to share.

Try to practice mindful speaking and mindful listening by waiting for the end of the bell sound before speaking or moving. Thank each member for her or his comment and participation.

Depending on the size of the group, this could take most of the session time.

Distribute wallet cards (see downloads at www.newharbinger.com/27831) or some small gift to each member, if desired.

· ·

· ·

OPTIONAL ACTIVITY: Message in a Bottle

Refer back to chapter 9 for the instructions for this activity.

· ·

Moving to Practice

Guide students in a short gratitude practice or a practice that the group members choose. Use the student-workbook page in the final theme E, "Tips to Take Away: Mindfulness Cues," to discuss ways to continue mindfulness practice after the program is over.

H

Part 4

Supplementary Information

Chapter 17

The Adolescent Period: Challenges and Opportunities

What is happening in the adolescent brain? Adolescence is a time of unique possibilities and challenges in development. Recent research has highlighted some dramatic transformations in the adolescent brain that bear directly on education (Blakemore & Frith, 2005). In adolescence, these changes mainly occur in the frontal and parietal cortices, which are the site of executive functions, a general term used to describe higher-order cognitive processes (Blakemore & Choudhury, 2006). Myelination of the frontal cortex, which allows for smooth and efficient processing of information, proceeds continuously over the course of adolescence but is not complete until early adulthood. During adolescence, the creation and myelination of new synaptic connections occur, as well as the pruning of unused, unpracticed connections. These activities are most pronounced in the prefrontal cortex, located right behind the forehead—which plays a role in self-control, judgment, and emotion regulation—and in the temporal lobes, serving language functions and contributing to emotion regulation (Sawyer et al., 2012; Casey, Giedd, & Thomas, 2000; Sowell, Thompson, & Toga, 2007).

Because the adolescent brain is, in many ways, rewiring itself depending on what is learned and experienced, this stage of synaptic reorganization may be particularly sensitive to inner and outer experiences related to emotions and social relationships (Blakemore, 2008). In the case of learning, mild stress can enhance memory, but chronic or excessive stress can result in damage to parts of the brain that are critical for new learning and memory consolidation (Sapolsky, 2004).

Concurrently, adolescents' risk-taking behavior is at an all-time high. However, the propensity toward risky behavior is not sufficiently kept in check by a well-functioning internal monitor (prefrontal cortex), a situation described by Dahl (2004) as "turbo-charging the engines of a fully mature car belonging to an unskilled driver." Thus, the pattern of neurobiological changes that occurs in adolescence may make adolescents especially sensitive to distress during this period (Walker, 2002), and many researchers now consider adolescence to be a *stress-sensitive period* of development (Steinberg, 2008). Compared to other stages of the life span, the changes in hormone levels that occur during adolescence are the most rapid (Fataldi et al., 1999). In addition to increases in pubertal sex hormones, greater activation of the HPA axis has also been demonstrated. Recent longitudinal studies have found that levels of cortisol rise gradually through middle childhood and increase rapidly around age thirteen (Walker & Bollini, 2002). Studies of adults have consistently linked increases in HPA reactivity, as measured by cortisol increases, with unipolar and bipolar disorders, schizophrenia, and post-traumatic stress disorder (Müller, Holsboer, & Keck, 2002; Post, 2007; Walker & Diforio, 1997). Some evidence suggests a similar pattern for adolescent disorders, notably depression (Birmaher & Heydl, 2001; Goodyer, Park, Netherton, & Herbert, 2001). Although all of the mechanisms are not completely understood, both hormonal changes and maturation of the HPA axis appear to influence how the brain gets reorganized (Romer & Walker, 2007; Walker, Sabuwalla, & Huot, 2004).

What is happening in the environment during adolescence? Contemporary adolescents also face a host of environmental challenges that can threaten their social and emotional well-being, including the poor fit between developmental needs and the structure and curricula of schools (Eccles, 2004), a decline in academic orientation and motivation starting in the early adolescent years (Gutman, Sameroff, & Cole, 2003), increasing psychological separation from parents (Darling, Cumsille, & Martinez, 2008), increasing susceptibility to peer influence (Sim & Koh, 2003), pressures of romantic relationships (Collins, 2003), participation in antisocial or risky behaviors (Reyna & Farley, 2006), and heavy exposure to media. Media messages serve as standards for social comparison that may undermine self-esteem, mold expectations for normative behavior, and amplify values that may be at odds with those of families and communities (Comstock & Scharrer, 2006). Increases in feelings of distress in early adolescence are largely attributable to increases in depressed mood (Garber, Keiley, & Martin, 2002; Hammen & Rudolph, 2003) and conflicts with parents (Larson & Richards, 1994; Laursen & Collins, 1994). Declines in positive emotionality have also been reported in adolescence (Collins & Steinberg, 2006), and the onset of depression is occurring at younger and younger ages (Cross-National Collaborative Group, 1992). A 1993 report by the American Academy of Pediatrics Committee on Psychosocial Aspects of Child and Family Health (2001) that provides a list of threats to adolescent well-being was recently updated to include the following items: school problems (including learning disabilities and attention difficulties), mood and anxiety disorders, adolescent suicide and homicide, firearms in the home, school violence, drug and alcohol abuse, HIV, and AIDS; and the effects of media on violence, obesity, and sexual activity were called the "new morbidities."

Why should we pay attention to adolescents' health and stress? The sheer number of challenges that adolescents face in navigating this developmental stage may overwhelm their available cognitive and emotional resources, especially for those who have experienced less-than-optimal conditions in infancy and childhood. One implication is that adolescence is a sensitive period for emotional development (Casey et al., 2008; Walker et al., 2004). "This developmentally normative mismatch between strong affective and behavioral impulses, and the adolescents' still-limited capacity to regulate them, and reduced adult monitoring, means that early-to-middle adolescence is a period of heightened vulnerability to problems associated with poor regulation of affect and behavior" (Yap, Allen, & Sheeber, 2007). The onset of many mental health problems, such as depression, anxiety, eating disorders, substance abuse, and schizophrenia, during adolescence highlights the need to take the well-being of youth very seriously (Paus, Keshavan, & Giedd, 2008). Although research suggests that the adolescent brain is vulnerable to permanent stress-related alterations in the context of pubertal neuroplasticity, this period also can be a time for "interventions and opportunities to reduce or reverse the adverse effects accumulated from earlier insults" (Romeo & McEwen, 2006).

Chapter 18

A Primer on Stress

What is stress? Stress derives from the individual's perception that internal or external events tax or exceed available coping resources and thus endanger well-being (Lazarus and Folkman, 1984). Recently, McEwen, and Gianaros (2010) described the central role of the brain, that perceiver in chief, in triggering the cascade of stress processes *and* in recovery from stress. This research points to the importance of how we perceive the world and our experience.

What happens under stress? I acknowledge that this is an oversimplified explanation, but it may be a helpful adjunct to your lessons on stress. Stress is an unavoidable part of life, and despite its negative connotation, it is not all bad. The happy anticipation of a new baby is, for many people, a form of positive stress, or *eustress* as defined by Selye (1978). This can be contrasted to *distress*, which refers to the kinds of frustrations, conflicts, pressures, and negative events that people experience in their lives either intermittently or chronically. The body has a typical way of handling stressors, which involves an initial outpouring of chemicals that mobilize the body's rapid-response system ("the stress response") and then recede once the threat has subsided. Other physical systems that are less important for survival are temporarily sidelined but come back online once the stress is over. In early animal studies of stress, Selye identified three stages: the alarm phase, during which the activity of the sympathetic nervous system and adrenal glands increases for fight, flight, or freeze responses; the resistance phase, during which the body's stress response is active as it continues to resist the effects of the stressor; and finally, the exhaustion phase, which occurs if the struggle persists to the point where the body's resources are depleted. Depression, illness, or even death can occur after severe, prolonged stress. Remember that the link between stress and this internal cascade is the brain's perception of something as stressful. Individuals differ in what they interpret as stressful. One person's stress may be another person's exciting challenge.

When confronted with a physical or psychological threat, important chemicals such as epinephrine (adrenaline) and norepinephrine (noradrenaline) are released. They send a burst of energy to those structures that are necessary for fighting or fleeing (for example, the heart and lungs) while diverting energy from less-necessary systems (for example, digestion and reproduction). Adrenaline is instrumental in causing the well-known effects of arousal, such as racing heart and sweaty palms.

Stress also activates a physiological system called the *hypothalamic-pituitary-adrenal* (HPA) *axis*. When a person experiences or anticipates stress, the prefrontal cortex and amygdala detect the danger and inform the hypothalamus, a small, centrally located region in the mid-brain. The chemical (CRF, corticotropin-releasing factor) message is picked up by the pituitary gland, which is read as a sign to release adrenocorticotropic hormone, or ACTH, into the bloodstream. ACTH then makes its way through the bloodstream to the adrenal glands, near the kidneys, which receive the message to release cortisol. Cortisol is a key stress hormone. Cortisol then travels back to the brain and binds to receptors on the amygdala and the hippocampus.

Cortisol acts to increase blood glucose levels and to suppress the immune response, after providing a short-term immunity boost. Under normal conditions, cortisol makes its way back to alert the HPA axis to shut down the system when it is no longer needed to respond to threats. Problems start when stress is prolonged, and there is no effective shut-off valve. Ultimately, the individual's stress-response system may become chronically activated, putting a great deal of wear and tear on the body and mind. Chronic hypervigilance, or scanning the environment for potential threats, creates conditions for emotional problems like anxiety and depression. Chronic activation of metabolic processes that release glucose into the bloodstream in anticipation of fighting or fleeing can set the stage for illnesses like diabetes. Chronic activation of immune processes in anticipation of infection can render this system less functional and more vulnerable to disease. This wear and tear is called *allostatic load* (McEwen, 2002). Allostatic load can result from unchecked, dysregulated, chronic stress. Growth hormone is suppressed. Long-term negative effects on many systems, including cardiovascular, nervous, and memory systems, can result.

How does stress affect the immune system? Although this stress-response process serves us well in emergency situations or in relatively short hormonal bursts, there are costs associated with chronic activation of the system. For example, during the acute phase of the body's stress response, immune-system functioning is depressed. The immune system operates through a process of inflammation to limit the spread of harmful pathogens and to repair their damage.

Chronically elevated levels of cortisol are linked to cardiovascular decline in middle-aged and older adults (Pahuja & Kotchen, 2011). High levels of cortisol can also dysregulate immune functions and reduce the body's capacity to protect itself against disease. You may have noticed, for example, that when you are dealing with some ongoing stressor, you might be more likely to catch a cold or flu, an example of the process of immunosuppression. This occurs because cortisol inhibits the proliferation or blunts the responses of certain types of cytokines. *Cytokines* are small protein molecules of many different varieties that are secreted by cells of the immune system and that help to regulate its functioning. Operating somewhat like neurotransmitters, cytokines are messenger molecules that communicate instructions to other cells to respond or to inhibit a response.

Another immune-system process, inflammation, is also affected when the body confronts chronic stressors. Inflammatory processes, which take their marching orders from cortisol, can be destructive to the body unless their force is regulated. Remember that these functions are temporarily suppressed when the body needs to respond to acute stressors and then, ideally, they return to baseline. The problem arises when the stressors become chronic. Chronic exposure not only increases cortisol production, but also desensitizes the immune cells' ability to respond to cortisol's instructions to inhibit inflammatory processes. Consequently, high concentrations of proinflammatory cytokines, which are related to maladaptive inflammation, go unchecked. Many disease conditions, such as cardiovascular disease, allergies, rheumatoid arthritis, and other autoimmune disorders, have been associated with unregulated inflammatory processes.

Psychological stressors, such as traumatic environmental events, operate on the body in much the same way as infectious agents. Stressors, both psychological and physical, produce the same kinds of immune-related symptoms that we see in the body's normal infection response. These include some combination of fever, increased sleep, reduction in eating and drinking, reduced exploration and activity, reduced aggression, reduction in social interaction, cognitive alterations, increased pain sensitivity, increased HPA activity, and depressed mood. Viewed from this perspective, certain types of depression are associated with hyperactivation of the immune response, even though the precise direction of these effects is still unclear. The important point in this discussion is the establishment of the connection between emotional experiences and the dysregulation of body mechanisms (like immune-system functioning).

Recent evidence (Quan & Banks, 2007) has clearly supported the existence of bidirectional communication processes between the brain and the immune system in relation to stressors, be they psychological or physical. Opiate receptors for the body's natural opiates, called *endorphins*, are present on the surface of cells in the immune system (spleen and thymus). This discovery uncovered the connections among the brain, the immune system, and the emotions, linking the mind and body in new and exciting ways. As we are learning, the brain and the immune system operate together in a highly orchestrated dance that maintains allostasis, or balance, within the systems of the body-mind. Originally, it was thought that the brain "talked" and the immune system responded. Now researchers (Quan & Banks, 2007) increasingly recognize that the brain also "listens" to the communication of the immune system, which sends its chemical messengers to various parts of the nervous system, including the brain. Findings such as these have helped usher in a new field, *psychoneuroimmunology*, the study of the interactions among the central nervous system, the immune system, and behavior.

Effects of chronic stress on other systems	Some purported mechanisms	Stress-related problems
Memory and learning problems.	Stress causes damage to and shrinkage of neurons in the hippocampus, which is highly important for memory and learning.	Difficulty in learning new information and remembering.
Increased damage to blood vessels and inflammation at branch points.	Adrenaline surges (and other sympathetic nervous system activities) increase force on blood vessels and increase chance of damage at delicate branch points (which stimulates inflammatory processes).	Hypertension, heart disease, atherosclerosis; material (such as fats in the bloodstream) sticks to inflamed areas, causing buildup. Also, stressed eating (encouraged by excessive cortisol) can lead to a high-fat diet with more circulating fats.
Increased appetite.	Cortisol stimulates appetite, especially for high-fat foods. When they stimulate fat deposition, stress hormones preferentially stimulate deposits in the abdomen.	Visceral belly fat.
Thinning of the stomach lining.	Too much cortisol interferes with digestion; stomach slacks off in building mucous protective layer; thin layer is overpowered by hydrochloric acid.	Risk for gastric ulcers increases.
Mobilizes glucose and fatty acids into the bloodstream.	Stress hormones promote insulin resistance, because the message is to mobilize (rather than store) glucose. Eventually, fat cells become less responsive to insulin.	Diabetes (type 2, or adult onset).
Thinning of bones.	Too much cortisol interrupts new bone growth.	Osteoporosis, fracture risk.

Interference with sleep and sleep quality.	Levels of cortisol (and other stress hormones) rise, and the sympathetic system gets more active. Sleep deprivation stimulates stress hormones, which compromise quantity and quality of deep (restorative) sleep.	Insomnia, sleep disorders.
Mental illness.	Excessive stress hormones disrupt neurotransmitter and cytokine systems.	Depression, anxiety, PTSD, and so on. Stress is implicated in virtually all diagnoses.
Accelerates aging process.	Cortisol damages hippocampus, which controls stress hormones; negative feedback loop causes cortisol excess.	Premature aging and age-related diseases.

Sources: Bremner, 2005; Goldstein, 2006; Sapolsky, 2004; and Sternberg, 2001.

Appendix A

Sample Assessments for Mindfulness Research with Youth

To assess the effectiveness of the program, various questionnaires may be used before and/ or after implementation. Instructors may choose to assess satisfaction with the program, effectiveness of the program on certain outcomes, or both. In addition to questionnaires, focus groups or open-ended questions can also be helpful in assessment of outcomes.

There are several questionnaires currently in use for measuring mindfulness, emotion, cognition, and health/mental health–related constructs. This is not an exhaustive list. The following references simply provide sample assessment measures that are currently available in the literature. Many of these instruments have been used with adolescents, although it is recommended that instructors review the scientific literature in making a selection based on their particular population and outcomes of interest in order to adopt measurements that best suit their needs.

Mindfulness (Children and/or Adolescents)

Brown, K. W., West, A. M., Loverich, T. M., & Biegel, G. M. (2011). Assessing adolescent mindfulness: Validation of an adapted Mindful Attention Awareness Scale in adolescent normative and psychiatric populations. *Psychological Assessment, 23*(4), 1023–1033.

Greco, L. A., Baer, R. A., & Smith, G. T. (2011). Assessing mindfulness in children and adolescents: Development and validation of the Child and Adolescent Mindfulness Measure (CAMM). *Psychological Assessment, 23*(3), 606–614.

Anxiety

March, J. S., & Parker, J. D. A. (1999). The multidimensional anxiety scale for children (MASC). In M. E. Maruish (Ed.), *The use of psychological testing for treatment planning and outcomes assessment* (2nd ed., pp. 299–322). Mahwah, NJ: Lawrence Erlbaum Associates.

Levels of Emotional Awareness

Bajgar, J., Ciarrochi, J., Lane, R., & Deane, F. P. (2005) Development of the Levels of Emotional Awareness Scale for Children (LEAS-C). *British Journal of Developmental Psychology, 23*(4), 569–586.

Rumination

Nolen-Hoeksema, S. (2001). The short version of the Ruminative Style Questionnaire. In Nolen-Hoeksema, S., & Davis, C. G. (1999). "Thanks for sharing that": Ruminators and their social support networks. *Journal of Personality and Social Psychology, 77*(4), 801–814.

Positive and Negative Affect

Watson, D., & Clark, L. A., & Tellegen, A. (1988). Development and validation of brief measures of positive and negative affect: The PANAS scales. *Journal of Personality and Social Psychology, 54*(6), 1063–1071.

Emotion Regulation

Gratz, K. L., & Roemer, L. (2004). Multidimensional assessment of emotion regulation and dysregulation: Development, factor structure, and initial validation of the difficulties in emotion regulation scale. *Journal of Psychopathology and Behavioral Assessment, 26*(1), 41–54.

Neumann, A., van Lier, P. A. C., Gratz, K. L., & Koot, H. M. (2010). Multidimensional assessment of emotion regulation difficulties in adolescents using the Difficulties in Emotion Regulation Scale. *Assessment, 17*(1), 138–149.

Phillips, K. F. V., & Power, M. J. (2007). A new self-report measure of emotion regulation in adolescents: The Regulation of Emotions Questionnaire. *Clinical Psychology and Psychotherapy, 14*(2), 145–156.

Behavior Ratings

Achenbach, T. M. (2001). *The Child Behavior Checklist and Youth Self-Report Form.* Burlington, VT: ASEBA, University of Vermont.

Spoth, R., Redmond, C., & Lepper, H. (1999). Alcohol initiation outcomes of universal family-focused preventive interventions: One- and two-year follow-ups of a controlled study. (The Risky Behavior Survey.) *Journal of Studies on Alcohol, Supplement. 13,* 103–111.

Executive Function

Hearts and Flowers

Davidson, M. C., Amso, D., Anderson, L. C. , & Diamond, A. (2006). Development of cognitive control and executive functions from 4 to 13 years: Evidence from manipulations of memory, inhibition, and task switching. *Neuropsychologia, 44* (11), 2037–2078.

Diamond, A., Barnett, W. S., Thomas, J., & Munro, S. (2007). Preschool program improves cognitive control. *Science, 318*(5855), 1387–1388.

Flanker Task

Eriksen, C. W. (1995). The Flankers Task and Response Competition: A useful tool for investigating a variety of cognitive problems. *Visual Cognition, 2*(2–3), 101–118.

Attention Network Test (ANT)

Fan, J., McCandliss, B. D., Sommer, T., Raz, A., & Posner, M. I. (2002). Testing the efficiency and independence of attentional networks. *Journal of Cognitive Neuroscience, 14*(3), 340–347.

Brief Rating Inventory of Executive Functions (BRIEF)

Gioia, G. A., Isquith, P. K., Guy, S. C., & Kenworthy, L. (2000). *BRIEF: Behavior Rating Inventory of Executive Function.* Luz, FL: Psychological Assessment Resources.

Self-Compassion

Neff, K. D. (2003). The development and validation of a scale to measure self-compassion. *Self and Identity, 2,* 223–250.

Health and Well-Being

Currie, C., Samdal, O., Boyce, W., & Smith, R. (Eds.). (2001). Health behaviour in school-aged children: A World Health Organization cross-national study (HBSC). Research protocol for the 2001/2002 survey. Health Policy for Children and Adolescents No. 4. Edinburgh, Scotland: University of Edinburgh.

Sample Learning to BREATHE Evaluation Questions

On a scale of 1 (not useful) to 10 (very useful), please circle the number that shows how useful and beneficial each of the following is to you.

Practice in breathing	1	2	3	4	5	6	7	8	9	10
Learning how to handle thoughts better	1	2	3	4	5	6	7	8	9	10
Learning how to handle feelings better	1	2	3	4	5	6	7	8	9	10
Learning about the body's stress system	1	2	3	4	5	6	7	8	9	10
Body-scan practice	1	2	3	4	5	6	7	8	9	10
Mindful movement practice	1	2	3	4	5	6	7	8	9	10
Loving-kindness practice	1	2	3	4	5	6	7	8	9	10
Group discussions	1	2	3	4	5	6	7	8	9	10
Workbook	1	2	3	4	5	6	7	8	9	10
Handouts and materials	1	2	3	4	5	6	7	8	9	10
Practice audio (downloads)	1	2	3	4	5	6	7	8	9	10
Overall satisfaction with the Learning to BREATHE program	1	2	3	4	5	6	7	8	9	10

1. What have you learned or gained from this program?

2. How often did you practice being mindful in your day-to-day life?

☐ Every day

☐ More than once a day

☐ Every week

☐ Several times a week

☐ Not at all

3. How often did you practice with the audio downloads?

☐ Every day

☐ More than once a day

☐ Every week

☐ Several times a week

☐ Not at all

4. What would you add to, or change about, this program?

5. Would you recommend this program to others? Why or why not?

Thanks for your participation and responses!

Appendix B

Links between L2B and Educational Laws and Standards

In order to find a place for the Learning to BREATHE program within school curricula, it may be helpful to link the goals of L2B to performance standards for existing subject areas or programs. This allows the L2B curriculum to be the vehicle for meeting objectives in areas such as health education, counseling, or study-skills or social-skills classes, just to name a few. The following standards simply provide some possibilities for these connections, but ultimately, the fit should be made wherever it's most reasonable and practical for the setting.

Laws and standards differ across countries and states. These are illustrations of linkages between the Learning to BREATHE program and standards.

Federal Law: No Child Left Behind (NCLB)

Although not directly aimed at teaching academic curricula, the Learning to BREATHE program is an "enabling component" (Zins et al., 2004, p. 19) that supports national standards-based educational initiatives like NCLB and the Safe and Drug-Free Schools and Communities Act goals. These goals include increasing academic success (Performance Goal 1) and improving learning environments (Performance Goal 4), which follow here (www.ed.gov/about/reports/strat/plan2011-14/draft-strategic-plan.pdf).

Performance Goal 1: By 2013–2014, all students will reach high standards, at a minimum attaining proficiency or better in reading/language arts and mathematics.

Performance Goal 4: All students will be educated in learning environments that are safe, drug-free, and conducive to learning.

Consistent with current emphases on empirical support, this is a research-based program with demonstrated effectiveness.

National Health Education Standards (NHES): Standard 7

See www.cdc.gov/healthyyouth/sher/standards/7.htm:

Demonstrate the ability to practice health-enhancing behaviors and avoid or reduce health risks.

Grades 9–12 Performance Indicators for Standard 7

7.12.1   Analyze the role of individual responsibility for enhancing health.

7.12.2   Demonstrate a variety of healthy practices and behaviors that will maintain or improve the health of self and others.

7.12.3   Demonstrate a variety of behaviors to avoid or reduce health risks to self and others.

National School Counseling Standards: Personal and Social Development for Grades 9–12

See http://static.pdesas.org/content/documents/ASCA_National_Standards_for_Students.pdf:

Standard 1. Students will acquire knowledge, attitudes, and interpersonal skills to help them understand and respect self and others.

Benchmark 1. The student will acquire and use self-knowledge.
1. Exhibits positive attitudes towards self and others.

2. Uses personal strengths and assets.

3. Understands how attitudes and choices affect behavior.

4. Understands change is a factor in growth and development.

5. Demonstrates appropriate social behavior.

6. Analyzes appropriate ways to take responsibility for themselves.

7. Identifies and uses school and community resources.

State Curriculum: Sample Application to PA Academic Standards for Health, Safety, and Physical Education

These standards require students to learn about mental and physical health, and coping strategies for anger management (www.lhup.edu/pballat/department_docs/PA.State.Standards.doc):

10. 1. Concepts of Health

Evaluate factors that impact the body systems and apply protective/preventive strategies.

☐ fitness level

☐ environment (e.g., pollutants, available health care)

☐ health status (e.g., physical, mental, social)

☐ nutrition

10.3. Safety and Injury Prevention

10.3.6 C. Describe strategies to avoid or manage conflict and violence.

☐ anger management

☐ peer mediation

☐ reflective listening and negotiation

Guidance and Career Education Policy for the Ontario Elementary and Secondary Schools (1999)

This is an example from "Interpersonal Development Competency for Grades 7 and 8" (www.edu.gov.on.ca/eng/document/curricul/secondary/choices/choicee.pdf):

Students will:

demonstrate the skills and knowledge necessary to manage their own behaviour (e.g., self-control, the role of emotions, anger management).

Guidance and Career Education Policy for the Ontario Elementary and Secondary Schools (2006)

This example is from "Applying Personal-Management Skills Competency for Grades 9 and 10" (www.edu.gov.on.ca/eng/curriculum/secondary/guidance910currb.pdf):

Students will:

use personal-management skills;

identify internal and external factors that affect behaviour and school performance (e.g., emotional stress, motivation, racism, peer attitudes, exclusion, physical distractions), and identify strategies for improving behaviour to enhance learning;

demonstrate behaviours that reflect self-motivation and self-reliance (e.g., taking initiative, being persistent in pursuing a goal, completing tasks independently);

explain how stress can positively and negatively affect learning performance (e.g., with regard to test taking and work completion), and demonstrate effective use of stress-management techniques to maximize performance.

Ontario Curriculum for Health and Physical Education for Grades 11 and 12

These examples are from the "Mental Health and Stress Management Competencies":

Students will:

describe the characteristics of an emotionally healthy person (e.g., positive self-concept, ability to manage stress effectively, ability to work productively);

demonstrate the skills that enhance personal mental health (e.g., coping strategies for stress management);

describe the positive and negative effects of stresses that are part of daily life; explain physiological responses to stress;

use appropriate strategies for coping with stress and anxiety (e.g., relaxation, meditation, exercise, reframing);

demonstrate an understanding of change and its impact on an individual's health.

Learning to BREATHE Student Workbook—Six-Session Version

"MINDFULNESS is paying attention in a particular way:
on purpose, in the present moment, and nonjudgmentally."

—Jon Kabat-Zinn

B	Listen to your **Body**
R	**Reflections** (thoughts) are just thoughts
E	Surf the waves of your **Emotions**
A	**Attend** to the inside and the outside
T	Try **Tenderness**—Take it as it is
H	Practice **Healthy** Habits of mind
E	Gain the inner Edge. Be **Empowered**!

This 6-session student workbook is available for download at www.newharbinger.com/27831.

Theme B: My Mindful/Mindless Life

What things (or activities) in your life do you do on automatic pilot (mindlessly)? What are the things you do that fully engage you (mindfully)? Fill in the boxes with as many examples as you can name. You can also write about how you feel when you do things mindfully (with attention) or mindlessly (without attention).

My Mindful Life...

_____

_____

_____

_____

_____

_____

_____

My Mindless Life...

_____

_____

_____

_____

_____

_____

_____

Theme B: Mindfulness in My Life

You can practice mindful attention in all of the moments of your day.

As an experiment, select an activity as "your practice": a simple daily activity that you choose to do mindfully on a regular basis. Pick one of these examples or come up with your own. Do this activity with awareness and interest; really "be there" for this simple activity. Try adding one new practice each week.

○ Washing your face

○ Going up and down stairs

○ Washing dishes

○ Getting dressed

○ Getting or preparing a snack

○ Eating breakfast

○ Answering a phone call

○ E-mailing

○ Driving to a certain place

○ Waiting at a red light

○ Walking down a hallway

○ Eating lunch

○ Opening and closing your locker

○ Walking a pet

○ Washing your hands

○ Texting

○ Standing in line

○ Waiting for a bus

○ Listening to someone

○ Brushing your teeth

○ Other _____

B My Home Practice: Theme B

1. Practice mindful breathing for at least three breaths at a time, three times per day.

2. Practice the "Body Scan" with audio (see audio downloads at www.newharbinger.com/27831) _____ times.

3. Try the "Three-Minute Body Scan," described next in this workbook, each day in school or in some other place.

4. Practice your own special activity mindfully (from theme B, "Mindfulness in My Life"). Note your observations and reflections in the box below.

Observations and Reflections:

_____

_____

_____

_____

_____

_____

_____

_____

_____

_____

_____

_____

_____

Theme B: Tips to Take Away: Three-Minute Body Scan

You can do a short "Body Scan" at any time, especially if you notice that you're feeling tense or anxious.

Try it:

- while seated in class
- before tests
- before athletic events
- before speaking in public
- before getting out of bed in the morning
- before falling asleep
- while standing in line
- during social events
- before an interview

How to do it:

1. Use your attention to find your breath in your body.

2. Starting from either your feet or your head, move your attention through your body and notice your experience. Scan for tension in your feet; lower back; stomach; shoulders; face, jaw, or forehead; or wherever you hold tension in your body.

3. As you scan each area, breathe into the area, releasing tension and bringing in new energy as you did in the "Body Scan."

4. Expand your awareness to your entire body and feel the breath move from your head to your feet.

Theme R: Big Event Circles

Story 1

Write your thoughts in the circle below.   Write how you're feeling in the circle below.

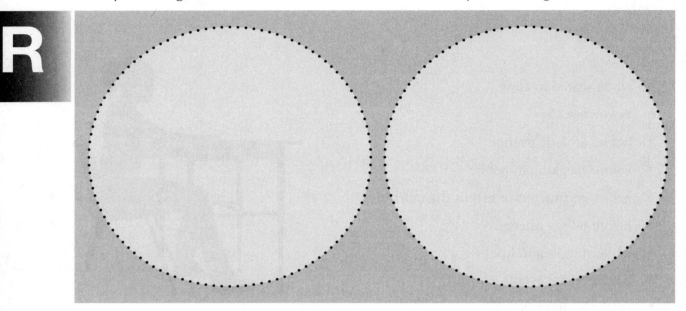

Story 2

Write your thoughts in the circle below.   Write how you're feeling in the circle below.

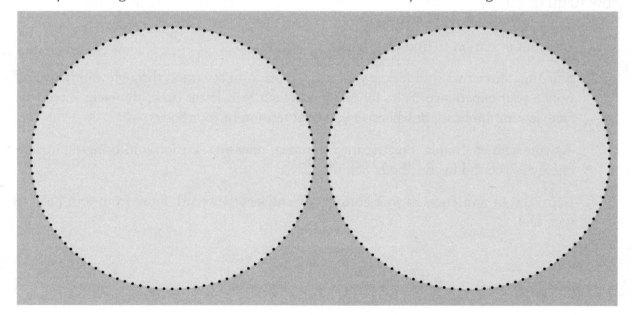

My Home Practice: Theme R

1. Practice mindful breathing for at least three breaths at a time, three times per day.

2. Practice a short period of mindfulness of thoughts (once a day, ideally; see audio downloads at www.newharbinger.com/27831).

3. Use the workbook activity on the next page, "Dealing with Troubling Thoughts," to help you when you practice.

4. Continue practicing mindfulness in your day-to-day life, especially in your personal-choice area (from "Mindfulness in My Life"). Note your observations and reflections in the box below.

Observations and Reflections:

_____

_____

_____

_____

_____

_____

_____

_____

_____

_____

_____

_____

Theme R: Tips to Take Away: Dealing with Troubling Thoughts

Notice the thoughts that are arising in your mind.

Try the mindful approach:

1. Become aware of what your mind is doing: *thinking*. It's generating thoughts. The thought is like a bubble that arises in the space of the mind. It's just what the mind does.

2. Step back and examine the thought with curiosity. How loud or soft is it in your mind? How strong is it? How long does it last? Can you notice sensations in your body when the thought arises? Don't try to push it out of your mind. Just observe.

3. Get in touch with your breath as you observe the thought. Remember, it's just a thought. Don't struggle with it, because that can make it stronger.

4. Watch the thought change in intensity. Return your full attention to your breath.

My Home Practice: Theme E

1. Practice mindful breathing for at least three breaths at a time, three times per day.

2. Do a short mindfulness practice on feelings (once a day, ideally; see the audio downloads at www.newharbinger.com/27831).

3. Begin to notice thoughts, feelings, and physical sensations as they arise throughout the day.

4. Practice being kind to yourself when uncomfortable feelings arise. Don't try to push them away. Just notice them and where they show up as sensations in your body.

5. Keep practicing mindfulness in your day-to-day life, especially in the practice of your choice (from theme B, "Mindfulness in My Life"). Note your observations and reflections in the box below.

E

Observations and Reflections:

_____

_____

_____

_____

_____

_____

_____

_____

_____

_____

Theme E: Tips to Take Away: Working with Anger

Anger is an emotion that has a long list of close relatives: irritation, frustration, impatience, rage, hatred, annoyance, resentment, irritability, crankiness, and so forth. Anger and its variations can cause us to "heat up." Notice the way we refer to angry feelings, for example, "boiling mad," "hotheaded," or "seeing red." Anger impairs our thinking and can feel overwhelming. It makes us lose our balance. Sometimes when we're angry, we act impulsively in ways that end up hurting ourselves and others. Shouting, threatening, fighting, rudeness, disrespect, and name-calling are a few examples. Sometimes we take out our anger in quieter ways by gossiping, excluding others, and making them feel bad. Most of all, anger can hurt our health, well-being, and social relationships. Chronic anger ramps up the stress response and reduces our own level of happiness.

Kick the anger habit!

Try a mindful approach to difficult emotions. When you feel yourself getting angry:

1. Stop and pay attention. Notice with interest where you are feeling the anger in your body. What does this experience feel like for you?

2. Turn your attention toward the feelings as they arise: Are they sharp, hard, soft, intense, fast, slow, burning? Are they moving around in your body? Are they centered in one place? Do they change as you observe them?

3. Experience the feelings of anger as waves, coming and going. Don't try to block them, avoid them, or get rid of them. Don't try to hold on to them or keep them going. Just don't act on the angry feelings right now. You can view anger as a strong energy in the body and mind, like a sudden storm.

4. Tune in to the breath and see if you can ride the waves of the anger and watch them get smaller and smaller.

Now you're in a better position to make a smart decision about how to act.

Remember:

You can use this approach to work with any difficult feelings. Just substitute the name of a feeling in the steps above. Surf the waves of your annoyance, boredom, sadness, disappointment, jealousy, and so on. Breathe and watch the feelings rise and fall. They're not fun, but they will pass. And you will become more empowered.

Theme A: What's the Best Balance?

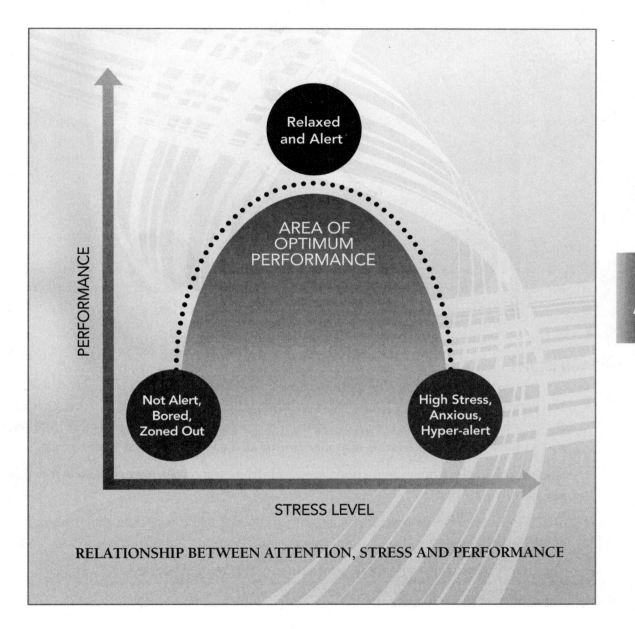

Relaxed
and Alert

AREA OF
OPTIMUM
PERFORMANCE

PERFORMANCE

Not Alert,
Bored,
Zoned Out

High Stress,
Anxious,
Hyper-alert

STRESS LEVEL

RELATIONSHIP BETWEEN ATTENTION, STRESS AND PERFORMANCE

A

Theme A: What's My Limit?

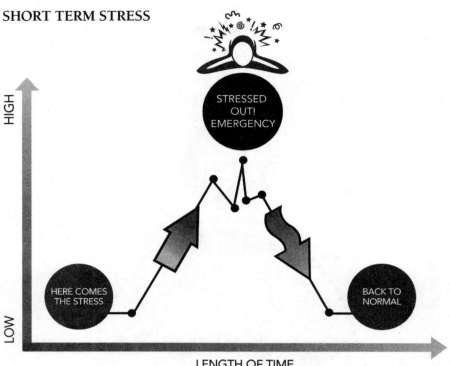

SHORT TERM STRESS

HIGH

STRESSED OUT! EMERGENCY

HERE COMES THE STRESS

BACK TO NORMAL

LOW

LENGTH OF TIME

Did you know?

- You can notice your body's stress response when it occurs because of the many physical changes involved. Your heart races, your palms sweat, your breath gets more shallow, and so forth. Your body's stress response is intended to help you deal with threats.

- Some foods (cola, coffee, tea, chocolate) and drugs (nicotine) also cause a stress-like reaction in your body.

- Our bodies respond to psychological stressors in the same way that they respond to physical threats.

- Our perceptions play a major role in whether or not we feel stressed.

Some interesting websites on stress:
www.stress.org
www.isma.org.uk
www.pbs.org/programs/killer-stress

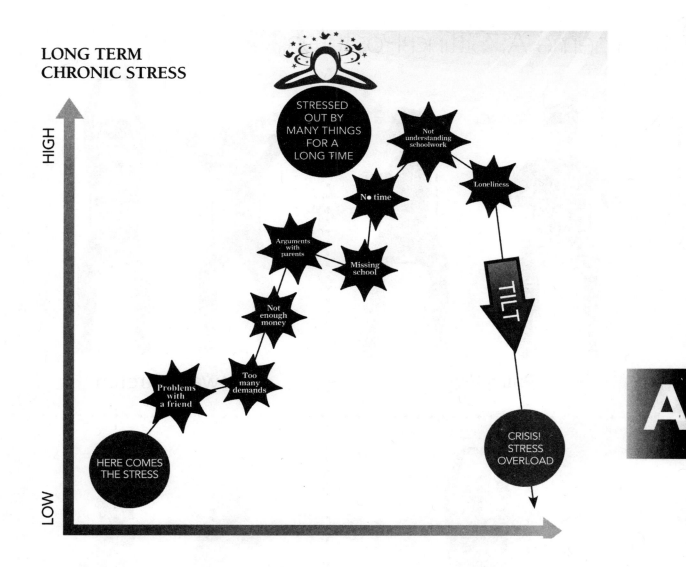

LONG TERM CHRONIC STRESS

HIGH

LOW

STRESSED OUT BY MANY THINGS FOR A LONG TIME

Not understanding schoolwork

Loneliness

No time

Arguments with parents

Missing school

Not enough money

Too many demands

Problems with a friend

HERE COMES THE STRESS

TILT

CRISIS! STRESS OVERLOAD

A

List your chronic stressors

1. _____ 6. _____

2. _____ 7. _____

3. _____ 8. _____

4. _____ 9. _____

5. _____ 10. _____

Circle your top three stressors.

Theme A: Sitting Postures:

Palm Press

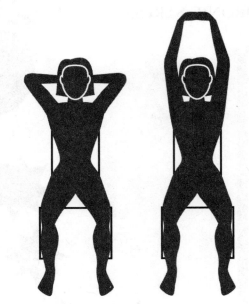

Upward Stretch

Seated Tree

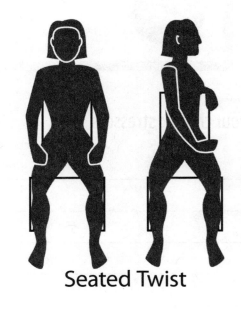

Seated Twist

Theme A: Standing Postures:

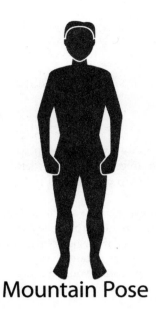

Mountain Pose

Upward Stretch

A

Reach Up

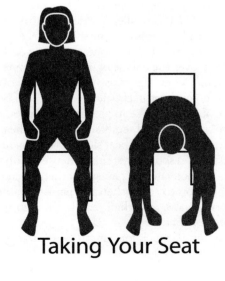

Taking Your Seat

Theme A: Memo from the Body-Mind

To:	Body-Mind Owners: All Makes and Models
From:	Your Stress-Response System
Re:	Your Stress
Message:	High Priority!

Dear Owner:

As the system primarily involved in your body-mind's stress response, we want to keep you informed about our operations so that you will be in a better position to keep us in good working order. Your body-mind's stress response came with your basic equipment. It is intended to prepare you to fight, flee, or freeze in case of a real emergency so that you can survive.

Specifically, we are a coordinated group that includes the *autonomic nervous system* (ANS) and the *hypothalamic-pituitary-adrenal axis* (HPA axis for short). Here's how we operate. You have a threat detector located deep inside your brain called the *amygdala*. When the amygdala registers the information that your safety is threatened or that there's something out there to worry about, the *sympathetic part* (SNS) of the *autonomic nervous system* (ANS) leaps into action to help protect you. Your brain immediately sends signals to the interior of the *adrenal glands*, which sit on top of your kidneys, telling them to release the hormone (and neurotransmitter) *adrenaline* into your bloodstream. Remember that hormones are chemical messengers that have powerful effects on your body-mind. If you can recall feeling your hair stand on end, your heart beginning to pound, your palms beginning to sweat, and your stomach turning (possibly when faced with a test you didn't expect), you know our power to get your system revved up to fight, freeze, or run away.

We also provide an additional homeland-security system called the HPA axis. Two of our components (*hypothalamus* and *pituitary*) are located deep in the brain. After a red alert from the amygdala, the hypothalamus gets this ball rolling by secreting hormones into the hypothalamic-pituitary circulatory system. The principal one is *CRH* (*corticotrophin-releasing hormone*), which triggers the pituitary to release *ACTH* (also called corticotrophin). ACTH jump-starts the adrenals to release another stress hormone, called *cortisol*, from their surface into the bloodstream. If you've ever been scared to death watching a horror movie alone at night, you know that adrenaline works within seconds, but cortisol backs it up over the course of minutes or hours. It takes about an hour for the effects of cortisol to leave the system. When the stressful situation is over and you have prevailed, the other arm of the ANS, called the *parasympathetic nervous system* (PNS), moves into action by relaxing your body-mind and allowing it to rebalance in preparation for the next threat. The *vagus nerve* that originates in the brain is part of the PNS and sends signals to the heart (and other organs) that regulate the heartbeat (among other things). The heartbeat slows down as a result of activation of the vagus nerve. It works like a brake on the stress-response system. When you inhale, you activate the sympathetic system, and when you exhale, you activate the parasympathetic system. That's why some relaxation practices teach extending the exhalation to strengthen the parasympathetic (or "cool-down") response. Let's try it. Take a deep breath right now, and then exhale through your mouth in a slow, long, smooth sigh. Whew! Thank goodness for that.

Anyway, so much for our trusty apparatus.

It has come to our attention that many owners are activating the stress-response system for extended periods of time without a break. Because owners might not realize the damage they do to their systems when they are under constant stress, we take the opportunity in this memo to present it in some detail.

We find it hard to believe that this constant activation is due to unceasing, real threats on owners' health and safety (such as constantly coming face-to-face with wild animals or other equally scary situations). We've been told that owners are activating their systems because of internal threats like worries, fears, anger, resentments, foiled expectations, disappointments, and so forth. Now we acknowledge that life can be really tough. We have the greatest sympathy for what owners are going through. However, we—the elements of your stress system—need to inform you of the fact that we are being overworked when the stressful events that keep us going are happening in owners' minds. In other words, owners who constantly ruminate, let problems fester, hold on to jealousy, or continually feed the fires of anger are really wearing us out!

Here's the view from the inside. Constant activation of the system results in too much cortisol pumping into the bloodstream. Too much cortisol dismantles your *immune system*. Remember the immune system? Immune system cells are constantly on patrol, killing invaders and saving you from illness. Without a well-functioning army of immune cells, your body isn't going to heal from invaders very well. If you get sick (low immunity) during exam time (high stress), don't say we didn't warn you.

Too much cortisol also damages and even kills cells in your brain (*hippocampus*) that are responsible for learning and memory. That's not going to help you graduate! Stress hormones like adrenaline cause the heart to pump blood faster, potentially resulting in high blood pressure and damage to your arteries because of the force of blood on the delicate vessels. Stress hormones like cortisol increase your appetite, especially for comfort food, because your body reads their chemical message as "Yikes! An emergency! Better store up some energy so I can run away when I need to." Stress hormones are related to stomach discomfort, and you know that's no fun either. Recall that it takes about an hour for the body to sop up the excess cortisol floating around in the bloodstream. If you have even one stress reaction per hour— well, *you* do the math. And remember, you probably don't really have to encounter some terrible threat like a wild animal on your way to school. Your body-mind, alas, doesn't know the difference between "real" and "mental" stress. That's what keeps us so overworked. Thinking about stressful things makes us work overtime. Your mind is the gateway to stress.

Did you realize that about 70 percent of cases of insomnia are caused by stress? Body-Mind Owners need their sleep to be on top of their game, so this can be a big problem. Lack of sleep can make you grouchy, not to mention pretty sad. The stress-related changes in your immune system also result in making too much of certain chemicals, called *cytokines*, that float to the brain and affect your moods. It's normal to feel pretty sad when bad things happen, but too much stress can make you depressed if you don't know how to roll with it.

Last, let's not forget the risk of addictions. We understand that stress seems to be temporarily reduced by taking an addictive substance or engaging in some stress-avoidance activity. The point here is that it's temporary. You can count on feeling a crash shortly afterward. This only increases anxiety and all those awful stress-related feelings.

We could go on and on, but we think we've made our point. We want to keep on working for you so that you'll have a happier, healthier life. Here's the bottom line: the things that stress you out in your life are not going away. You need to learn how to relate to your stress in ways that don't harm your system. Working with your mind and your mental attitude is a great place to start. Please, keep up the good work.

Yours truly,
Your Body-Mind Team

A

My Home Practice: Theme A

1. Practice mindful breathing for at least three breaths at a time, three times per day.

2. Do a short mindful-movement practice (once a day, ideally; see audio downloads at www.newharbinger.com/27831). Use the illustrations for "Sitting Postures" and "Standing Postures".

3. Continue to notice thoughts, feelings, and physical sensations as they arise throughout the day.

4. Continue practicing mindfulness in your day-to-day life, especially in the area you chose in theme B, "Mindfulness in My Life." Add the practice of kindness to yourself and others.

5. Use workbook pages "More Ways to Practice Mindfulness in Action" and "Eating Awareness Calendar" to help with mindful-walking and mindful-eating practices.

6. Note your observations and reflections in the box below.

Observations and Reflections:

_____

_____

_____

_____

_____

_____

_____

_____

_____

_____

_____

Theme A: Tips to Take Away: More Ways to Practice Mindfulness in Action

Mindful Eating

- Break out of eating on "automatic pilot."

- Experiment with eating mindfully by paying attention to all the sensations of eating.

- Try eating a snack or a meal in silence.

- Look at the food on your plate with curiosity: notice colors, textures, shapes, aromas, and so on.

- Slow down the pace of eating.

- Before chewing, experience what the food feels like in your mouth.

- As you chew, notice all the sensations.

- Try practicing gratitude for all the people whose work made it possible for you to eat this food.

Mindful Walking

- Pay attention to all the sensations of movement as you walk.

- Notice the contact of your feet with the floor or the ground.

- Notice the sequence of each step by slowing down your walking in the following way: Lift your right foot, place the heel down, and then place the upper part of the foot down. Repeat with the other foot.

- As you move from place to place, use the transition as a time to be in your body by experiencing the sensations of walking.

- Feel the movements of your body as you walk up stairs.

- Choose a period of time to practice mindful walking. Select an area or path (even in your bedroom) where you can practice undisturbed. Begin by slowing down your pace and focusing your full attention on an aspect of walking (for example, your feet, the movement of your legs, and so on). When your mind wanders, just bring your attention back to the experience of walking.

Theme A: Eating Awareness Calendar

Practice mindful eating by choosing one experience of eating each day and trying to become aware of that experience while it is happening.

Record in detail your responses to the questions below after the period of eating.

	What was the experience? (for example, snack, meal)	Were you aware of the experience while it was happening? (yes or no)	How did your body feel during the experience? Describe the sensations in detail.	What moods, feelings, and thoughts came along with this experience?
Day 1				
Day 2				
Day 3				
Day 4				
Day 5				
Day 6				
Day 7				

A

Theme T: Ways We Take Care of Ourselves

Observations and Reflections:

Thoughts

Actions

Feelings

T

Theme T: Ways We Don't Take Care of Ourselves

Observations and Reflections:

Thoughts

Actions

Feelings

My Home Practice: Theme T

1. Practice mindful breathing for at least three breaths at a time, three times per day.

2. Try to do a short loving-kindness practice (once a day, ideally; see audio downloads at www.newharbinger.com/27831). Change the language to suit yourself.

3. Begin to notice thoughts, feelings, and physical sensations as they arise throughout the day. Pay particular attention to thoughts and feelings that are related to self-criticism or criticism of others. Try offering yourself and others kindness instead.

4. Continue practicing mindfulness in your day-to-day life, especially in your practice area. Note your observations and reflections in the box below.

Observations and Reflections:

T

Theme T: Tips to Take Away: Dial Up the Gratitude

Positive emotions provide many benefits to physical, intellectual, emotional, and social well-being. In particular, gratitude can be an effective antidote to anger, hostility, and irritation, which are bad for your health. We are used to thinking of gratitude as a feeling that comes and goes. But gratitude is also a *practice*. Recent scientific studies show that you can cultivate positive emotions like gratitude. You might have heard that researchers who studied lottery winners found that these instant millionaires often ended up much less happy than they were before they won huge sums of money. How can you explain this? It appears that happiness doesn't come exclusively from what's outside us. It's really more a matter of what's happening inside us. Daily practice of gratitude can increase your happiness in real and long-lasting ways.

Try these techniques

1. Pay mindful attention to good things in your day, no matter how small they are.

2. Keep a daily log of things that you are grateful for. Make this a regular routine by adding to the list each night before you go to bed.

3. Turn things around and practice gratitude for the things that seem less desirable. Do you hate homework? Practice being grateful that you can go to school.

4. When you're feeling low or upset, practice looking for the blessings. Stop. Tune in to your breath. Look around and find three things that you're grateful for.

5. Say thank you or write a letter of gratitude to someone who has helped you.

6. Notice the kindness of others, and say thank you often.

7. Experience the feelings of gratitude in your body, around the area of your heart. Tune in to this feeling several times each day.

8. Try writing in your journal about gratitude. Here are some questions to get you started:

Select something in your life for which you are grateful. It could be a person, object, activity, memory, and so on. Write in your journal your responses to the following questions: *Why am I grateful for this? How does it enrich my life? How would I feel if I lost it? How could I show my gratitude for this?*

My Home Practice: Theme H

1. Practice mindful breathing as often as possible throughout the day.

2. Make a plan to practice a mindfulness activity of your choice (mindful breathing, body scan, loving-kindness, mindful eating, mindful walking, and so on) each day.

3. Note your observations and reflections in the box below.

Observations and Reflections:

H

Theme E: Tips to Take Away

Mindfulness Cues

You can enhance your practice of mindfulness by using cues to remind yourself to pay attention in order to be really present for your one and only life.

* Put a note on your computer screen or your mirror reminding yourself to "BREATHE."

* Drive or walk with the music turned off, for a change, to notice your surroundings.

* Take three slow, mindful breaths as you get up in the morning and before you go to sleep.

* When you talk to a friend, really listen. Gently let your own thoughts and preoccupations go, and tune in to what this person is saying.

* Download a bell sound to your computer, and set it to ring at random moments. Each time it rings, take a mindful breath.

* Choose a path or street that you walk or run down regularly. Make that your "mindful walking or running path" and practice mindful walking or running each time you go there.

* Go outside at night for three minutes and really look at the stars.

* Go outside during the day for three minutes and really look at something beautiful in nature.

* Exercise mindfully. Pay attention to the movement of your body.

* Practice taking a mindful breath before responding to an e-mail or text message.

* Center your attention by taking five mindful breaths before you start your homework.

* Continue to expand on your "Mindfulness in My Life" activity in theme B.

Appendix D

Learning to BREATHE Student Workbook— Eighteen-Session Version

"MINDFULNESS is paying attention in a particular way:
on purpose, in the present moment, and nonjudgmentally."

—Jon Kabat-Zinn

B	Listen to your **Body**
R	**Reflections** (thoughts) are just thoughts
E	Surf the waves of your **Emotions**
A	**Attend** to the inside and the outside
T	Try **Tenderness**—Take it as it is
H	Practice **Healthy** Habits of mind
E	Gain the inner Edge. Be **Empowered**!

This 18-session student workbook is available for download at www.newharbinger.com/27831.

B Mindfulness

is a way of paying attention to our experience that helps us live our lives in a healthy way.

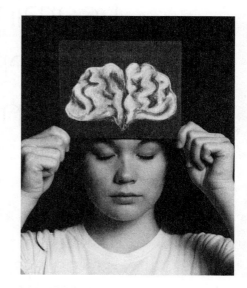

1. **ON PURPOSE** (or really meaning to pay attention to the *inside* and the *outside*)

2. **IN THE PRESENT MOMENT** (knowing right now what's going on *inside* and *outside*)

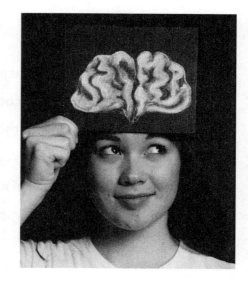

3. **WITHOUT JUDGMENT** (treating yourself kindly, regardless of what your *inside* or *outside* experience is—without getting all caught up in it)

Theme B: My Mindful/Mindless Life

What things (or activities) in your life do you do on automatic pilot (mindlessly)? What are the things you do that fully engage you (mindfully)? Fill in the boxes with as many examples as you can name. You can also write about how you feel when you do things mindfully (with attention) or mindlessly (without attention).

My Mindful Life…

_____

_____

_____

_____

_____

_____

My Mindless Life…

_____

_____

_____

_____

_____

_____

B Mindfulness in My Life

You can practice mindful attention in all of the moments of your day. As an experiment, select an activity from the list below as "your choice": an activity that you choose to do with mindfulness on a regular basis. (If you wish to do activities that are not listed, you may write them in boxes 16, 17, and 18.)

1. Playing a game at recess	2. Going up or down stairs	3. Brushing your teeth
4. Getting dressed	5. Listening to someone	6. E-mailing or texting
7. Eating a meal or a snack	8. Walking down a hallway	9. Spending time at your locker
10. Washing your hands	11. Doing schoolwork or homework	12. Standing in line
13. Waiting for the bus	14. Packing your books for school	15. Changing classes
16.	17.	18.

You can cut out the squares and put them in a box. Select a new one each day. Continue to add new opportunities for mindfulness to your collection.

Now write what you will bring attention to as you do your chosen activity, or draw a picture of the activity that you've chosen to do in a mindful way.

Mindfulness in My Life Activity (Write):

Sensations _____

_____

_____

Thoughts/Reflections _____

_____

_____

Emotions _____

_____

_____

Mindfulness in My Life Activity (Draw):

B My Home Practice: Theme B

1. Practice mindful breathing for at least three breaths at a time, three times per day.

2. Practice the "Body Scan" with audio (see audio downloads at www.newharbinger. com/27831) _____ times.

3. Do the "Mindfulness in My Life" practice.

4. Write about your experience in the box with lines, or draw your experience in the box without lines.

My Experience (Write):

_____

_____

_____

_____

_____

My Experience (Draw):

Tips to Take Away: Three-Minute Body Scan

You can do a short "Body Scan" at any time, especially if you notice that you're feeling tense or anxious.

Try it:

- while seated in class

- before tests

- before athletic events

- before speaking in public

- before getting out of bed in the morning

- before falling asleep

- while standing in line

- during social events

- before an interview

How to do it:

1. Use your attention to find your breath in your body.

2. Starting from either your feet or your head, move your attention through your body and notice your experience. Scan for tension in your feet; lower back; stomach; shoulders; face, jaw, or forehead; or wherever you hold tension in your body.

3. As you scan each area, breathe into the area, releasing tension and bringing in new energy as you did in the "Body Scan."

4. Expand your awareness to your entire body and feel the breath move from your head to your feet.

Theme R: Big Event Circles

Story 1

Write your thoughts in the circle below.   Write how you're feeling in the circle below.

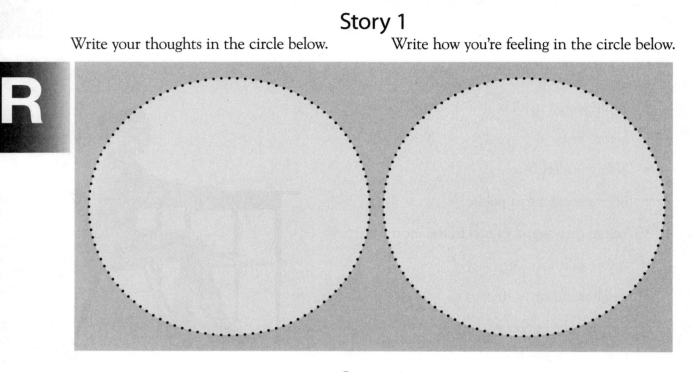

Story 2

Write your thoughts in the circle below.   Write how you're feeling in the circle below.

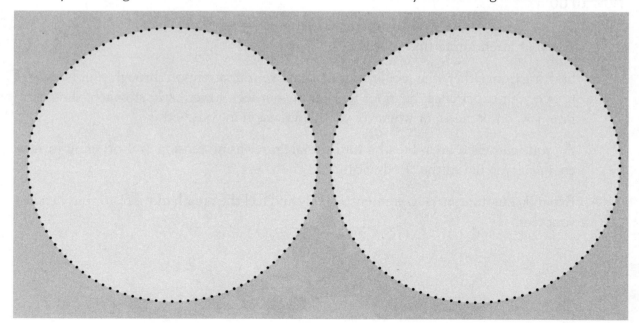

R

Theme R: All Kinds of Thoughts

They're just thoughts. Can you be mindful of all of them?

My Home Practice: Theme R

1. Practice mindful breathing for at least three breaths at a time, three times per day.

2. Practice a short period of mindfulness of thoughts (once a day, ideally; see audio downloads at www.newharbinger.com/27831).

3. Do the "Mindfulness in My Life" activity from theme B.

4. Write about your experience in the box with lines, or draw your experience in the box without lines.

My Experience (Write):

_____

_____

_____

_____

_____

My Experience (Draw):

Theme R: Tips to Take Away: Dealing with Troubling Thoughts

Notice the thoughts that are arising in your mind.

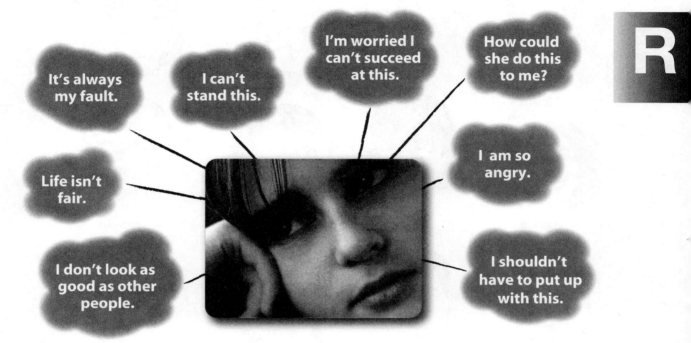

It's always my fault.

I can't stand this.

I'm worried I can't succeed at this.

How could she do this to me?

Life isn't fair.

I am so angry.

I don't look as good as other people.

I shouldn't have to put up with this.

R

Try the mindful approach:

1. Become aware of what your mind is doing: THINKING. It's generating thoughts. The thought is like a bubble that arises in the mind. It's just what the mind does.

2. Examine the thought with curiosity. How loud or soft is it in your mind? Does it yell to be heard, or is it quiet, like a whisper? How strong is it? Is it pleasant, unpleasant, or neutral? How long does it last? Don't try to push the thought out of your mind.

3. Get in touch with your breath as you observe the thought. Remember, it's just a thought. Don't struggle with it because that can make it stronger.

4. Watch the thought fade away. Return your full attention to your breath.

Emotion Faces

Anxious

Embarrassed

Surprised

Lonely

Hopeful

Shy

Frustrated

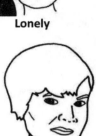

Mischievous

Enraged

Suspicious

Jealous

Sad

Disgusted

Confident

Guilty

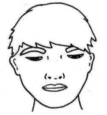

Exhausted

Happy

Overwhelmed

Bored

Confused

My Home Practice: Theme E

1. Practice mindful breathing for at least three breaths at a time, three times per day.

2. Do a short mindfulness practice on feelings (once a day, ideally; see audio downloads at www.newharbinger.com/27831) once a day.

3. Continue with the daily mindfulness practice of your choice. Or continue your "Mindfulness in My Life" practice from theme "B."

4. Write about your experience in the box with lines, or draw your experience in the box without lines..

My Experience (Write):

_____

_____

_____

_____

_____

My Experience (Draw):

Tips to Take Away: About Anger and Other Uncomfortable Emotions

Everyone gets angry. Anger has many different names: irritation, frustration, impatience, rage, hatred, annoyance, resentment, irritability, and moodiness. Sometimes anger in the body feels like "heat." Sometimes people say, "I am boiling mad," or that others are "hotheaded." Other times it can feel hard or stone cold. Anger can make us feel tense and tight. Anger makes us feel out of control. Anger makes us feel jumpy. Anger interrupts our thinking and interferes with our decision making. Sometimes when we are angry, we act impulsively in ways that hurt others or ourselves. Shouting, threatening, fighting, being rude or disrespectful, and name-calling are a few examples.

Kick the anger habit! We can think of anger as just energy in the body.

When you feel yourself getting angry:

- *Stop:* Pay attention.

- *Notice:* Where is the anger in your body?

- *Allow:* Let the feelings of anger be waves, coming and going. Don't try to block them or get rid of them. Don't try to hold on to them or keep them. Anger can be viewed as a strong energy in the body and mind.

- *Breathe:* Focus on the breath. See if you can ride the waves of the anger and watch them get smaller and smaller.

- *Say:* "I can feel this anger and care for myself without hurting others."

Remember:

You can use this approach to work with any difficult feelings. Surf the waves of your annoyance, boredom, sadness, disappointment, jealousy, and so on. Breathe and watch the feelings rise and fall. They're not fun, but they will pass. And you will become stronger and more balanced.

A Stressed-Out Case

What's My Limit?

SHORT TERM STRESS

STRESSED OUT! EMERGENCY

HIGH

LOW

HERE COMES THE STRESS

BACK TO NORMAL

LENGTH OF TIME

Did you know?

- Your body's fight-or-flight response is intended to help you deal with stress.

- Your body gets a temporary boost of energy in an emergency, which helps you cope.

- Some foods (cola, coffee, tea, chocolate) and drugs (nicotine) also cause a stress-like reaction in your body.

- Our bodies respond to mental stress in the same way that they respond to physical threats.

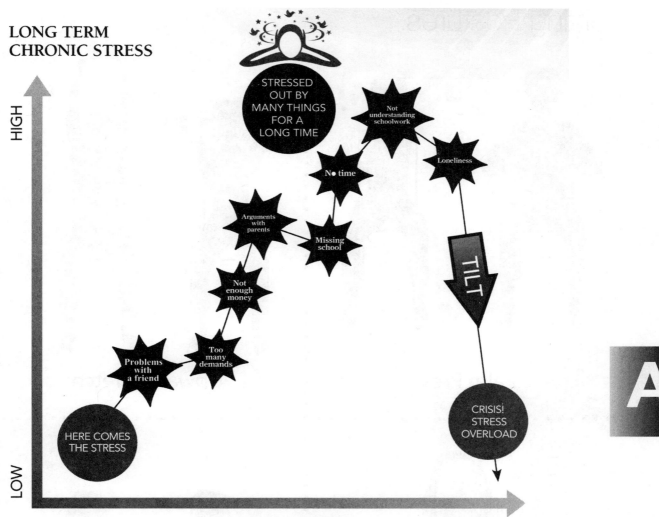

LONG TERM CHRONIC STRESS

HIGH

LOW

STRESSED OUT BY MANY THINGS FOR A LONG TIME

Not understanding schoolwork

No time

Loneliness

Arguments with parents

Missing school

Not enough money

Too many demands

Problems with a friend

TILT

HERE COMES THE STRESS

CRISIS! STRESS OVERLOAD

LENGTH OF TIME

List your chronic stressors

List your chronic stressors. "Chronic" means that they happen a lot.

1. _____
2. _____
3. _____
4. _____
5. _____

6. _____
7. _____
8. _____
9. _____
10. _____

Circle your top three stressors.

Sitting Postures:

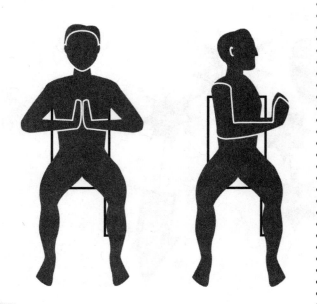

Palm Press

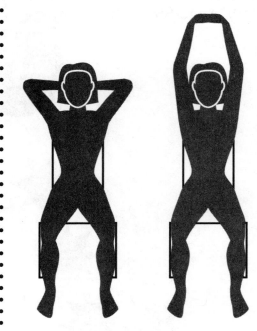

Upward Stretch

Seated Tree

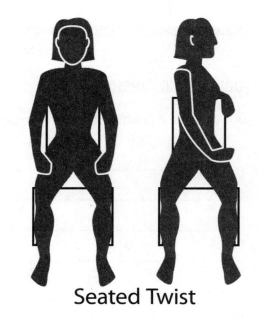

Seated Twist

Standing Postures:

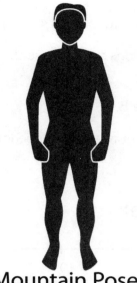

Mountain Pose

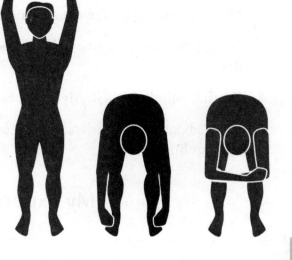

Upward Stretch

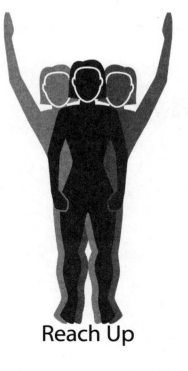

Reach Up

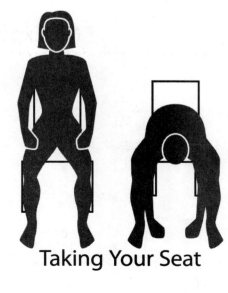

Taking Your Seat

My Home Practice: Theme A

1. Practice mindful breathing for at least three breaths at a time, three to six times per day.

2. Practice mindful movements or mindful walking each day.

3. Begin to notice thoughts, feelings, and physical sensations as they arise throughout the day.

4. Do the "Mindfulness in My Life" practice from theme B.

5. Write about your experience in the box with lines, or draw your experience in the box without lines.

My Experience (Write):

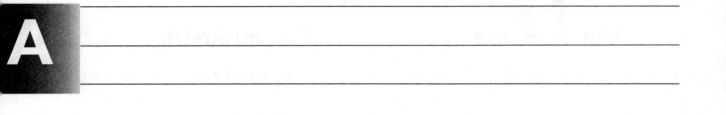

A

My Experience (Draw):

Tips to Take Away: Mindful Eating

PRACTICE 1

1. Pick a food or snack. Pretend that you have never eaten this food before and that this is a new and interesting experience.

2. Look at the food with curiosity. Notice color, textures, shapes, smells, sounds.

3. Before chewing, experience what the food feels like in your mouth.

4. As you chew, notice all the movement and sensations. Swallow more slowly than usual.

5. Slow down the pace of eating.

PRACTICE 2

Try eating a snack or a meal in silence.

A

PRACTICE 3

Try practicing gratitude for all the people whose work made it possible for you to eat this food.

Eating Awareness Experiment

Practice mindful eating by choosing one experience of eating each day and trying to become aware of that experience while it is happening. Record in detail your responses to the questions below, after the experience.

What did you eat? (Feel free to draw a picture.)

A

How aware were you of eating (chewing, swallowing, tasting) while it was happening (very aware, mostly unaware)?

How did your body feel while you were eating? Describe the sensations using your five senses.

What feelings or thoughts did you notice while eating?

Tips to Take Away: Mindful Walking

Pay attention to all the sensations of movement as you walk.

1. Choose a period of time to practice mindful walking. Select an area or path (even in your bedroom) where you can practice without interruption.

2. Notice the contact of your feet with the floor or the ground when you stand.

3. As you begin to walk, slow down your pace and focus your full attention on walking.

4. Notice:

    • Weight shifting from one foot

    • Lifting of the foot

    • Moving the foot forward

    • Placing the foot on the floor

5. Be mindful of fifteen to twenty steps in one direction. Stop and feel the sensations in your feet. Mindfully turn around and pay attention to fifteen to twenty steps in the other direction. Stop and repeat several times.

6. When your mind wanders, just bring your attention back to the sensations of walking.

You can do mindful walking:

• **As you move from place to place.** Use the transition as a time to be in your body by experiencing the sensations of walking.

• **As you walk up stairs.** Feel the movements of your body and the changing sensations.

• **Instead of rushing.** Try slowing down to pay attention.

Ways We Take Care of Ourselves

Write or draw your ideas here:

Thoughts

Actions

Feelings

Ways We Don't Take Care of Ourselves

Write or draw your ideas here:

Thoughts

_____

_____

_____

_____

_____

Actions

_____

_____

_____

_____

_____

T

Feelings

_____

_____

_____

_____

_____

My Home Practice: Theme T

1. Practice mindful breathing for at least three breaths at a time, three to six times per day.

2. Do a short loving-kindness practice _____ times. Change the language to suit yourself, if desired.

3. Begin to notice thoughts, feelings, and physical sensations as they arise throughout the day. Pay particular attention to thoughts and feelings that are related to self-criticism or criticism of others.

4. Write about your experiences in the box with lines, or draw your experiences in the box without lines.

My Experience (Write):

_____

_____

_____

T

_____

_____

My Experience (Draw):

A Recipe for Positive Emotions: Daily Doses of Gratitude

Gratitude helps make us happier and more resilient, because when we're grateful, we notice and appreciate all that we have. We're more likely to remember these good things when things get hard. Gratitude is more than just a nice feeling; it is a **practice**. **Gratitude is both a noun and a verb.** We practice gratitude in order to cultivate it and help it grow. The recipe for gratitude is practicing grateful thoughts, grateful feelings, and grateful actions. By practicing gratitude each day, we can get our daily recommended dose. Cut the squares and place them in a box or an envelope. Try choosing one activity each day as your special practice. Add to the squares by making your own suggestions.

Write a gratitude note to someone to thank that person for something he or she did for you.	Keep a notebook where you list some things you're grateful for each night before you go to bed.	Notice something that a relative does for you, and thank that person.	What foods are you grateful for? Eat one of them mindfully.
Write down five things about yourself (your talents, skills, and so on) that you are grateful for.	Be mindful that people you don't know very well often show you kindness. Say "thank you" often.	While riding in a car, try to identify ten things that you see that make you grateful.	When you watch a TV show, notice whether the characters have an attitude of gratitude. How do they show it?
Be mindful of the good things that happen in your day, even if they are small. What's the tiniest good thing you can notice? The biggest?	Notice something a friend does for you, and thank that person. Make an effort to repay the favor.	Notice how having kindness, compassion, and gratitude toward others feels in your body (maybe in your heart or face).	What music are you grateful to be able to listen to? Listen to it mindfully.
Read a story about gratitude. Read or write a poem about gratitude.	Offer loving-kindness practice to a friend as a way of showing your appreciation for that person.	Notice something a teacher does for you, and thank that person.	Think of your pet or an animal you like. Consider how much the animal makes you happy.
Try to do a favor for someone you appreciate without their noticing (for example, putting something away). Can you keep this a secret?	Make a gratitude collage of pictures of things and people you're grateful for. Hang it in your room to remind you to practice gratefulness.	Try to say something good about a person who becomes the subject of a conversation.	When you see someone who is sick, sad, or angry, send that person kindness.
When you are feeling sad, upset, or angry, notice and stop. Pay attention to your breath. Think of three things you are grateful for.	What sports are you grateful to be able to play? Play mindfully.	Notice something good about a classmate you don't know well. Notice that you can feel gratitude for having this person in your life.	Pick something that you usually take for granted (like water, trees, your house, and so on), and make a list of reasons why you're grateful for it.

My Home Practice: Theme H

1. Practice mindful breathing as often as possible throughout the day.

2. Practice being mindful in your daily life.

3. Note your observations and reflections in the box below.

Write how you plan to practice mindfulness in your daily life:

_____

_____

_____

_____

_____

_____

Draw how you plan to practice mindfulness in your daily life:

Designed to "Re-Mind"

By: _____

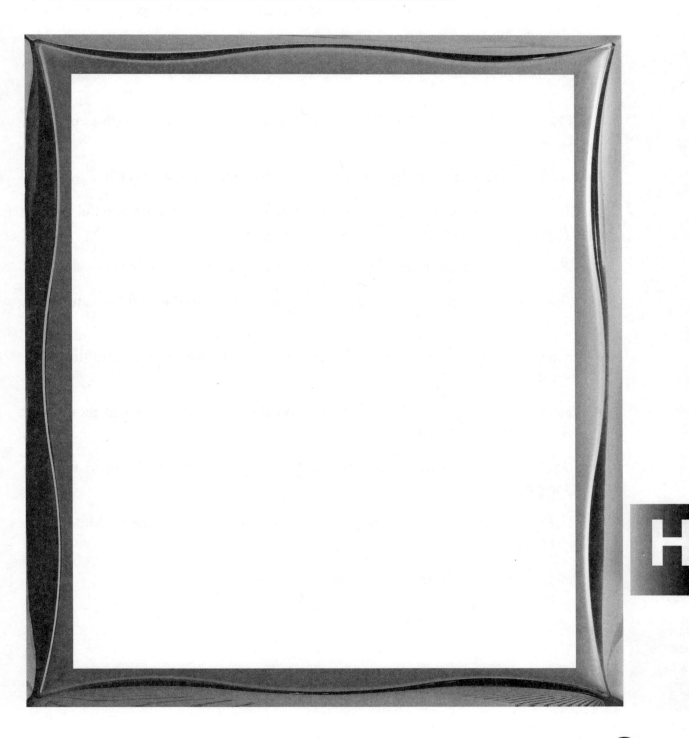

H

Tips to Take Away: *Mindfulness Cues*

* Ride in a car or walk with the music turned off, for a change, to notice your surroundings.

* Take three slow, mindful breaths as you get up in the morning and before you go to sleep.

* When you talk to a friend, really listen. Gently let go of your own thoughts and ideas, and tune in to what the person is saying.

* Each time you hear a bell ring (at home or school), take a mindful breath.

* Choose a path or street that you walk or run down regularly. Practice mindful walking or running each time you go there.

* When you are outside at night, really look at the stars for a minute or two.

* When you go outside during the day, really look at something beautiful in nature for a minute or two.

* Exercise or play a game mindfully. Pay attention to thoughts, feelings, and the movement of your body.

* Practice taking a mindful breath before responding to an e-mail or text message, or before answering a question.

* Focus your attention by taking five mindful breaths before you begin to work on something.

* Continue to expand on your chosen mindfulness practice from theme B, "Mindfulness in My Life."

* Practice kindness to yourself and others at least once a day.

E

BREATHE Wallet Card Template and BREATHE Acronym Posters

B – Listen to your Body. **R** – Reflections (thoughts) are just thoughts. **E** – Surf the waves of your Emotions. **A** – Attend to the inside and the outside. **T** –Try Tenderness – Take it as it is. **H** – Practice Healthy Habits of mind. **E** – Gain the inner Edge. Be Empowered!	**B** – Listen to your Body. **R** – Reflections (thoughts) are just thoughts. **E** – Surf the waves of your Emotions. **A** – Attend to the inside and the outside. **T** –Try Tenderness – Take it as it is. **H** – Practice Healthy Habits of mind. **E** – Gain the inner Edge. Be Empowered!
B – Listen to your Body. **R** – Reflections (thoughts) are just thoughts. **E** – Surf the waves of your Emotions. **A** – Attend to the inside and the outside. **T** –Try Tenderness – Take it as it is. **H** – Practice Healthy Habits of mind. **E** – Gain the inner Edge. Be Empowered!	**B** – Listen to your Body. **R** – Reflections (thoughts) are just thoughts. **E** – Surf the waves of your Emotions. **A** – Attend to the inside and the outside. **T** –Try Tenderness – Take it as it is. **H** – Practice Healthy Habits of mind. **E** – Gain the inner Edge. Be Empowered!
B – Listen to your Body. **R** – Reflections (thoughts) are just thoughts. **E** – Surf the waves of your Emotions. **A** – Attend to the inside and the outside. **T** –Try Tenderness – Take it as it is. **H** – Practice Healthy Habits of mind. **E** – Gain the inner Edge. Be Empowered!	**B** – Listen to your Body. **R** – Reflections (thoughts) are just thoughts. **E** – Surf the waves of your Emotions. **A** – Attend to the inside and the outside. **T** –Try Tenderness – Take it as it is. **H** – Practice Healthy Habits of mind. **E** – Gain the inner Edge. Be Empowered!
B – Listen to your Body. **R** – Reflections (thoughts) are just thoughts. **E** – Surf the waves of your Emotions. **A** – Attend to the inside and the outside. **T** –Try Tenderness – Take it as it is. **H** – Practice Healthy Habits of mind. **E** – Gain the inner Edge. Be Empowered!	**B** – Listen to your Body. **R** – Reflections (thoughts) are just thoughts. **E** – Surf the waves of your Emotions. **A** – Attend to the inside and the outside. **T** –Try Tenderness – Take it as it is. **H** – Practice Healthy Habits of mind. **E** – Gain the inner Edge. Be Empowered!
B – Listen to your Body. **R** – Reflections (thoughts) are just thoughts. **E** – Surf the waves of your Emotions. **A** – Attend to the inside and the outside. **T** –Try Tenderness – Take it as it is. **H** – Practice Healthy Habits of mind. **E** – Gain the inner Edge. Be Empowered!	**B** – Listen to your Body. **R** – Reflections (thoughts) are just thoughts. **E** – Surf the waves of your Emotions. **A** – Attend to the inside and the outside. **T** –Try Tenderness – Take it as it is. **H** – Practice Healthy Habits of mind. **E** – Gain the inner Edge. Be Empowered!

BODY

LISTEN!
YOUR BODY IS TRYING
TO TELL YOU SOMETHING.

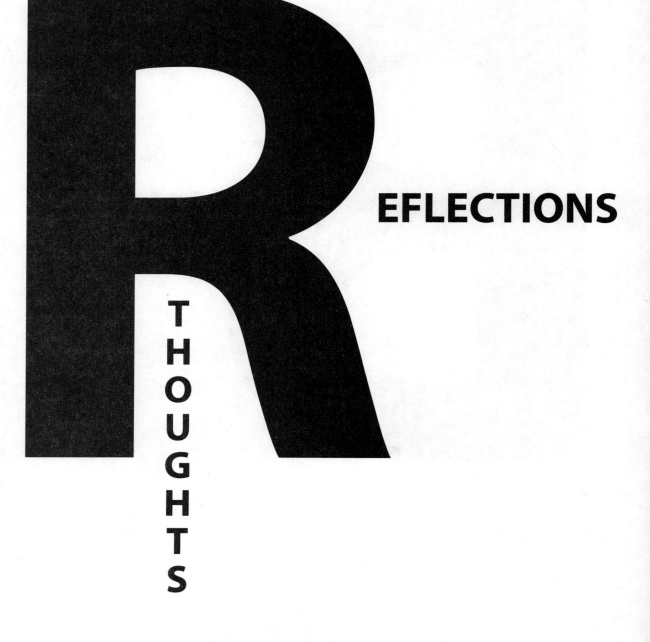

REFLECTIONS

THOUGHTS

THOUGHTS ARE JUST THOUGHTS.

EMOTIONS

SURF THE WAVES
OF YOUR EMOTIONS.

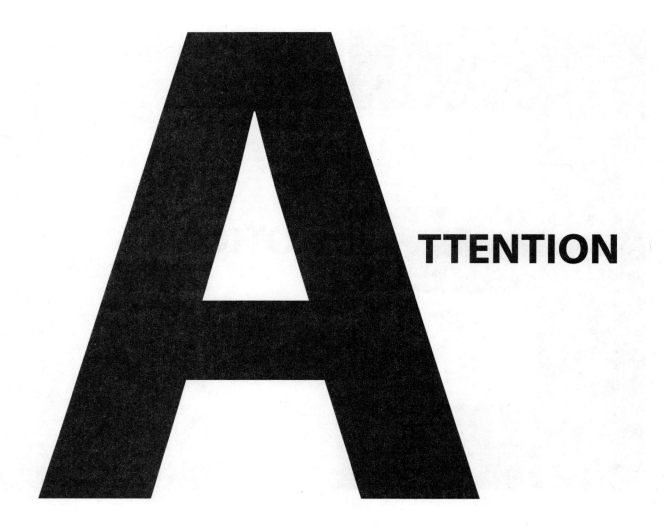

ATTENTION

ATTENTION TO BODY, THOUGHTS, AND FEELINGS IS GOOD STRESS REDUCTION.

TENDERNESS

Take it as it is.

LEARN TO BE KIND
TO YOURSELF.

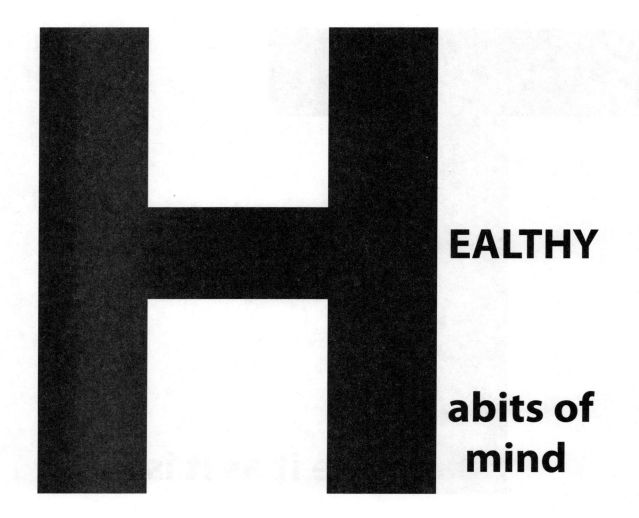

HEALTHY abits of mind

FINDING WAYS TO PRACTICE MINDFULNESS IN YOUR LIFE REDUCES STRESS AND INCREASES INNER STRENGTH.

**MPOWERMENT**

GAIN THE
INNER EDGE!

Recommended Reading on Mindfulness, Affective Neuroscience, and Education

Davidson, R. J. (2012). *The emotional life of your brain: How its unique patterns affect the way you think, feel, and live—and how you can change them.* With S. Begley. New York: Hudson Street Press.

Jennings, P. A. and M. T. Greenberg (2009). The prosocial classroom: Teacher social and emotional competencies in relation to student and classroom outcomes. *Review of Educational Research, 79*(1), 491–525.

Kabat-Zinn, J. (1990). *Full catastrophe living: Using the wisdom of your body and mind to face stress, pain, and illness.* New York: Delacorte Press.

Kabat-Zinn, J. (1994). *Wherever you go, there you are: Mindfulness meditation in everyday life.* New York: Hyperion.

Kaiser-Greenland, S. (2010). *The mindful child: How to help your kid manage stress and become happier, kinder, and more compassionate.* New York: Free Press.

Lantieri, L. (2008). *Building emotional intelligence: Techniques to cultivate inner strength in children.* Boulder, CO: Sounds True.

Mason, J. (2002). *Researching your own practice: The discipline of noticing.* London: Routledge Falmer.

Ryan, T. (2012). *A mindful nation: How a simple practice can help us reduce stress, improve performance, and recapture the American spirit.* Carlsbad, CA: Hay House.

Schoeberlein, D. (2009). *Mindful teaching and teaching mindfulness: A guide for anyone who teaches anything.* With S. Sheth. Somerville, MA: Wisdom Publications.

Siegel, D. J. (2007). *The mindful brain: Reflection and attunement in the cultivation of well-being.* New York: W. W. Norton and Company.

Zajonc, A. (2009). *Meditation as contemplative inquiry: When knowing becomes love.* Great Barrington, MA: Lindisfarne Books.

Web-Based Resources
for Teachers

The Center for Contemplative Mind in Society: www.contemplativemind.org

Center for Courage and Renewal: www.couragerenewal.org

Center for Mindfulness at UMASS Medical School: www.umassmed.edu/cfm/index.aspx

Collaborative for Academic, Social, and Emotional Learning (CASEL): www.casel.org

Garrison Institute: www.garrisoninstitute.org

Learning to BREATHE: www.learning2breathe.org

Mind & Life Institute: www.mindandlife.org

Mindfulness in Education Network: www.mindfuled.org

References

Akinbami, L. J., & Schoendorf, K. C. (2002). Trends in childhood asthma: Prevalence, health care utilization, and mortality. *Pediatrics, 110*(2, pt. 1), 315–332.

American Academy of Pediatrics Committee on Psychosocial Aspects of Child and Family Health. (2001). The new morbidity revisited: A renewed commitment to the psychosocial aspects of pediatric care. *Pediatrics, 108*(5), 1227–1230.

American Diabetes Association. (2011). Diabetes basics: Diabetes statistics—Data from the 2011 National Diabetes Fact Sheet. Retrieved March 13, 2011, from www.diabetes.org/diabetes-basics/diabetes-statistics.

American School Counselor Association. (2005). *The ASCA national model: A framework for school counseling programs* (2nd ed.). Alexandria, VA: ASCA.

Beck, A. T. (1979). *Cognitive therapy and the emotional disorders.* New York: Penguin Books.

Begley, S. (2007). *Train your mind, change your brain: How a new science reveals our extraordinary potential to transform ourselves.* New York: Ballantine Books.

Birmaher, B., & Heydl, R. (2001). Biological studies in depressed children and adolescents. *International Journal of Neuropsychopharmacology, 4*(2), 149–57.

Blakemore, S. J. (2008). Development of the social brain during adolescence. *Quarterly Journal of Experimental Psychology, 61*(1), 40–49.

Blakemore, S. J., & Choudhury, S. (2006). Development of the adolescent brain: Implications for executive function and social cognition. *Journal of Child Psychology and Psychiatry, 47*(3–4), 296–312.

Blakemore, S. J., & Frith, U. (2005). *The learning brain: Lessons for education.* Malden, MA: Blackwell Publishing.

Brantley, J. (2003). *Calming your anxious mind: How mindfulness and compassion can free you of anxiety, fear and panic.* Oakland, CA: New Harbinger Publications.

Bremner, J. D. (2005). *Does stress damage the brain? Understanding trauma disorders from a mind-body perspective.* New York: W. W. Norton and Company.

Broderick, P. C., & Blewitt, P. (in press). *The life span: Human development for helping professionals* (4th ed.). Upper Saddle River, NJ: Pearson Education.

Broderick, P. C., & Korteland, C. (2004). A prospective study of rumination and distraction in early adolescence. *Clinical Child Psychology and Psychiatry, 9*(3), 383–394.

Burns, D. D. (1999). *Feeling good: The new mood therapy.* New York: HarperCollins.

Campos, J. J., Frankel, C. B., & Camras, L. (2004). On the nature of emotion regulation. *Child Development, 75*(2), 377–394.

CASEL (2003). Safe and sound: An educational leader's guide to evidence-based social and emotional learning (SEL) programs. Chicago: Collaborative for Academic, Social, and Emotional Learning.

CASEL (2011). What is SEL? Skills and competencies. Chicago: Collaborative for Academic, Social, and Emotional Learning. casel.org/why-it-matters/what-is-sel/skills-competencies/.

Casey, B. J., Getz, S., & Galvan, A. (2008). The adolescent brain. *Developmental Review, 28*(1), 62–77.

Casey, B. J., Giedd, J. N., & Thomas, K. M. (2000). Structural and functional brain development and its relation to cognitive development. *Biological Psychology, 54,* 241–257.

Cohn, M. A., & Fredrickson, B. L. (2010) In search of durable positive psychology interventions: Predictors and consequences of long-term positive behavior change. *Journal of Positive Psychology, 5*(5), 355–366.

Cole, P. M., Michel, M. K., & Teti, L. O. (1994). The development of emotion regulation and dysregulation: A clinical perspective. *Monographs of the Society for Research in Child Development, 59*(2–3), 73–102.

Collins, W. A. (2003). More than myth: The developmental significance of romantic relationships during adolescence. *Journal of Research on Adolescence, 13*(1), 1–24.

Collins, W. A., & Steinberg, L. (2006). Adolescent development in interpersonal context. In N. Eisenberg (Vol. Ed.), W. Damon & R. M. Lerner (Series Eds.), *Handbook of child psychology: Vol. 3—Social, emotional, and personality development* (6th ed., pp. 1003–1067). Hoboken NJ: John Wiley and Sons.

Comstock, G., & Scharrer, E. (2006). Media and popular culture. In K. A. Renninger & I. E. Sigel (Vol. Eds.), W. Damon & R. M. Lerner (Series Eds.), *Handbook of child psychology: Vol. 4—Child psychology in practice* (6th ed., pp. 817–863). Hoboken, NJ: John Wiley and Sons.

Crane, R. S., Kuyken, W., Hastings, R. P., Rothwell, N., & Williams, J. M. G. (2010). Training teachers to deliver mindfulness-based interventions: Learning from the UK experience. *Mindfulness, 1*(2), 74–86.

Cross-National Collaborative Group (1992). The changing rate of major depression: Cross-national comparisons. *Journal of the American Medical Association, 268*(21), 3098–3105.

Czaja, J., Rief, W., & Hilbert, A. (2009). Emotion regulation and binge eating in children. *International Journal of Eating Disorders, 42*(4), 356–62.

Dahl, R. E. (2004). Adolescent brain development: A period of vulnerabilities and opportunities. *Annals of the New York Academy of Sciences, 1021,* 1–22.

Damasio, A. R. (1994). *Descartes' error: Emotion, reason, and the human brain.* New York: Putnam.

Darling, N., Cumsille, P., & Martinez, M. L. (2008). Individual differences in adolescents' beliefs about the legitimacy of parental authority and their own obligation to obey: A longitudinal investigation. *Child Development, 79*(4), 1103–1118.

Davidson, R. J. (2012). *The emotional life of your brain: How its unique patterns affect the way you think, feel, and live—and how you can change them.* With S. Begley. New York: Hudson Street Press.

Davidson, R. J., Kabat-Zinn, J., Schumacher, J., Rosenkranz, M., Muller, D., Santorelli, S. F., Urbanowski, F., Harrington, A., Bonus, K., & Sheridan, J. F. (2003). Alterations in brain and immune function produced by mindfulness meditation. *Psychosomatic Medicine, 65*(4), 564–70.

Degnan, K. A., Henderson, H. A., Fox, N. A., & Rubin, K. H. (2008). Predicting social wariness in middle childhood: The moderating roles of child care history, maternal personality, and maternal behavior. *Social Development, 71*(3), 471–487.

Durlak, J. A., Weissberg, R. P., Dymnicki, A. B., Taylor, R. D., & Schellinger, K. B. (2011). The impact of enhancing students' social and emotional learning: A meta-analysis of school-based universal interventions. *Child Development, 82*(1), 405–432.

Eccles, J. S. (2004). Schools, academic motivation, and stage-environment fit. In R. M. Lerner & L. Steinberg (Eds.), *Handbook of adolescent psychology* (2nd ed., pp. 125–153). Hoboken, NJ: John Wiley and Sons.

Elias, M. J., Wang, M. C., Weissberg, R. P., Zins, J. E., & Walberg, H. J. (2002). The other side of the report card: Student success depends on more than test scores. *American School Board Journal, 189*(11), 28–30.

Ellis, A., & Harper, R. A. (1975). *A new guide to rational living.* Englewood Cliffs, NJ: Prentice-Hall.

Fataldi, M., Petraglia, F., Luisi, S., Bernardi, F., Casarosa, E., Ferrari, E., Luisi, M., Saggese, G., Genazzani, A. R., & Bernasconi, S. (1999). Changes of serum allopregnanolone levels in the first 2 years of life and during pubertal development. *Pediatric Research, 46*(3), 323–327.

Fredrickson, B. L., Cohn, M. A., Coffey, K. A., Pek, J., & Finkel, S. M. (2008). Open hearts build lives: Positive emotions, induced through loving-kindness meditation, build consequential personal resources. *Journal of Personality and Social Psychology, 95*(5), 1045–1062.

Garber, J. (2006). Depression in children and adolescents: Linking risk research and prevention. *American Journal of Preventive Medicine, 31*(6, Suppl. 1), 104–125.

Garber, J., Keiley, M. K., & Martin, C. (2002). Developmental trajectories of adolescents' depressive symptoms: Predictors of change. *Journal of Consulting and Clinical Psychology, 70*(1), 79–95.

Goldstein, D. S. (2006). *Adrenaline and the inner world: An introduction to scientific integrative medicine.* Baltimore, MD: The Johns Hopkins University Press.

Goleman, D. (2003). *Destructive emotions: How can we overcome them?* New York: Bantam Dell.

Goleman, D. (2006). *Social intelligence: The new science of human relationships.* New York: Bantam Books.

Goodyer, I. M., Park, R. J., Netherton, C. M., & Herbert, J. (2001). Possible role of cortisol and dehydro-epiandrosterone in human development and psychopathology. *British Journal of Psychiatry, 179,* 243–249.

Greenberg, M. T., Weissberg, R. P., O'Brien, M. U., Zins, J. E., Fredericks, L., Resnik, H., et al. (2003). Enhancing school-based prevention and youth development through coordinated social, emotional, and academic learning. *American Psychologist, 58*(6–7), 466–474.

Gross, J. J., & Muñoz, R. F. (1995). Emotion regulation and mental health. *Clinical Psychology: Science and Practice, 2*(2), 151–164.

Gutman, L. M., Sameroff, A. J., & Cole, R. (2003). Academic growth curve trajectories from 1st grade to 12th grade: Effects of multiple social risk factors and preschool child factors. *Developmental Psychology, 39*(4), 777–790.

Hammen, C., & Rudolph, K. D. (2003). Childhood mood disorders. In E. J. Mash & R. A. Barkley, *Child Psychopathology* (2nd Ed., pp. 233–278). New York: The Guilford Press.

Hayes, S. C., Strosahl, K. D., & Wilson, K. G. (1999). *Acceptance and commitment therapy: An experiential approach to behavior change.* New York: The Guilford Press.

Kabat-Zinn, J. (1990). *Full catastrophe living: Using the wisdom of your body and mind to face stress, pain, and illness* (hardcover ed.). New York: Delacorte Press.

Kabat-Zinn, J. (1994). *Wherever you go, there you are: Mindfulness meditation in everyday life.* New York: Hyperion.

Kessler, R. C., Avenevoli, S., Costello, J., Green, J. G., Gruber, M. J., McLaughlin, K. A., Petukhova, M., Sampson, N. A., Zaslavsky, A. M., & Merikangas, K. R. (2012). Severity of 12-month *DSM-IV* disorders in the National Comorbidity Survey Replication Adolescent Supplement. *Archives of General Psychiatry, 69*(4), 381–389.

Kok, B. E., & Fredrickson, B. L. (2010). Upward spirals of the heart: Autonomic flexibility, as indexed by vagal tone, reciprocally and prospectively predicts positive emotions and social connectedness. *Biological Psychology, 85*(3), 432–436.

Larson, R., & Richards, M. H. (1994). *Divergent realities: The emotional lives of mothers, fathers, and adolescents.* New York: Basic Books.

Laursen, B., & Collins, W. A. (1994). Interpersonal conflict during adolescence. *Psychological Bulletin,* 115(2), 197–209.

Lazarus, R. S., & Folkman, S. (1984). Stress, appraisal, and coping. New York: Springer Publishing Company.

Linehan, M. M. (1993). *Cognitive-behavioral treatment of borderline personality disorder.* New York: The Guilford Press.

McEwen, B. S. (2002). *The end of stress as we know it.* With E. N. Lasley. Washington, DC: Joseph Henry Press.

McEwen, B. S., & Gianaros, P. J. (2010). Central role of the brain in stress and adaptation: Links to socio-economic status, health, and disease. *Annals of the New York Academy of Sciences, 1186,* 190–222.

Merikangas, K., Avenevoli, S., Costello, J., Koretz, D., & Kessler, R. C. (2009). National comorbidity survey replication adolescent supplement (NCS-A): I. Background and measures. *Journal of the American Academy of Child and Adolescent Psychiatry, 48*(4), 367–369.

Mihalic, S., Irwin, K., Fagan, A., Ballard, D., & Elliott, D. (2004). Successful program implementation: Lessons from blueprints. *Juvenile Justice Bulletin* NCJ204273. Washington, DC: US Department of Justice.

Morrow, J., & Nolen-Hoeksema, S. (1990). Effects of responses to depression on the remediation of depressive affect. *Journal of Personality and Social Psychology, 58*(3), 519–527.

Müller, M., Holsboer, F., & Keck, M. E. (2002). Genetic modification of corticosteroid receptor signalling: Novel insights into pathophysiology and treatment strategies of human affective disorders. *Neuropeptides, 36*(2–3), 117–131.

National Scientific Council on the Developing Child. (2004). Children's emotional development is built into the architecture of their brains. Working Paper 2. Cambridge, MA: Harvard University Center on the Developing Child. Retrieved December 15, 2006, from www.developingchild.net/reports.shtml.

Neff, K. D. (2003). Self-compassion: An alternative conceptualization of a healthy attitude toward oneself. *Self and Identity, 2*(2), 85–102.

Pahuja, R., & Kotchen, T. A. (2011). Salivary cortisol predicts cardiovascular mortality. *Current Hypertension Reports, 13*(6), 404–405.

Paus, T., Keshavan, M., & Giedd, J. N. (2008). Why do many psychiatric disorders emerge during adolescence? *Nature Reviews Neuroscience* 9(12), 947–957.

Post, R. M. (2007). Kindling and sensitization as models for affective episode recurrence, cyclicity, and tolerance phenomena. *Neuroscience and Biobehavioral Reviews, 31*(6), 858–873.

Quan, N., & Banks, W. A. (2007). Brain-immune communication pathways. *Brain, Behavior, and Immunity, 21*(6), 727–735.

Reyna, V. F., & Farley, F. (2006). Risk and rationality in adolescent decision making: Implications for theory, practice, and public policy. *Psychological Science in the Public Interest, 7*(1), 1–44.

Romeo, R. D., and McEwen, B. S. (2006). Stress and the adolescent brain. *Annals of the New York Academy of Sciences, 1094,* 202–214.

Romer, R., & Walker, E. (Eds.) (2007). *Adolescent psychopathology and the developing brain: Integrating brain and prevention science.* New York: Oxford University Press.

Rosenthal, L. (1971). Some dynamics of resistance and therapeutic management in adolescent group therapy. *Psychoanalytic Review, 58*(3), 353–366.

Sapolsky, R. M. (2004). *Why zebras don't get ulcers* (3rd ed.). New York: Henry Holt and Company.

Sawyer, S. M., Afifi, R. A., Bearinger, L. H., Blakemore, S. J., Dick, B., Ezeh, A. C., & Patton, G. C. (2012). Adolescence: A foundation for future health. *Lancet, 379*(9826), 1630–1640.

Segal, Z. V., Williams, J. M. G., & Teasdale, J. D. (2002). *Mindfulness-based cognitive therapy for depression: A new approach to preventing relapse.* New York: The Guilford Press.

Seligman, M. E. P. (2002). *Authentic happiness: Using the new positive psychology to realize your potential for lasting fulfillment*. New York: The Free Press.

Selye, H. (1978). *The stress of life* (rev. ed.). New York: McGraw-Hill.

Sher, K. J., & Grekin, E. R. (2007). Alcohol and affect regulation. In J. J. Gross (Ed.), *Handbook of emotion regulation* (pp. 560–580). New York: The Guilford Press.

Siegel, D. J. (1999). *The developing mind: Toward a neurobiology of interpersonal experience*. New York: The Guilford Press.

Siegel, D. J. (2007). *The mindful brain: Reflection and attunement in the cultivation of well-being*. New York: W. W. Norton and Company.

Silvia, P. J. (2002). Self-awareness and emotional intensity. *Cognition and Emotion, 16*(2), 195–216.

Sim, L., Adrian, M., Zeman, J., Cassano, M., & Friedrich, W. N. (2009). Adolescent deliberate self-harm: Linkages to emotion regulation and family emotional climate. *Journal of Research on Adolescence, 19*(1), 75–91.

Sim, T. N., & Koh, S. F. (2003). A domain conceptualization of adolescent susceptibility to peer pressure. *Journal of Research on Adolescence, 13*(1), 57–80.

Sowell, E. R., Thompson, P. M., & Toga, A. W. (2007). Mapping adolescent brain maturation using structural magnetic resonance imaging. In D. Romer & E. F. Walker (Eds.), *Adolescent psychopathology and the developing brain: Integrating brain and prevention science* (pp. 55–84). New York: Oxford University Press.

Sroufe, L. A., Egeland, B., Carlson, E. A., & Collins, W. A. (2005). *The development of the person: The Minnesota study of risk and adaptation from birth to adulthood*. New York: The Guilford Press.

Steinberg, L. (2008). A social neuroscience perspective on adolescent risk-taking. *Developmental Review, 28*, 78–106.

Sternberg, E. M. (2001). *The balance within: The science connecting health and emotions*. New York: W. H. Freeman.

US Department of Health and Human Services, US Department of Education, & US Department of Justice. (2000). *Report of the Surgeon's General's Conference on Children's Mental Health: A national action agenda*. Washington, DC: US Department of Health and Human Services.

Walker, E., & Bollini, A. M. (2002). Pubertal neurodevelopment and the emergence of psychotic symptoms. *Schizophrenia Research, 54*(1), 17–23.

Walker, E. F. (2002). Adolescent neurodevelopment and psychopathology. *Current Directions in Psychological Science, 11*(1), 24–28.

Walker, E. F., & Diforio, D. (1997). Schizophrenia: A neural diathesis-stress model. *Psychological Review, 104*(4), 667–685.

Walker, E. F., Sabuwalla, Z., & Huot, R. (2004). Pubertal neuromaturation, stress sensitivity, and psychopathology. *Development and Psychopathology, 16*(4), 807–824.

Wang, M. C., Haertel, G. D., Walberg, H. J. 1993. Toward a knowledge base for school learning. *Review of Educational Research, 63*(3), 249–94.

Weck, F., Bohn, C., Ginzburg, D. M., & Stangier, U. (2011). Treatment integrity: Implementation, assessment, evaluation, and correlations with outcome. *Verhaltenstherapie, 21*(107), 99–107.

Wegner, D. M. (1989). *White bears and other unwanted thoughts: Suppression, obsession, and the psychology of mental control*. New York: Viking.

Weinstein, C. S. (2007). *Middle and secondary classroom management: Lessons from research and practice* (3rd ed.). Boston: McGraw-Hill.

Weisz, J. R., Jensen-Doss, A., & Hawley, K. M. (2006). Evidence-based youth psychotherapies versus usual clinical care: A meta-analysis of direct comparisons. *American Psychologist, 61*(7), 671–689.

Yap, M. B., Allen, N. B., & Sheeber, L. (2007). Using an emotion regulation framework to understand the role of temperament and family processes in risk for adolescent depressive disorders. *Clinical Child and Family Psychology Review, 10*(2), 180–196.

Zins, J. E., Weissberg, R. P., Wang, M. C., & Walberg, H. J. (Eds.). (2004). *Building academic success on social and emotional learning: What does the research say?* New York: Teachers College Press.

Patricia C. Broderick, PhD, is a research associate at the Prevention Research Center for the Promotion of Human Development at Penn State University and founder of the Stress Reduction Center at West Chester University of Pennsylvania. She is a licensed clinical psychologist, a certified school psychologist and counselor for grades K 12, and she is a graduate of the Mindfulness based stress reduction (MBSR) advanced practicum at the Center for Mindfulness at UMASS. In addition, she is the author of The Life Span: Human Development for Helping Professionals, a textbook for graduate level students and mental health professionals.

Foreword writer **Myla Kabat Zinn, RN, BSN**, spent a number of years assisting at births both in the hospital and at home. During those years she also taught childbirth education classes based on mindful awareness. She is the coauthor, with her husband Jon, of *Everyday Blessings: The Inner Work of Mindful Parenting*. She has lead workshops on mindful parenting in the U.S. and in Europe.

Foreword writer **Jon Kabat Zinn, PhD**, is internationally known for his work as a scientist, writer, and meditation teacher engaged in bringing mindfulness into the mainstream of medicine and society. He is professor of medicine emeritus at the University of Massachusetts Medical School and author of numerous books, including *Full Catastrophe Living, Arriving at Your Own Door*, and *Coming to Our Senses*.

Register your **new harbinger** titles for additional benefits!

When you register your **new harbinger** title—purchased in any format, from any source—you get access to benefits like the following:

- Downloadable accessories like printable worksheets and extra content

- Instructional videos and audio files

- Information about updates, corrections, and new editions

Not every title has accessories, but we're adding new material all the time.

Access free accessories in 3 easy steps:

1. Sign in at NewHarbinger.com (or **register** to create an account).

2. Click on **register a book**. Search for your title and click the **register** button when it appears.

3. Click on the **book cover or title** to go to its details page. Click on **accessories** to view and access files.

That's all there is to it!

If you need help, visit:

NewHarbinger.com/accessories

new harbinger
CELEBRATING
40 YEARS